Am

Biologically Inspired Neural Networks

Ammar Belatreche

Biologically Inspired Neural Networks

Models, Learning, and Applications

VDM Verlag Dr. Müller

Impressum/Imprint (nur für Deutschland/ only for Germany)

Bibliografische Information der Deutschen Nationalbibliothek: Die Deutsche Nationalbibliothek verzeichnet diese Publikation in der Deutschen Nationalbibliografie; detaillierte bibliografische Daten sind im Internet über http://dnb.d-nb.de abrufbar.
Alle in diesem Buch genannten Marken und Produktnamen unterliegen warenzeichen-, marken- oder patentrechtlichem Schutz bzw. sind Warenzeichen oder eingetragene Warenzeichen der jeweiligen Inhaber. Die Wiedergabe von Marken, Produktnamen, Gebrauchsnamen, Handelsnamen, Warenbezeichnungen u.s.w. in diesem Werk berechtigt auch ohne besondere Kennzeichnung nicht zu der Annahme, dass solche Namen im Sinne der Warenzeichen- und Markenschutzgesetzgebung als frei zu betrachten wären und daher von jedermann benutzt werden dürften.

Coverbild: www.ingimage.com

Verlag: VDM Verlag Dr. Müller Aktiengesellschaft & Co. KG
Dudweiler Landstr. 99, 66123 Saarbrücken, Deutschland
Telefon +49 681 9100-698, Telefax +49 681 9100-988
Email: info@vdm-verlag.de
Zugl.: Londonderry, University of Ulster, Diss, 2007

Herstellung in Deutschland:
Schaltungsdienst Lange o.H.G., Berlin
Books on Demand GmbH, Norderstedt
Reha GmbH, Saarbrücken
Amazon Distribution GmbH, Leipzig
ISBN: 978-3-639-22826-7

Imprint (only for USA, GB)

Bibliographic information published by the Deutsche Nationalbibliothek: The Deutsche Nationalbibliothek lists this publication in the Deutsche Nationalbibliografie; detailed bibliographic data are available in the Internet at http://dnb.d-nb.de.
Any brand names and product names mentioned in this book are subject to trademark, brand or patent protection and are trademarks or registered trademarks of their respective holders. The use of brand names, product names, common names, trade names, product descriptions etc. even without a particular marking in this works is in no way to be construed to mean that such names may be regarded as unrestricted in respect of trademark and brand protection legislation and could thus be used by anyone.

Cover image: www.ingimage.com

Publisher: VDM Verlag Dr. Müller Aktiengesellschaft & Co. KG
Dudweiler Landstr. 99, 66123 Saarbrücken, Germany
Phone +49 681 9100-698, Fax +49 681 9100-988
Email: info@vdm-publishing.com

Printed in the U.S.A.
Printed in the U.K. by (see last page)
ISBN: 978-3-639-22826-7

To my parents, for their constant encouragement and inspiration.

To my wife, Habiba, for her understanding and love.

To Adam, our beautiful and lively son.

Contents

CHAPTER 1

Introduction

1.1 Background

To date, artificial neural networks have been researched extensively and have successfully been used in a wide range of applications. The use of neural networks is motivated by the astonishing computing capabilities shown by humans (and animals) when performing sensory perception tasks. For example, the human brain can reliably recognise a person's familiar face in a changing environment where conventional computers might fail. Also the human brain is able to store and recall a variety of information and more importantly acquire new knowledge through learning, a feature that conventional computers lack. However the models used in these applications and most of the existing commercial and freely available tools are based on a high abstraction of real biological neurons found in different areas of the brain. Therefore they do not capture all aspects of the biological nervous systems, i.e. the complex structure of the brain (which contains approximately 10^{10}-10^{11} highly interconnected neurons) and the rich dynamics of networks of neurons and their connecting synapses, nor do they explain the means by which the brain represents and process information or perform fast and accurate decisions about the perceived environment. In these abstract models, the output of a neuron is represented by a continuous analogue value indicating its average activity. Examples of such models include the McCulloch-Pitts circuits, feedforward multilayer perceptrons (MLPs) with backpropagation-based supervised learning, Kohonen self-organising maps (SOM) with unsupervised competitive learning, radial basis functions (RBFs) which combines both supervised and unsupervised learning, and recurrent neural networks such as Hopfield networks, etc.

However, it has been shown since the 1920s that biological neurons respond with one or more action potentials (Adrian, 1926; Adrian and Adrian Zotterman, 1926a,b; Adrian, 1928), called spikes, instead of a continuous value as it was and is still widely used nowadays in most of existing neural networks. The neural models whose dynamics are based on the spike generation mechanisms are called spiking neurons and they offer a better representation of real biological neurons when compared to traditional artificial neural networks (ANNs). This plausible type of neuron has been classified as a third generation (Maass, 1997) of neurons which comes after the first and second generations representing the McCulloch-Pitts neurons which use threshold logic units (TLUs) and the multi-layer perceptron (MLPs) with continuous outputs, respectively. Within this new generation, many spiking neuron models have been proposed and studied by neuroscientists ranging from the more complex and detailed model of Hodgkin and Huxley and its derived reduced versions, to more abstract and less complex models such as the Integrate-and-Fire (IF) and the Spike Response model (SRM) (Gerstner and Kistler, 2002; Arbib, 1995). Besides the variety of neuron models, two different hypotheses have been put forward as to how the brain represents information, i.e. what is the neural code? The first hypothesis is based on rate coding and it suggests that the brain needs to average neural spikes temporally and/or spatially to obtain a firing rate which is then interpreted and communicated between interconnected neurons. According to this hypothesis, individual action potentials do not represent information and are generated simply for the need of propagating the rate information across populations of neurons. The other hypothesis gives more importance to individual spikes and argues that the speed at which the brain computes suggests that the spike averaging process is implausible and there is not much time to determine such an average over time or across populations of neurons and then interpreting it. According to this hypothesis, the brain uses temporal encoding and it is the timing of individual spikes considered in single (e.g. time to first spike) or in groups of neurons (e.g. correlation and synchronisation of their spike trains or their temporal activities) that matters for information representation and processing. There are recent experiments, in favour of this hypothesis, which state that learning of synaptic strengths (i.e. synaptic plasticity) depends on the precise timings of pre- and post-synaptic spikes (instead of firing rates) such as the spike-timing-dependent plasticity (STDP) which is an unsupervised learning rule (Bi and Poo, 1998; Song, et al., 2000; Yao and Dan, 2001; Gerstner and Kistler, 2002; Panchev and Wermter, 2004).

With the above in mind, a natural question arises. Why should we study spiking neural networks when classical ANNs have already proved to work perfectly on a wide range of problems and have successfully been applied in many fields? Actually, despite the significant understanding gained so far about the basic dynamics of biological neurons and their different plausible models and learning paradigms, the question of how the brain computes and performs different perceptual tasks is far from being answered.

Research in neural networks is multidisciplinary in nature, and artificial neural networks are built and studied by many research groups for several reasons. For example, biologists and neuroscientists attempt to understand how the brain works by studying neurons at the low and high levels and building networks of neurons which best mimic the detailed dynamics of those found in the nervous system. This could help unravel the detailed dynamics of neural activity, understand the interaction between neurons in different areas of the brain and explain what happens to the connections between neurons when presented with different stimuli or when different patterns are learned or memorised and new knowledge is discovered. This could also help understand what happens when different areas of the brain are partially or totally damaged and how such damage affects the perception of different sensory modalities. On the other hand, computer scientists and engineers attempt to build and simulate neuro-inspired systems and implement different aspects of the brain dynamics in order to equip machines with the brain unmatched capabilities in performing many tasks for which there is no algorithmic solution or the current computer systems fail to solve or have shown very poor performance. That is, the objective is to build computing systems that are able to perform those difficult tasks that are carried out by the brain efficiently and with apparent ease, such as object recognition, scene segmentation and analysis, speech and speaker recognition, odour recognition, learning and reasoning, consciousness, …etc.

Within the framework of existing neural models and encoding schemes, the work presented in this book shows that it is possible to develop new efficient learning and computing systems using different models of spiking neural networks and therefore help further our understanding of their dynamics, increase their applicability in solving computing and engineering problems and make steps forward towards devising new computing systems with similar performance of the brain.

1.2 Objectives of this book

The remarkable computational and perceptual capabilities of the brain have motivated researchers to investigate the possibilities of creating neuro-inspired systems which draw inspiration from biological principles of the nervous system. Although the computing power of the brain is still a mystery and far from being deciphered and despite that research in the multidisciplinary field of neuroscience is in its infantile stage, there is some basic understanding of the underlying principles and dynamics of the computing elements. A number of neural models were suggested and different hypotheses about the means of information encoding and processing in the brain were put forward. Also, based on physiological experiments some unsupervised learning rules, based on the temporal activities of coupled neurons, were formulated. However, despite the variety of neural models, learning mechanisms and neural architectures created so far, there is still a lack of efficient training mechanisms which increase their usefulness and applicability and also help further our understanding of how different perceptual tasks are carried out by the nervous system efficiently and with apparent ease. This work treats the ideas of using different biologically plausible models of neurons and synapses and explores new training approaches which allow us to build spiking neural networks that are able to perform useful computations based on the spike timings of both individual neurons and populations of neurons as a means of information encoding and processing. The first motivation of this work is based on the belief that using these biologically plausible models may help further our understanding of how the brain works and build new computational systems which will either outperform classical approaches or provide systems with similar performance and les resources requirements. The second motivation is that biologically plausible models which differ from classical artificial neurons (1st and 2nd generations) are interesting in their own right and worth being explored. It is important to note that the strategy adopted in this work is to use different biologically plausible neural models and encoding schemes and build learning possibilities and architectures that do not necessarily match the exact low level physiological details of real biological models. As a computer scientist, the author believes that the use of 'biologically plausible' or "biologically inspired" instead of being limited to those 'biologically precise' models may suffice for capturing the essential computing aspects of the brain and gaining insights into its computing nature. With this and the discussion provided in the background section in mind, the main objectives set out in this work are as follow:

- Explore the existing biologically plausible neural models and gain an understanding of their dynamics and the properties of individual neurons. The different levels of abstraction are examined which start with the cell level, then to the neuron level and finally to the network level.

- Explore the encoding schemes used by these plausible models to represent and process the features of real objects in a perceived environment. The effects of encoding paradigms on the accuracy and speed of perception are also examined.

- Explore the existing learning mechanisms and assess their efficiency and applicability.

- Simulate the main biologically plausible models, analyse their dynamics and compare the advantages and disadvantages of each model.

- Explore new possibilities of supervised training and computing with spiking neurons using different neural models, synaptic models, encoding schemes and architectures.

- Investigate possible applications of spiking neurons and compare their potential with classical approaches in terms of efficiency and computational paradigm.

The above-mentioned objectives required an in depth investigation of the multidisciplinary field of computational neuroscience and the broad area of intelligent systems represented by a large body of research literature. This investigation encompassed many details which will be presented in the body of this book. In order to achieve these objectives, the following sequence of research was carried out and is grouped into three phases.

Phase 1

This is the starting phase where the classical models of neural networks are reviewed along with their different architectures, learning mechanisms and applications. Also at this stage, besides the review of more biologically plausible neurons and temporal encoding scheme, the simulation and analysis of their models were carried out. The different steps involved in this phase are summarised below.

- Review the existing literature related to classical abstract artificial neural networks, their models, learning mechanism and different architectures. The high abstraction of this generation of artificial neural networks was highlighted and their biological plausibility and limitations were pointed out.

- Investigate the recent generation of more biologically plausible neurons, identify the existing models, simulate and analyse the mainly used models and highlight the advantages and disadvantages of each model.

- Identify the existing hypotheses about the different possibilities used by the brain to encode and process different sensory information.

- Identify the existing learning mechanisms and highlight their plausibility, their strengths and weaknesses and more importantly their applicability to solve real world problems.

Phase 2

In this phase, new training alternatives were explored, developed and tested and the following steps were involved:

- Explore other possibilities for efficient supervised training of spiking neural networks. This stage led to the investigation of the suitability of evolutionary strategies for supervised training of spiking neural networks with different neural and synaptic models.

- Develop a supervised training approach for spiking neural networks with spike response model-based neurons and static synapses.

- Demonstrate its efficiency on the classification of selected samples of non-linearly problems and compare the obtained performance with existing approaches.

- Investigate the suitability of evolutionary strategies to train spiking networks based on more detailed models of synapses and the integrate-and-fire neurons and demonstrate its performance on the classification of selected benchmark datasets.

Phase 3

In this phase, the focus was directed towards the application of spiking neurons in solving real world problems and this required to:

- Identify suitable neuron models and architectures that can be applied to solve real world problems with the particular focus, in this work, on computer vision applications.

- Develop a system for colour image segmentation and highlight the main advantages and limitations of the obtained biologically inspired system when compared with its traditional algorithmic counterparts.

The outcomes of these investigations are presented in detail in the subsequent chapters.

1.3 Contributions

This work presents a description of the research carried out to investigate learning and computing with different models of spiking neural networks. The outcome of this research is summarised as follows:

- Proposal of an evolutionary strategy-based supervised training for spiking neural networks, with static weights, spike response model neurons and a linear temporal encoding scheme.
- Extension of the proposed evolutionary supervised training approach to spiking neural networks with integrate-and-fire neurons and dynamic synapses, which represent a more detailed model of synapses whose strengths depend on the structure of impinging spike trains.
- Proposal of a colour image segmentation system based on the combination of networks of neural oscillators, another biologically plausible neural model whose dynamics are different from the previous two models, and a devised self-organising map-based colour reduction method.

These contributions will be presented in more detail in chapters 5, 6 and 7 and are briefly described in the following paragraphs:

The proposed evolutionary strategy-based training approach was applied to spiking neurons which are based on the spike response model and are connected in a feed-forward architecture using static synapses, each of which consists of a synaptic weight representing the synaptic strength and a time delay representing the synaptic delay. It is the synaptic parameters that underlie the learning process and therefore are adjusted in order to learn a specific task. In contrast to the existing unsupervised training methods based on the correlation between pre and post synaptic timings, the newly proposed supervised training approach is very useful for training spiking neural networks when a priori knowledge is available about the processed data. The proposed method approaches the training process as a continuous optimisation problem and evolutionary strategies (ESs) were applied to iteratively search for the spiking network best free parameters (i.e. synaptic weights and delays) which learn a classification task, i.e. a mapping between a given set of temporal inputs which encode the real world features and temporal outputs which represent the selective temporal response of output neurons to a specific input pattern. Besides the sparse coding, a simple temporal encoding scheme is proposed and its usefulness is demonstrated on classification tasks in terms of accuracy obtained and scalability. The efficiency of the proposed approach has been demonstrated on the classification of benchmark datasets, namely the nonlinearly separable XOR problem, the IRIS and the Breast Cancer datasets.

Moving from spike response models and static synapses, the possibilities of training and computing with integrate-and-fire neurons and dynamic synapses were investigated. In contrast to static synapses represented by constant scalar weights, dynamic synapses (DS) represent a more plausible model of biological synapses where the synaptic strength is represented by a dynamic entity whose value changes upon the arrival of spike trains. The behaviour of dynamic synapses was simulated and analysed and viable training approaches of feedforward spiking networks of integrate-and-fire neurons and dynamic synapses were explored. First, spike-timing-dependent plasticity (STDP), a biologically plausible unsupervised training method, was applied but without success as the trained network failed to learn desired mapping between the inputs and output data sets. The proposed evolutionary training approach was then extended to such spiking networks and proved successful in searching the optimal network parameters for a given mapping between input and output datasets. In this approach, a different encoding scheme is used at the output layer where the timing of the maximum postsynaptic neuron response (PSR) is used (instead of the firing time) to signal a particular pattern. Also the network free parameters were reduced to the time constants of inactivation process of dynamic synapses (this parameter and other dynamic synapse parameters will be explained in detail in Chapter 6). The efficiency of the proposed approach was also demonstrated on classification of benchmark datasets.

The third contribution consists of the investigation of computing with another biologically plausible neural model that is observed in a variety of biological phenomena and more importantly in cortical neurons and different areas of the brain. This model is called neural oscillators and its dynamics were simulated and analysed in both temporal space and phase plane (see details in Chapter 7). Based on the emerging synchronisation of the activity of coupled neural oscillators and inspired by the temporal correlation theory used to explain the feature binding problem, a system for colour image segmentation was proposed. Whereas the previous two models (presented in chapters 5 and 6) used the timing of the network output neurons to perform the recognition of a pattern, the model in this system (presented in chapter 7) uses the temporal synchronisation of a population of neurons to implement the segmentation of coherent objects in a given image. Also, in contrast to the feedforward architecture used in the two previous contributions, a grid of neural oscillators, which are laterally connected through excitatory synapses and globally inhibited by a common inhibitor, is used this time where each neural oscillator is assigned to a single pixel of the input image. The correlation of the oscillators' temporal activities is exploited as a means of segmentation of existing objects where an object is defined as a coherent region, i.e. contiguous pixels with similar features. Segmentation occurs through the synchronisation of neural oscillators that are mapped to pixels of the same object, and the desynchronisation with other neural oscillators which belong to other objects in the image. No supervised training is applied in this case, as the activities of neural oscillators is self-organised. However, before assigning each neural oscillator to a pixel in the colour image, a colour reduction approach is applied. This devised approach uses Kohonen self-organising maps in order to map the original image colour space (space of RGB triplets) into a new reduced space of representative colours. Each colour in the new space is represented by an index which is eventually assigned to a neural oscillator. Also the original RGB image is first converted to the HSV (Hue, Saturation, Value) space which is chosen due to its suitability for digital image processing applications.

1.4 Outline

The book consists of eight chapters which present a logical progression of the research carried out according to the abovementioned objectives. A brief overview of the remaining chapters is presented below:

- **Chapter 2** reviews the first and second generations of neural networks. An historical background is provided, different classical models of neural networks are presented and the various architectures with their associated learning methods are discussed and compared. Also, applications of artificial neural networks are reviewed and their biological plausibility is discussed.

- **Chapter 3** reviews the third generation of artificial neural networks. Their biological foundation is presented, the main spiking neural models are simulated and their dynamics analysed. These models are compared in term of their biological plausibility and their level of abstraction. The question of which model to use and why is addressed. The existing encoding schemes are covered and classified based on either the use of spike timings or firing rates and their role in performing computational tasks is highlighted. The existing learning paradigms are introduced and their biological plausibility and their applicability are discussed.

- **Chapter 4** reviews the concepts of evolutionary computations, covers the plethora of evolutionary algorithms used in optimisation problems and define the class of optimisation algorithms to which belong evolutionary strategies (ES), which have been used in the subsequent two chapters for supervised training of spiking networks. The different classes of evolutionary algorithms are introduced and the suitability of each class to optimise different types of problems is discussed. The main elements and operators of an evolutionary algorithm are presented and their different implementations are outlined. The synergy between evolutionary algorithms and neural networks is presented and the advantages of using evolutionary algorithms in the optimisation of artificial neural network connectivity, learning rules and architecture is discussed.

- **Chapter 5** presents the proposed evolutionary strategies-based supervised training approach of spiking neural networks. The question of using supervised or unsupervised training is discussed and the advantages of using supervised learning rules are pointed out. The existing gradient based supervised training is briefly reviewed and its drawbacks are highlighted. The proposed network model and architecture are presented and the use of evolutionary strategies (ES) in order to optimise the network parameters is explained in detail. The proposed mapping between a spiking network (phenotype) and its genetic representation (genotype) is illustrated and the iterative optimisation process is presented. The proposed temporal encoding scheme is illustrated and contrasted with the spare encoding scheme. The efficiency of the proposed approach is demonstrated on classification of nonlinearly separable benchmark problems and conclusions and discussions of the obtained results are presented.

- **Chapter 6** presents the extension of the proposed training approach to spiking networks with integrate-and-fir neurons and dynamic synapses. The concept of dynamic synapse is presented and its difference with the traditional concept of a synapse is outlined. The dynamics of a biological chemical synapse are presented and illustrated. The behaviour of an integrate-and-fire neuron coupled with other neurons through dynamic synapses is simulated and the neuron response to different spike trains with different onset times is analysed. Based on this analysis, a devised temporal encoding scheme for the neurons at the output layer is presented and illustrated. The failure of the STDP algorithm in finding the optimal parameters that learn a given mapping between input and output neurons is pointed out, then the extension of evolutionary strategies-based approach to supervised training of this network model is presented. The network adjustable parameters are defined, and the implementation of the evolutionary strategy is presented. The proposed approach is demonstrated on the classification of benchmark datasets and conclusions and discussion of the obtained results are presented.

- **Chapter 7** presents the proposed system for colour image segmentation based on another biologically plausible neural model called neural oscillators and a different spiking network architecture. The neural oscillator model is presented; its presence in different brain areas and its plausibility are discussed. A mathematical model, represented by a system of differential equations, of neural oscillators is simulated and its dynamics are analysed both in time domain and phase plane space. Also dynamics of coupled neural oscillators are simulated and examined and the emerging synchronisation/desynchronisation behaviour is illustrated both in temporal domain and phase plane space. An important part of these simulations and analyses are included in Appendix A. The feature binding problem and its relation with image segmentation are discussed. The dynamics of arrays of neural oscillators that are locally connected through excitatory synapses and globally inhibited by a common inhibitor are presented and the mechanism of grey scale image segmentation using such networks is illustrated. Numerical simulations of networks of oscillators are carried out using discrete step by step integration for small size images and an algorithmic approach, which captures the essential dynamics of a neural oscillator, is used for larger images in order to reduce the computing time resulting from the integration of a large number of differential equations. The application of networks of oscillators to colour images and the devised colour reduction approach are presented in detail. The proposed system is demonstrated on selected samples of colour images and the conclusions and discussions of the obtained results are presented.

CHAPTER 2

Artificial neural networks

2.1 Introduction

Biologically inspired artificial neural networks offer a different and interesting computational and information processing paradigm. Artificial neural networks computations are inspired from the biological neural system with the aim of reproducing some of the flexibility and power of the human brain for solving problems that are intractable or difficult for traditional sequential computers. With the ability of experience-based learning performed by humans and animals, artificial neural networks can outperform the enormous computation power of the computer, based on the Von Neumann computing paradigm. This is evidenced by the advances made in applying artificial neural networks for solving real world problems and engineering tasks.

Artificial neural networks (ANNs) are defined as a class of mathematical algorithms, since a network can be regarded essentially as a graphic notation for a large class of algorithms. Such algorithms produce solutions to a number of specific problems (Zurada, 1992). Another definition is that ANNs are synthetic networks that emulate the biological neural networks found in biological living organisms. An important feature of artificial neural networks is their new structure used for information processing. It allows these networks to solve real world problems for which an algorithmic approach does not necessarily exist. Algorithmic approaches are used by conventional computers to solve any given problem for which a solution is represented in the form of instructions that a computer needs to execute. Unless a solution is presented in the form of a specific set of instructions (steps), a computer cannot provide a solution. Without a specific set of steps (instructions) being known to the computer, it cannot compute. Artificial neural networks consist of a large number of neurons that are interconnected in a feed-forward or recurrent structure and perform parallel computations to solve a problem. These neurons (also called processing elements PE) are wired together using weighted connections which mimics the biological synapses in the nervous system. The network learns by examples through the adjustment of the connecting weights and generalises to other unknown data it might encounter.

This chapter provides an overview of classical artificial neural networks ANNs, their evolution, learning paradigms and their applications. Section 2.2 discusses the history of neural networks and presents the development of research in this field. Section 2.3 presents the mathematical neural models and their link to the real biological neurons that form the building unit of the nervous system. Section 2.4 discusses the existing neural architectures and a categorisation of learning paradigms is presented in Section 2.5. Section 2.6 presents and compares the existing learning rules. Section 2.7 discusses in detail the multilayer perceptron, backpropagation training algorithm and the importance of local minima when training such networks. Additional types of networks and training methods are presented in Section 2.8 where attractor networks, self-organising maps and radial basis functions are discussed. Section 2.9 discusses some applications of artificial neural networks in solving real world problems.

2.2 History of neural networks

The history of neural networks can be traced back to the year 1943, which is often considered the initial year in the development of artificial neural networks. It started with the work of McCulloch (a neurophysiologist) and Pitts (a mathematician) in which they studied the underlying mechanisms of neurons and used electrical circuits for modelling a simple neural network. Their devised model included all the necessary elements to perform logic operations, and therefore could function as an arithmetic logic-computing element. Other work was carried out by Donald Hebb in 1949, and presented in his book *'Organization of Behaviour'* (Hebb, 1949). He presented a description of a physiological learning rule for synaptic alteration for the first time. Hebb's book, particularly his formulation of the synaptic learning mechanism has been an inspiration for the development of computational models of learning and adaptive systems. His stated rule (will be discussed later in the section on unsupervised learning) has even been adapted with the most recently studied neural models which are believed to be more plausible in representing the biological neurons' behaviour. These models are called spiking neuron models and will be the focus of the next chapter.

During the 1950s, the first neuro-computers (Minsky, 1954) which adapted connections automatically were built and tested. In 1958, a new approach to the pattern recognition problem was introduced by Rosenblatt in his work on the *perceptron*, a novel method of supervised learning. It was a trainable machine capable of learning to classify certain patterns by modifying connections to the threshold elements (Rosenblatt, 1958). The idea caught the imagination of engineers and scientists and laid the groundwork for the basic machine learning algorithms that are still used today.

In the early 1960s, the ADALINE and MADALINE models were developed by Bernard Widrow and Marcian Hoff. They have also developed a new learning rule called the *Widrow-Hoff learning* (Widrow and Hoff, 1960). These models are based on Multiple ADAptive LINear Elements and were used to solve real world problems such as pattern recognition, weather forecasting, and adaptive controls. During the 1960s, it was believed that perceptron-based neural networks could do anything. But then came the book by Minsky and Papert (1969), who mathematically demonstrated that there are fundamental limits on the computing capabilities of single-layer pereceptrons. The stated limitations of the perceptron-class were made public and the challenge, however, was not answered until the mid-1980s. Meanwhile, the mainstream of research flowed towards other areas, and research activity in the neural network field, called at that time *cybernetics*, sharply decreased.

Back-propagation was first developed by Werbos in 1974, a supervised learning algorithm that made solving n-separable problems possible. However it went unnoticed at that time. It was later rediscovered by Parker in 1985, then by Rumelhart and McClelland in 1986 (Rumelhart and McClelland, 1986), who are now considered the inventors of the algorithm. Back-propagation is a supervised training algorithm which allowed the construction and training of percepetron-based multilayer networks. The alteration of connection weights is based on the current or actual output and a desired output given as a supervision signal. As suggested by the training algorithm name, the alteration of the weights is carried out backwards, starting from the output layer and working backwards towards the input layer. Associative memory research has been pursued by, among others, Tuevo Kohonen (Kohonen, 1977) and James A. Anderson (Anderson, 1977). Stephen Grossberg (1976, 1982, and 1988) and Gail Carpenter have introduced a number of neural architectures and developed the theory of adaptive resonance theory ART. In 1982, Hopfield (Hopfield, 1982) used an energy function to model the computation carried out by recurrent networks. Another important development in 1982 was the publication of Kohonen's paper on self-organising maps using a one- or two-dimensional lattice structure (Kohonen, 1982).

Today, neural networks discussions are occurring in several fields and hybrid systems using other Artificial Intelligence (AI) techniques are used to improve the performance of ANNs. For example artificial neural networks are combined with fuzzy logic in order to optimise the network performance and to embed or extract meaningful rules in their weights (Ishibuchi et al., 1993, 1995; Buckley and Ayashif, 1994; Zhenquan et al., 2002; Freisleben and Kunkelmann, 19993; Nauck, 1994; Arabshahi et al., 1992; Halgamuge et al., 1994; Xu et al., 1992; Kosko, 1991). The resulting fuzzy neural networks (FNNs) systems are used in different applications such controller design and pattern recognition (a section will be devoted to applications of neural networks). Also, genetic algorithms (GAs) have been used with artificial neural networks for optimising their weights (Grossberg, 1988; Fukuda and Ishigami, 1993; Gupta and Ding, 1994; Buckley et al., 1996; Yao,

1999; Leung et al., 2003). These references are only a selection of a very large body of research related to the combination of fuzzy logic and global optimisation techniques with artificial neural networks. The number of applications of such hybridisation is continuously increasing every year.

More recently, a new generation of artificial neural networks, called spiking neural networks (SNNs), has attracted the attention of researchers both in the field of neuroscience and computing (Abeles, 1991; Arbib, 1995; Mark et al., 1996; Maass, 1997; Gerstner, 2002). Due to their detailed models, spiking neurons are believed to better capture the dynamics of real biological neurons and will therefore offer more powerful computing paradigms when compared to classical abstract artificial neurons whose chronological evolution was reviewed above. While this chapter will only focus on classical ANNs, spiking neurons will be addressed in Chapter 3 where their differences with classical ANNs are highlighted, their models are simulated and analysed and their learning mechanisms are discussed.

2.3   Models of artificial neural networks

An artificial neuron is modelled as a computing unit with many inputs and one output. It is the information-processing element (PE) in an artificial neural network.

2.3.1   Neuron model

Three basic neuronal elements are identified:

• A set of weights, which characterise the strength of the synapse linking a neuron to another. Synaptic weight linking a neuron 'j' to a neuron 'i' is identified by w_{ij} (see Figure 2-1). A weight can take either a positive or a negative value, which represent the excitatory or the inhibitory effect of a synapse.

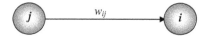

Figure 2-1 The connection strength between two neurons is represented by a real scalar number called weight and denoted by w_{ij}.

• An adder for summing the receiving neuron's inputs modulated by the respective connection weights.

• An activation function, which is applied on the input summation for limiting the amplitude of the neuron's output.

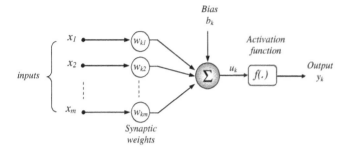

Figure 2-2 Abstract model of an artificial neuron. The inputs are modulated by the neuron synaptic weights, then summed up with an external bias. The total is then fed to an activation function whose output determines the neuron output.

A neuronal model is described in Figure 2-2 where an external bias is included. The bias b_k can affect the input value of the activation function, depending on its value being positive or negative. Mathematically, the neuronal model is described by the following equations:

$$u_k = \sum_{j=1}^{m} w_{kj} x_j$$ **Equation 2.1**

$$y_k = f(u_k + b_k)$$ **Equation 2.2**

where $x_1, x_2, ..., x_m$ represent the input features;

$w_{k1}, w_{k2}, ..., w_{km}$ are the synaptic weights of the neuron k;

u_k is the linear summation of the input features;

b_k is the bias;

$f(.)$ is the activation function which can take several forms; details of these functions will follow in later sections;

y_k is the neuron output.

By including the bias in the linear summation of the input features, the combination of the previous equations could be reformulated as follows:

$$v_k = \sum_{j=0}^{m} w_{kj} x_j, \text{ and } y_k = f(v_k)$$ **Equation 2.3**

In the previous equation a new synapse is added, its input is $x_0 = +1$ and its weight is $w_{k0} = b_k$.

In addition to these properties of individual neurons, a neural network is also characterised by global properties such as:

The network topology: The topology of the network is the pattern of connections between the individual neurons. Details of different topologies will follow in the followings.

The learning algorithm used: Learning is essential to these different neural topologies. It consists of adjusting the network connectivity so that a processing unit is capable of adapting its input/output behaviour depending on any possible changes in the surrounding environment.

The encoding scheme: This includes the interpretation placed on the data to the network and the results of its processing.

2.3.2 Types of activation functions

The behaviour of an artificial neural network is a result of its connection weights and the activation function used for its units. Several forms of activation functions could be considered: threshold function, linear function and sigmoid function, among others.

2.3.2.1 Threshold function

Also called step function or Heaviside function, it is defined with the following equations:

$$f(v) = \begin{cases} 1 & if\ v \geq 0 \\ 0 & if\ v < 0 \end{cases}$$
Equation 2.4

If a neuron k is considered, its output employing such a threshold function is given by:

$$f(v_k) = \begin{cases} 1 & if\ v_k \geq 0 \\ 0 & if\ v_k < 0 \end{cases}$$
Equation 2.5

where $v_k = \sum_{j=0}^{m} w_{kj} x_j$ as defined previously.

The graph of this function is shown in Figure 2-3.

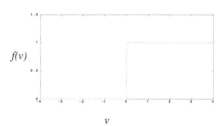

v

Figure 2-3 The shape of a Heaviside function. Positive inputs are mapped to the step value of '1'. Negative values are mapped to '0'.

Such a neuron is referred to in literature as McCulloch-Pitts (McCulloch and Pitts, 1943) model, in recognition of their pioneering work in 1943. The output of a neuron takes on a binary value (0 or 1) based on whether the linear summation of its inputs has a positive or a negative sign.

16

Another anti-symmetric function is referred to as the *signum function*. Its output ranges from (-1 to 1) instead of (0 to 1) which is sometimes desirable for some applications, the shape of this function is shown in Figure 2-4.

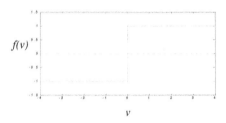

Figure 2-4 The shape of a signum function. Positive inputs are mapped to the step value of '1' while negative values are mapped to '-1'.

2.3.2.2 Piecewise-linear function

The output y_k is a non-linear function of the activation v_k, defined by:

$$f(v_k) = \begin{cases} 0 & v_k \leq -0.5 \\ v+0.5 & -0.5 < v_k < 0.5 \\ 1 & v_k \geq 0.5 \end{cases}$$

Equation 2.6

Thus, for this activation function described in Figure 2-5, the output y_k of the neuron is no longer a binary and can take values from 0 to 1.

Two situations can be considered as special cases of the piecewise-linear function:

- A linear combiner: if the linear region is maintained without running into saturation
- Threshold function: if the slope of the linear function is made infinitely large.

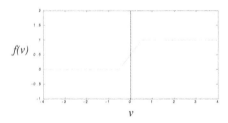

Figure 2-5 The shape of a piecewise-linear function. Input values between in the interval]-0.5, +0.5[are linearly mapped to their image values. outside this interval, values are mapped to either a value of '1' (positive inputs) or a nil value (negative inputs).

2.3.2.3 Sigmoid function

It has an s-shaped curve, and it is the most used activation function in the design of multilayer perceptrons (MLPs). It is a monotonically increasing function and offers a balance between linear and non-linear behaviour. It is defined by:

$f(v) = \dfrac{1}{1+e^{-av}}$, where '$a$' is a parameter that represents the slope of the sigmoid function.

Graphically the sigmoid function is illustrated in Figure 2-6 shown below.

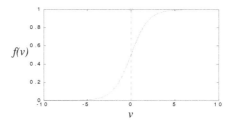

Figure 2-6 The shape of a sigmoid function. It can be see how all input values are non-linearly mapped to the interval [0,1]. Because of its effect on the input values, it is function is sometimes referred to as a 'squashing' function.

Different sigmoid functions are obtained when 'a' is varied as shown .Figure 2-7

Unlike the threshold function, the sigmoid function is differentiable, which present an important feature for learning algorithms, as detailed in subsequent sections.

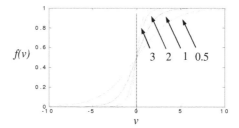

Figure 2-7 The variation of the parameter 'a' produces different sigmoid curves with different slopes (a varied 0.5, 1, 2, 3). The slope of the sigmoid becomes steeper as the value of the parameter 'a' is increased. A sigmoid function with a large value of 'a' will resemble a step function (Heaviside function).

2.4 Network architectures

A neural network can also be defined as an interconnection of neurons, such that neuron outputs are connected, through weights, to all other neurons including themselves; both lag-free and delay connections are allowed (Zurada, 1992). Generally, there is a link between the chosen network

18

architecture and the training/learning rule. As different structures are explained the associated learning rules are outlined in subsequent sections. This section focuses on network architectures (topologies), which are fundamentally identified in three different classes as follows:

2.4.1 Single layer feedforward networks

This class represents the simplest form of a layered network, in which neurons are organised in the form of layers.

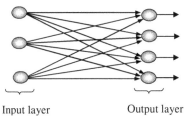

Input layer   Output layer

Figure 2-8 A single layer feedforward network. The input layer serves as a source of inputs which are modulated and fed to the neurons of the output layer.

A single layer feedforward network consists of an input layer of sources that feed an output layer of neurons (processing units). The name feedforward came from the fact that neuron interconnections are acyclic, i.e. input neurons are connected to output neurons, but not vice versa. Figure 2-8 illustrates a single layer feedforward network with three input neurons and four output neurons. The input layer of source neurons is not considered as a layer since there is no computation performed at this level.

2.4.2 Multilayer feedforward networks

This class consists of one or more hidden layers which propagate the neurons responses at the input layer forward to the network output layer. These hidden layers also help the network in extracting high order statistics from the input data (Haykin, 1999). In multiplayer feedforward networks, the input neurons supply input features to the first hidden layer whose outputs constitute the inputs to the second hidden layer and so forth. The outputs of the final (output) layer of the network represent the overall response of the network to the inputs fed by the input neurons of the input layer.

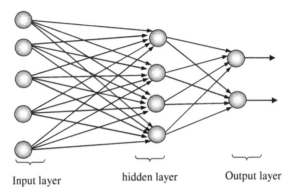

Input layer   hidden layer   Output layer

Figure 2-9 An example of a multilayer feedforward neural network with three layers, namely an input, hidden and output layer.

The structure of this topology is described in Figure 2-9 and the network is referred to as a 5x4x2 network since it has five neurons in the input layer, four neurons in the hidden layer and two neurons in the output layer. Thus this network contains 5*4 + 4*2=28 synaptic connections. The network is said to be *fully connected* if every neuron in each layer of the network is connected to all the neurons in the adjacent forward layer (Haykin, 1999). If some of connections are missing, the network is referred to as *partially connected*.

2.4.3 Recurrent networks

A recurrent network, also called feedback network, is a network which contains at least one feedback loop. A feedback network can be obtained from the feedforward network shown in Figure 2-8 by connecting the neurons' outputs to their inputs. The result is depicted in Figure 2-10 shown below. The essence of closing the feedback loop is to enable control of outputs, which has a strong effect on the learning capability of the network. The network structure depicted in Figure 2-10 below does not contain *self-feedback* loops, which refer to a situation where the output neuron is fed back to its own input. This structure does not contain hidden neurons as well. However, feedback loops involve the use of delay elements which are denoted by the symbol (Δ) in Figure 2-10 .

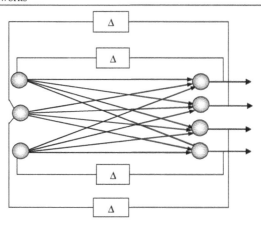

Figure 2-10 An example of a recurrent network with delay elements. The neurons outputs are re-entered to the input neurons with a certain delay denoted by (Δ).

2.5 Learning and adaptation

Learning and adaptation are crucial features of connectionist paradigms. The ability to learn from the surrounding environment and then adapt and generalise to new occurring events make neural networks a distinguished paradigm from the classical algorithmic approaches where a set of instructions is predefined. In general, learning is a relatively permanent change in behaviour brought about by experience (Zurada, 1992). Learning in human beings and animals is an inferred process; we cannot see it happening directly however we can assume that it has occurred by observing changes in performance. In the context of neural networks, a definition of learning, adapted from (Mendel and McLaren, 1982), has been given by (Haykin, 1999) which is quoted below:

"Learning is a process by which the free parameters of a neural network are adapted through a process of simulation by the environment in which the network is embedded. The type of learning is determined by the manner in which the parameter changes take place."

This definition implies that, for learning, a neural network needs to be embodied in an environment, and then it undergoes changes in its free parameters which allow its adaptation to this environment. The manner in which neural networks learn, i.e. its free parameters are changed, is called the *learning rule* or *learning algorithm*. A variety of learning rules have been used in the literature, each of which has advantages of its own and is suitable for specific learning tasks. In the following sections, different classes of learning are presented, and then several learning rules are presented in more details.

2.5.1 Supervised learning

In a supervised learning approach, the inputs and the outputs are provided to the network which then tries to associate a set of outputs to a set of inputs. The set of the presented input/output is referred to as a "training set". Therefore, the weights are adjusted such that the network responds to any input to generate the desired output or with an accepted accuracy or a small error. This process, illustrated in Figure 2-11, occurs repeatedly as the weights are continually altered. During the weight alteration process, the network is fed with the same data set till the network performance converges to a certain acceptable error. The network, however, may not converge when only few data are presented or if the qualities of input data are not specific enough to allow the network to derive the existing association between its inputs and outputs data and therefore will not learn the data statistical model.

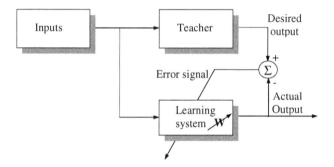

Figure 2-11 Illustration of the supervised learning. The system free parameters (denoted by W) are adjusted based on the teacher (supervision) signal.

Ideally, the network requires sufficient data to be split into two parts. A training part used for adjusting the network weight during the training process and another part, called the test set, which should be held separately in order to test the generalisation abilities of the network to new unseen data. The generalisation test determines whether the network has learned the data model efficiently or rather has memorised the presented data in a non-significant way. If the network fails to generalise, i.e it has failed to solve the problem, then it needs to be redesigned by reviewing several factors that could affect the network convergence/performance. These factors are:

- the activation function,
- the training method,

- the weight initialisation method,
- number of hidden layers and neurons in each layer,
- and the connections.

There are no rules available for creating a network that could successfully learn a particular data set. It is rather based on trial and error.

2.5.2 Unsupervised learning

As opposed to supervised training, no desired output is provided to the network (See illustration in Figure 2-12). Therefore no explicit error is calculated to determine the network performance. The network must self-adjust its weights in order to group (or cluster) the input data based on its features and thus learn the its global structure/distribution. This process is also referred to as self-organisation. An important network with self-organising capability has been created and developed by Tuevo Kohonen where data clusters are discovered through the unsupervised alteration of neuron weights which are arranged in simple structures such as grids, hexagonal structures, and other geometrical shapes (Kohonen, 1982, 1993, 1995, 1996). This network will be discussed in detail later in this chapter.

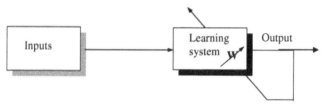

Figure 2-12 Illustration of the unsupervised learning paradigm. The tuning of the system free parameters (W) is based on the output values only.

2.5.3 Reinforcement learning

Reinforcement Learning is an interactive learning where the network weight alteration is based only on whether the network outputs are right and then they are rewarded or wrong and then punished, i.e. the network performance is refined through a process of trial and error. No specific outputs or actions are given to the network, it rather needs to interactively discover the actions that are most rewarded and avoid the ones that are not. The aim of reinforcement learning is to achieve a certain goal through the interaction with its environment. It differs from supervised learning where a defined set of examples is provided a priori by a supervisor. This type of learning is inadequate for problems where interactive learning is required, as it is not always feasible to provide correct examples of all correct actions an agent has to perform. It is important though to note that different and more detailed definitions of reinforcement learning can be found. Some of them classify reinforcement learning as another unsupervised learning simply because there is no desired output provided to the network. A definition by Haykin (Haykin, 1999) is quoted here:

"If an action taken by a learning system is followed by a satisfactory state of affairs, then the tendency of the system to produce that particular action is strengthened or reinforced. Otherwise, the tendency of the system to produce that action is weakened".

2.6 Neural networks learning rules

Based on the presence or absence of a teacher, two classes of learning paradigms can be found in the literature, namely supervised and unsupervised learning algorithms. The weights of the adaptive element, that is the neuron, are modifiable depending on the input signal it receives, its output value, and the associated teacher response. In some cases the teacher signal is not available and no error information can be used, thus the weights modification is based only on the input and/or output. This is the case of unsupervised learning as explained previously. The following sections describe the way in which the neurons' weights are adjusted with respect to each learning rule. The trained network is shown in Figure 2-13 where a vector w_i (weight vector) and its components w_{ij} connecting the jth input with the ith. It is clear that the jth input can be an output of another neuron or an external input.

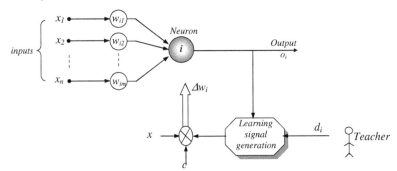

Figure 2-13 Illustration of the learning mechanism which consists of adding a small change to the neurons weights. In its general form, this change depends on the inputs, the current weight values and sometimes a teacher signal (when the learning is supervised).

In this section single neuron and single layer networks are covered. Multilayer feedforward networks and additional networks with their corresponding learning rules will be covered in section 2.7 and section 2.8. The following general learning rule is adopted in neural network studies:

The change Δw_i in the weight vector $w_i = [w_{i1} \ w_{i2} \dots w_{in}]^t$ is proportional to the product of input x and the output learning signal r. In general, the learning signal is a function of the vector weight, the input and sometimes of the teacher's signal.

From Figure 2-13 we have the learning signal r given by:

$$r = r(w_i, x, d),$$

Equation 2.7

Where x is the input vector and d is a desired output. The change in the weight vector according to the general learning rule at step k is given by:

$$\Delta w_i^k = c. \ r[w_i^k, x^k, d^k]. \ x^k,$$

where c is a positive scalar called *learning rate*. The resulting vector weight at the next step $(k+1)$ is

$$w_i^{(k+1)} = w_i^k + \Delta w_i^k$$

Equation 2.8

2.6.1 Hebbian learning

As mentioned in previous sections, the best known Hebb rule is the first learning rule presented by Donald Hebb in 1949 in his famous book '*The Organization of Behavior*'. Hebb verified that if one neuron repeatedly excited another, the communication between them was facilitated by repeated excitation, which means that repeated excitation lowered the threshold or, equivalently that the excitation effect of the first neuron was amplified. This rule implements the interpretation of the classic Hebb's statement (Hebb, 1949):

'*When an axon of cell A is near enough to excite a cell B and repeatedly or persistently takes part in firing it, some growth process or metabolic change takes place in one or both cells such that A's efficiency, as one of the cells firing B, is increased*'.

The Hebbian learning rule has been adopted as a supervised and unsupervised training algorithm. When used in an unsupervised way, the actual output is considered for weights changing. However the Hebbian principle can be combined with supervised learning by making the weights adjustment in this case depend on the desired output.

2.6.1.1 Unsupervised Hebbian learning

In the unsupervised rule, the neuron's output is considered as the learning signal as follows:

$$r = f(w_i^t x) = o_i \ ;$$

Equation 2.9

where f is the neuron's activation function.

The increment Δw_i of the weight vector becomes

$$\Delta w_i = c\, o_i\, x;$$

Equation 2.10

and the single weight is adapted using the following increment :

$$w_{ij} = c\, o_i\, x_j$$

Equation 2.11

2.6.1.2 Supervised Hebbian learning

The Hebbian rule principle is adapted to a supervised learning situation if the learning signal is replaced by the desired output instead of the actual output as follows:

The learning signal is $r = d_i$; the increment of the weight vector $\Delta w_i = c\, d_i\, x$; and the individual weight adjustment $\Delta w_{ij} = c\, d_i\, x_j$.

2.6.1.3 Anti-Hebbian learning

Another modification of the Hebbian learning rule is to modify the weight adjustment by including a minus sign as follows

$$\Delta w_i = -\, c\, o_i\, x; \quad \text{therefore} \quad \Delta w_{ij} = -\, c\, o_i\, x_j .$$

2.6.2 Perceptron learning rule

In late 1950s, Frank Rosenblatt introduced a network composed of units that were an enhanced version of McCulloch-Pitts Threshold Logic Unit (TLU) model. Rosenblatt's model of neuron, a *perceptron* (Rosenblatt, 1958), was the result of merger between two concepts from the 1940s, the McCulloch-Pitts model of an artificial neuron and the Hebbian learning rule of adjusting weights. The learning signal is simply the difference between the desired output and the actual or current one. Thus learning is supervised and the learning signal is equal to $r = d_i - o_i$; where $o_i = \text{sgn}(w_i^t\, x)$, which represent the threshold function and d_i is the desired output as described in Figure 2-14 shown below. The change in the vector weight is obtained as follows:

$$\Delta w_i = c[d_i - o_i]\, x.$$

Equation 2.12

Obviously, since the response is either +1 or −1, the weight increment reduces to $\Delta w_i = \pm 2cx$; where a plus sign is applicable when $d_i = 1$ and $\text{sgn}(w_i^t\, x) = -1$, and a minus sign is applicable when $d_i = -1$, and $\text{sgn}(w_i^t\, x) = 1$. No weight adjustment happens when $d_i = \text{sgn}(w_i^t\, x)$, that is, when the desired output and the actual response agree.

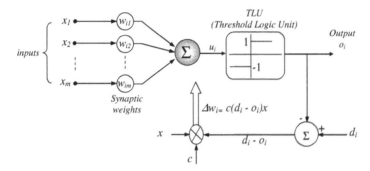

Figure 2-14 Illustration of the perceptron learning rule. The diagram shows the change in the weight vector and the signals involved.

2.6.3 Delta learning rule

A straightforward way to generalise the perceptron network is to replace its hard limiting (threshold) function with other continuous types of activation functions. The delta learning rule applies only to continuous activation functions and is used in a supervised mode. This rule was introduced by McClelland and Rumelhart (Rumelhart and McClelland, 1986). The delta rule is one of the most important training algorithms for continuous activation functions.

The learning signal (called *delta*) is defined by

$$r = [d_i - f(w_i^t x)] f'(w_i^t x) ;$$ Equation 2.13

where $f'(w_i^t x)$ represents the derivative of the activation function. The delta learning rule can be derived from the condition of least squared error between the actual and the desired output s, o_i and d_i, respectively defined by

$$E = \frac{1}{2} (d_i - o_i)^2$$ Equation 2.14

The gradient vector with respect to w_i is calculated and obtained as follows

$$\frac{dE}{dw_{ij}} = -(d_i - o_i) f'(w_i^t x) x$$ Equation 2.15

The minimisation of the error requires that the changes in the weights be in the direction of the negative gradient component, therefore:

$$\Delta w_{ij} = -c[-(d_i - o_i) f'(u_i) x] = c[(d_i - o_i) f'(u_i) x]$$ Equation 2.16

where u_i is the linear summation of the neuron's inputs.

2.6.4 Widrow-Hoff learning rule

The Widrow-Hoff learning rule, developed in (Widrow and Hoff, 1960), is classified as a supervised learning algorithm. It does not depend on the activation function as it minimises the squared error between a neuron activation value ($u_i=w_i^t x$) and its desired output, which represents a linear summation of the neuron inputs. In this case, the learning signal is defined by

$$r = d_i - w_i^t x;$$

Equation 2.17

and the weight vector adjustment under this rule is defined by

$$\Delta w_i = c\ [d_i - w_i^t x_i]\ x$$

Equation 2.18

This rule is considered as a special case of the delta learning rule explained in the previous section, where the activation function is replaced simply by the identity function $f(w_i^t x_i) = w_i^t x_i$ and therefore the derivative of the activation function is reduced to $f'(w_i^t x_i) = 1$. Thus the delta rule is reduced to Widrow-Hoff learning rule, which also is called LMS (least mean square) learning rule.

2.6.5 Winner-take-all learning rule

The winner-take all algorithm acts on the single neuron in a layer of neurons that responds most strongly. It is substantially different from the learning rules described previously as it represents an example of competitive learning. This learning is considered as an unsupervised algorithm in that the winner is determined by maximum activation test. The weight vector of the winner is rewarded by bringing its components closer to those of the input vector. The weight changes are restricted to the winner neuron as described in Figure 2-15 shown below.

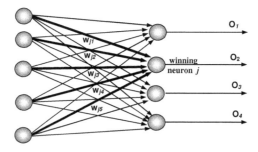

Figure 2-15 Illustration of the Widrow-Hoff competitive learning rule. Only the weights of the winning output neuron are adjusted in each iteration (in this example, the current iteration show that the output neuron O_2 is the winning neuron).

The vector weight increment of the winning neuron is given by $\Delta w_i = c[x - w_i]$. This rule corresponds to finding the weight vector that is closest to the input x since only the winning neuron fan-in weights are adjusted.

2.6.6 Outstar learning rule

This is another supervised learning rule that is better explained when neurons are arranged in a layer. It is used to produce a desired response d of the layer of p neurons as shown in Figure 2-16, (Grossberg, 1976, 1982, 1988; George and William, 1998). The rule is used to provide learning of repetitive and characteristic properties of input/output mapping relationships. This Grossberg outstar layer has been combined with a Kohonen network (a competitive network used by Tuevo Kohonen (Kohonen, 1996) and will be covered later in this chapter). The resulting network was called a *counter-propagation* network (CPN) and it was first used by Robert Hecht-Nielsen (Hecht-Nielsen, 1988).

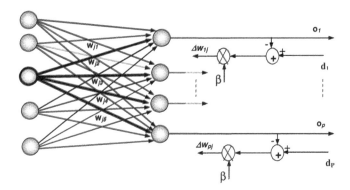

Figure 2-16 illustration of the Grossberg's outstar learning rule, a supervised learning where the fanning-out weights of a given neuron (indexed by j in the example shown here) are adjusted in order to map the output response to a certain desired vector $d = (d1,...,dp)$.

The weight adjustments in this rule are computed as follows

$$\Delta w_j = \beta [d - w_j],$$

Equation 2.19

or the individual weight adjustments are

$$\Delta w_{mj} = \beta [d_m - w_{mj}] , \text{ for } m = 1, 2, ..., p;$$

Equation 2.20

in contrast to any learning rule discussed so far, the adjusted weights are fanning out of the jth node and the weight vector in Figure 2-16 is defined accordingly as $w_j = [w_{1j} \; w_{2j} \; ... \; w_{pj}]^t$.

2.7 Multilayer perceptrons (MLP)

The Multilayer Perceptron (MLP) network is the most widely used neural classifier today; it has also been extensively analysed and for which many learning algorithms have been developed. An MLP network consists of a number of nonlinear neurons arranged into several layers. Typically it requires one or more hidden layers of processing nodes as illustrated in Figure 2-17. They have been demonstrated to be universal approximators, as they can approximate any given nonlinear function provided they have hidden neurons and sufficient training data. Their computational complexity depends on the number of layers and the number of neurons in each layer. Besides function approximation, they have also been applied in classification tasks. The use of hidden layers allows them to efficiently solve non-linearly separable problems. A simple example of this classification problem is the XOR function which is referred to as the *XOR problem*, which the single layer perceptron network has been proved unable to solve.

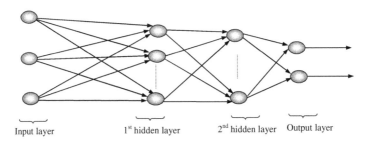

Input layer   1st hidden layer   2nd hidden layer   Output layer

Figure 2-17 The structure of a multilayer perceptron network (MLP) with two hidden layers. The input layer serves as a source of inputs and the network outputs are collected at the output layer.

The introduction of the multi-layer perceptron required a new training method adequate for such a multi-layer based architecture. The back-propagation algorithm was then developed to train different layer weights, based on the error at the output layer between the actual and desired output.

2.7.1 Backpropagation training algorithm

The Backpropagation Algorithm (BP), a supervised learning rule, offers a solution to the problem of MLP training. During this training, the responses of the output neurons are first calculated. Then, based on the error between the desired outputs and the actual outputs being calculated, the connection weights at the output layer are altered according to the gradient descent principle. In order to determine the weight increase/decrease for the hidden layers, the error calculated at the output layer is propagated backwards to the hidden layer whose weights are being changed. This weight alteration process is repeated each time a data sample is presented to the network. A cycle during which the whole training data set is fed to the network is referred to as an epoch. The following description of the Backpropagation algorithm is based on the descriptions in (Gurney, 1997; Duda et al., 2001; Zurada, 1992; Haykin, 1999). This description is related to the MLP illustrated in Figure 2-18, which consists of n neurons in the input layer, p neurons in the hidden layer, and m neurons in the output layer.

2.7.1.1 Hidden-to-output weights

When a pattern is presented to the input layer, an error is calculated between the desired output which is known a priori, d_k, and the actual or current output z_k . The SSE (sum squared error) is used to as the error function and is given by:

$$E(w) = \frac{1}{2}\sum_{k=1}^{m}(d_k - z_k)^2 = \frac{1}{2}\|d - z\|^2 \qquad \textbf{Equation 2.21}$$

where d and z are the target and the network output vectors of length c respectively;
w represents all the weights of the network. As stated before, the Backpropagation Algorithm is based on the gradient descent principle. The weights are randomly initialised, and then hanged in the negative direction of the error gradient in order to minimise the error function at the output layer. Thus the increment in the weight vector is

$$\Delta w = -\eta \frac{\partial E}{\partial w} \qquad \textbf{Equation 2.22}$$

or in terms of the individual weights

$$\Delta w_{jk} = -\eta \frac{\partial E}{\partial w_{jk}} \qquad \textbf{Equation 2.23}$$

where η is the learning rate, which indicates the relative magnitude of change in weights. The previous equations indicate that a step in the weight space is taken to lower the objective (error) function until the learning process converges to a final solution (network). The iterative changes in the network weights are described by this recurrent formula:

$$w(m+1) = w(m) + \Delta w(m) \qquad \textbf{Equation 2.24}$$

where m indexes the particular pattern presentation. Because the error function does not explicitly depend on w_{jk}, the chain rule is used for differentiation

31

$$\frac{\partial E}{\partial w_{kj}} = \frac{\partial E}{\partial net_k} \frac{\partial net_k}{\partial w_{kj}} = -\delta_k \frac{\partial net_k}{\partial w_{kj}}$$

Equation 2.25

where δ_k describes the variation of the overall error changes with the neuron's activation net_k. The neuron's activation function $f(.)$ is assumed to be differentiable, therefore:

$$\delta_k = -\frac{\partial E}{\partial net_k} = -\frac{\partial E}{\partial z_k} \frac{\partial z_k}{\partial net_k} = (d_k - z_k) f'(net_k)$$

Equation 2.26

and

$$\frac{\partial net_k}{\partial w_{kj}} = y_j .$$

Equation 2.27

Taken together, these equations express update in connection weights for the hidden-to-output layer weights as follows:

$$\Delta w_{kj} = \eta \delta_k y_j = \eta (d_k - z_k) f'(net_k) y_j$$

Equation 2.28

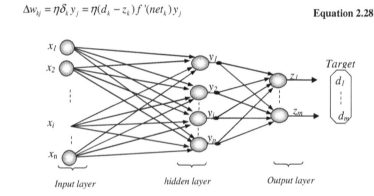

Figure 2-18 The backpropagation learning algorithm (BP).

2.7.1.2 Input-to-hidden weights

Using the chain rule again, the learning rule for the input-to-hidden neurons is calculated by

$$\frac{\partial E}{\partial w_{ji}} = \frac{\partial}{\partial w_{ji}} \left\{ \frac{1}{2} \sum_{k=1}^{m} (d_k - z_k)^2 \right\}, \quad \frac{\partial E}{\partial w_{ji}} = \frac{\partial E}{\partial y_j} \frac{\partial y_j}{\partial net_j} \frac{\partial net_j}{\partial w_{ji}} ;$$

and the hidden layer weight adjustment is given by

$$\Delta w_{ji} = \eta \left[\sum_k w_{kj} \delta_k \right] f'(net_j) x_i \text{ where } \delta_j \text{ is: } \delta_j = \left[\sum_k w_{kj} \delta_k \right] f'(net_j)$$

2.7.1.3 Learning protocols

In general, supervised learning consists in presenting the inputs in the training set whose corresponding outputs are known (desired outputs or targets), calculating the network output and then adjusting the weights such the actual output get closer to the desired target values. The ways in which the data samples are fed to the networks determine the learning protocol in which the network learns its environment. The most used protocols are: *stochastic, batch,* and *on-line*. In stochastic training, patterns are chosen randomly from the training set, and the network weights are adjusted for each pattern presentation. In batch training, all patterns are presented to the network before the learning takes place (Duda et al., 2001). In most cases, several passes through the training set are needed before the weights converge. In online training, each pattern is presented once and only once; there is no use of memory for storing patterns (Duda et al., 2001).

During the learning process, the word 'epoch' is used to refer to the cycle where the entire training data set is presented to the neural network. The backpropagation learning process is described by the first two protocols, that is, stochastic and batch protocols as shown in Figure 2-19 . The following symbols are used to describe the network parameters as follows:

w: network weights; θ: the stop criterion; η: learning rate; m: actual iteration; r: epoch; E: error; x^m: a given sample vector,

Stochastic protocol:
Initialise w, θ, η,
$m=0$;

do
$m=m+1$;
x^m=randomly chosen pattern
$w_{ji} = w_{ji} + \eta \delta_j x_i$;
$w_{kj} = w_{kj} + \eta \delta_k y_j$;

until E<=θ

return w;

Batch protocol:
Initialise w, θ, η, $m=0$; $r=0$;

do
r=r+1 ;//increment epoch
$m=0$;
$\Delta w_{ji}=0$; $\Delta w_{kj}=0$;

    do
    $m=m+1$;
    x^m=select pattern
    $\Delta w_{ji}= \Delta w_{ji} + \eta \delta_j x_i$;
    $\Delta w_{kj}= \Delta w_{kj} + \eta \delta_k y_j$;
    until m==n; // *n: size of training*
            // *set*.
$w_{ji}= w_{ji} +\Delta w_{ji}$;
$w_{kj}= w_{kj} + \Delta w_{kj}$;
until E<=θ
return w;

Figure 2-19 Two possible protocols for the application of backpropagation. (Left) stochastic protocol. (Right) batch protocol.

2.7.2 Importance of multiple minima

The goal of the Backpropagation rule is to find the set of weights for which the network error is at its minimum when different inputs are fed. The presence of local minima is one reason that the network is trained in a gradient descent-based iterative gradient descent way, since analytic methods are highly unlikely to find a single global minimum, especially in high dimensional weight spaces (Duda et al., 2001). In practice, the goal of the training algorithm is to avoid being stuck in a local minimum with a high training error, which indicate that the network has not learnt the key features of the problem. However, for many problems, convergence to a non-global minimum is acceptable, provided the error is fairly low. Furthermore, the commonly used stopping cause the training process to halted before the desired optimum is obtained, and therefore the convergence towards the global minimum is not necessarily required to obtain the desired network performance. Generally, the presence of multiple minima does not present difficulties in training networks, and a few simple heuristics can often overcome the problem of being trapped in such local minima.

2.7.3 Improving Backpropagation

The popularity of gradient descent is based more on its simplicity (it can be computed with multiplications and additions for weight change) than on its search power (Principe et al., 2000). Nevertheless, a naïve application of this learning rule can lead to very slow convergence or other unsatisfactory results such as getting stuck at a local minimum and therefore obtaining a bad configuration of the network (which implies poor performance of the network). Thus several techniques have been applied to improve the backpropagation algorithm performance with the aim to avoid being caught in local minima or to make the algorithm convergences faster. Some of these techniques explained in the following sections:

2.7.3.1 Learning rates

The learning rate should be kept small so that the convergence of training process can be ensured. When a small enough value is chosen, its magnitude can affect the network convergence speed. The final obtained weights are however not affected. In practice, it is found that a learning rate of $\eta=0.1$, is often adequate as a first choice (Duda et al., 2001). It should be decreased in case a divergence of the network error is observed during the training. The effect of learning rate is illustrated in Figure 2-20.

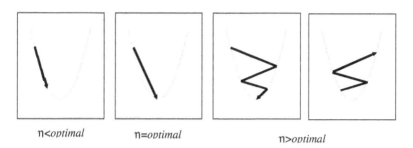

| η<optimal | η=optimal | η>optimal |

Figure 2-20 Effect of learning rate on back-propagation convergence. Small values guarantee the convergence of the algorithm to local optimum but at the cost of speed. On the other hand, big values might be useful at the start as they speed up the convergence process, but they result in oscillations around the local minimum later or to a divergence.

The optimal learning rate leads the algorithm to a one step convergence, and a very small learning rate lead to a very slow convergence. However a relatively big learning rate will lead the learning process to either an oscillation towards the minimum or to divergence, which is not desired.

2.7.3.2 Momentum

Momentum learning is an improvement to the gradient descent search in the sense that a memory term (the past increment to the weight) is used to speed up and stabilise convergence (Principe et al., 2000). The weight increment is then adjusted to include some fraction α of the previous weight update, therefore it becomes

$$w(m+1) = w(m) + (1-\alpha) \Delta w(m) + \alpha \Delta w(m-1);$$ **Equation 2.29**

where $\Delta w(m-1) = w(m) - w(m-1)$ is the past weight change.

The fraction α should not be negative, and for stability it must be less than 1.0. normally it should be set between 0.5 and 1.0. if $\alpha=0$, the algorithm is reduced to the standard backpropagation. This rule is called momentum learning due to the form of the last term, which resembles the momentum in mechanics. Thus the weights are changed *proportionally* to how much they were updated in the last iteration. Therefore, if the search is going down the hill and finds a flat region, the weights are still changed, *not because of the gradient*, but because of the rate of change in the weights. The effect of the momentum is illustrated in Figure 2-21 (left panel) where a ball representing the weight vector position is stuck in the shown valley when no momentum was used. In contrast, by

35

using the momentum term, the ball will continue past this local minimum as shown in Figure 2-21 (right panel).

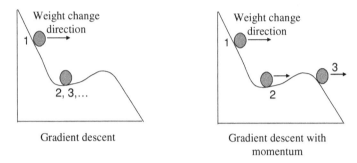

Gradient descent

Gradient descent with momentum

Figure 2-21 Learning with momentum. An enhanced version of the backpropagation algorithm where its speed and stabilisation are improved.

2.7.3.3 Hidden layers

The number of input and output neurons are simply determined by the dimensionality of the feature vectors and the number of classes/values a network is expected to find, respectively. However, the number of hidden neurons is not an obvious parameter to set out; if the patterns are easily separable then few hidden neurons can be sufficient to learn the problem. If the patterns are drawn from a more complicated distribution, however, more hidden neurons are needed.

There is no agreed method for finding the right number of hidden units. Most of the time, a rule of thumb is used, starting with fewer number, and then growing and pruning neurons appropriately. Another approach is combining genetic algorithms (Gas) or any other global optimisation techniques (e.g. Simulated annealing, Tabu search) for searching for the best number of hidden units and also to adjust the network weights. This technique has been used by several researchers using different encoding schemes and different mechanisms (Yao, 1999; Hintz and Spofford, 1990; Leung et al., 2003; Foster et al., 1999; Gonzalez, 1992).

2.8 Additional networks and training methods

2.8.1 Attractor networks or 'memories'

In an associative memory system, information that is stored through the weight distribution between different neurons can be recalled and accessed by content. Two types of associative memories are found and distinguished by the way they store information:

Autoassociative:

In which each object is stored and associated with itself. In order to train an associative memory network to store a certain object, the same object is presented to both the input and output layers. This type of associative memories is applied in handwritten characters recognition and cleaning. A very well known network of this class of associative memories is the so-called Hopfield network (Hopfield, 1982), which is also called an attractor network. These networks are used to recall patterns that fed into them, which make them useful to restore degraded objects.

Heteroassociative:

Where each stored object is associated with another different object, such as one object is presented at the input layer and another object is recalled at the output layer. The network weights are trained during the presentation of different patterns encoding each stored object and its corresponding 'cue' object.

2.8.2 Self-Organising Maps (SOM)

Self-organizing maps (SOMs) are used for data dimensionality reduction, data clustering and visualization. Devised by by Professor Teuvo Kohonen and based on self-organizing neural networks, they are used to reduce a high dimensional space into a low dimensional map usually represented by one or two dimensions. This mapping simplifies the visualisation of high dimensional data, a problem that humans find very difficult to solve. Therefore, SOM represent a powerful tool for understanding the distribution of high dimensional data. The attraction of SOMs is their ability to convert a complex, nonlinear statistical and high-dimensional data into a simple and low-dimensional display while preserving topological and metric relationships (Kohonen, 1995; Duda et al., 2001; Gurney, 1997).

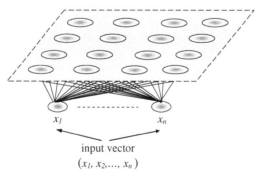

Figure 2-22 Kohonen Self-organising map (SOM). The neurons weights are tuned in an unsupervised way and the high-dimensional inputs can be visualised in a two dimensional map.

Two main tasks are performed by SOMs; dimensionality reduction and similarity visualisation. The basic structure of Kohonen SOMs is illustrated in Figure 2-22. The input units of SOM correspond in number to the dimension of the feature vectors and the output neurons act as prototypes. The neurons in an SOM are organised in a regular low-dimension grid, usually of 1- or 2-dimensionality, as shown in Figure 2-23 . Higher dimensionalities are allowed but their visualisation is problematic. Hexagonal and rectangular grids are the most used forms of neuron organisation.

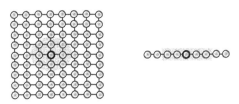

Figure 2-23 Example of map topologies with neighbour neurons around the best matching units highlighted, default 2D-grid (left hand side) and simple 1-D map (right hand side).

The learning in an SOM belongs to the competitive algorithms class, where the network aim is to find the best matching node through the interaction of all neuron nodes (Kohonen, 1995). The SOM training algorithm resembles vector quantisation (VQ) algorithms, such as k-means. The important distinction is that in addition to the best matching unit (BMU), also its topological neighbours on the map are updated, such that the region around the best matching node is changed towards the current presented training sample, as shown in Figure 2-24. At the end of training, the neurons on the grid become ordered, i.e. neighbouring neurons have similar weight vectors.

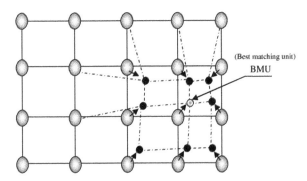

Figure 2-24 Updating of the BMU and its neighbouring units. The search for the best matching unit is a time consuming operation particularly if a large map is used.

The SOM is trained iteratively, such that at each training step t, a sample data vector x_i is chosen from the training set. Distances between x_i and all the prototype vectors are computed. The best-matching unit (BMU) denoted here by b_i, is the neuron with weight vector closest to x_i. It is important to note that searching for the best matching unit is the most time consuming operation in the training of self-organising maps.

$$bi = arg\,\min_{j}\left\{\left\|x_i - w_j(t)\right\|\right\}$$

Equation 2.30

Next, the prototype vectors are updated by moving them toward x_i, as illustrated in Figure 2-24. The update rule for the prototype vector j is:

$$w_j(t+1) = w_j(t) + \alpha(t) h_{b,j}(t)[x_i \quad w_j(t)]$$

Equation 2.31

where t is the training step index, $\alpha(t)$ is learning rate and h_{bi} is a neighbourhood kernel centred on the winner unit. The kernel gets its biggest value for the winner unit, and decreases monotonically with increasing distance on the map grid $d_j = \|r_{bi} - r_j\|$, calculated between the BMU or neuron b_i and neighbouring unit j. r_{bi} and r_j are positions of both neurons b_i and j on the map. The kernel can take different shapes, such as Gaussian, rectangular, circular ...etc, as shown in Figure 2-25. For a Gaussian shape, the kernel function is expressed as follows:

$$h_{b,j}(t) = e^{(-d_j^2/2\sigma^2(t))}$$

Equation 2.32

where $\sigma^2(t)$ is a neighbourhood radius. Both the learning rate and the kernel radius decrease monotonically during training, that is learning rate decreases to zero and the neighbouring radius to some suitable non zero value, typically one.

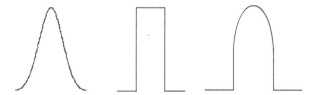

Figure 2-25 Different neighbourhood functions used for updating the weights of the BMU neighbouring neurons, from the left 'Gaussian' ,'Rectangular' and 'Cut-gauss'.

2.8.3 Radial basis function networks

Radial basis functions (RBF), introduction by Broomhead and Lowe (Broomhead and Lowe, 1988), have been widely used for nonlinear function approximation.

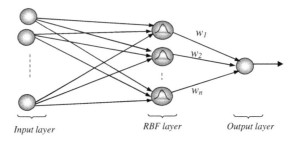

Figure 2-26 Radial basis function (RBF) network. The activation function of the hidden layer neurons is a radial basis function such as a Gaussian function.

The basic structure of RBFs (see Figure 2-26) is also feed-forward, but have only one hidden layer. Like MLPs, RBFs can also learn arbitrary mappings between multidimensional spaces. Each neuron in the RBF layer calculates the distance between its weight vector (a prototype vector) and the input vector from the input layer. The obtained distance is then fed to the activation function of the neurons of the RBF layer which is a radial basis function. The latter is a function whose response is characterised by a monotonic decrease (or increase) with the distance from its central point.

A typical radial basis function is the Gaussian function $e(-\frac{(x-c)^2}{r^2})$, where c is the centre and r is the radius) whose response decrease with distance from its centre (see

Figure 2-27 where it is depicted by a dotted line). Although the Gaussian function is widely used and the most popular as the activation function of the RBF neurons, other radial basis functions such as the inverse quadratic $(\frac{1}{1+(x-c)^2})$ (see

Figure 2-27 where it is depicted by a thick solid line) and the inverse multi-quadratic ($\frac{1}{\sqrt{r^2+(x-c)^2}}$) (see

Figure 2-27 where it is depicted by a thin solid line) are also of particular interest in the study of RBF networks. In a study by Rojas et al. (2000), the influence of using different radial basis functions on the behaviour the RBF network has been analysed. The outputs from the RBF layer are passed to the neurons in the output layer after being multiplied by different weights. The network outputs are simply a linear combination of the inputs to the output layer neurons.

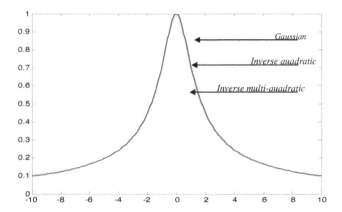

Figure 2-27 different types of radial basis functions can be used as the activation function of the hidden units in an RBF network. The dotted line represents a Gaussian with $r=3$ and $c=0$. The thick line represents the inverse quadratic with $c=0$ and the thin solid line represents the inverse multi-quadratic with $r=1$ and $c=0$.

The learning in RBF networks can be divided into two stages. First, the centres and the widths for the radial basis functions are determined by examining the training set where only the input data is used and no target data involved. Unsupervised methods such as the K-means clustering algorithm and the k-nearest neighbour algorithm are learning candidates for this stage. Then, the weights of the output layer are trained in the second stage. The determination of these weights requires the solution of a linear system which is relatively fast. The training of an RBF network is generally faster than the training of a comparable sized MLP.

2.8.4 Comparison between RBFs and MLPs

As discussed in the previous section, RBF networks offer another alternative for function approximation and solving classification problems with a training procedure that is faster than the backpropagation trained MLPs which have been discussed previously. This might create at a first instance confusion as to which type of networks one should use and why would anyone use MLPs since RBF network play similar roles and with the advantage of fast training. This section draws a detailed comparison between the two types and highlights the advantages and disadvantages of each model.

Similarities

In terms of architectures, both MLPs and RBF networks use a feedforward topology as no cycles exist in their connectivity. Also they are both considered as universal approximators and can be used in the approximation of non-linear functions, interpolation, classification and the approximation of non-linear mappings between multidimensional spaces. Moreover, both models share the same principle of mapping between the input and output data, they both use compositions of single variable functions to express the input-output mapping.

Differences

Although MLPs and RBFs share the similar feedforward architecture, their particular structure is very different. More than one hidden layer can be used in MLPs, which produce leads to an architecture with a complex pattern of connectivity. The structure of RBFs is, however, kept simple with only two layers. A radial basis function layer, which consists of the weights and centres of the basis functions, and an output layer which consists of linear combinations of the outputs of the hidden layer (i.e. the activation values of the radial basis functions). Apart from the number of layers allowed in each type of network, they also differ in term of the type units and the training procedures. These differences are listed below:

- The hidden units of MLPs use a sigmoid activation function that is applied to the linear summation of weighted inputs (i.e. the dot product between the input and the neuron weights). However, RBFs use a Gaussian activation function applied to the Euclidian distance between the neuron weights (i.e. a prototype vector) and the inputs.

- The difference in the hiddent units in MLPs and RBFs lead to different decision boundaries (or regions). While the MLP units produce a hyper-plane (or a line in a 2D space), RBFs produce a hyper-sphere (or a circle in a 2D space).

- The decision boundaries of the MLP hidden units cover an infinite area of the input space, in contrast the RBFs coverage is local (concept of receptive field) and is limited to a small area of the input space.

- Also as a result of the difference in the hidden layer units of both networks, the MLP network form a distributed representation of the input space because many hidden units contribute to the determination of the output. The training of the network adjusts the hidden layer weights such that the linear combinations of the functions they represent produce the desired outputs for a certain set of inputs. In contrast, RBFs form a local representation of the input space due to the limited receptive fields of the hidden units activation functions (i.e. the radial basis functions or Gaussians as they are used in most cases). For a given input, the use of radial basis functions as activation functions leads to only few hidden units having significant activation.

- In terms of the difference in the training algorithms, the weights of an MLP network are trained using local (such as a gradient descent-based) or a global optimisation technique (e.g. Genetic Algorithms) where the entire set of weights are adjusted together at the same time. This training uses both the input and the target data (i.e. class labels). On the other hand, RBFs are trained in two separate stages where the weights of the hidden layer are trained first using unsupervised methods and only the input data is employed (i.e. no need for target data), then the weights of the output layer are determined using fast linear supervised techniques.

2.8.5 RBFs or MLPs; which one to choose?

Based on comparison above and since both types of networks can be applied to solve the same problems, a question of which type of network to use then arises. It has been shown that MLPs and RBfs use different types of hidden units which results in two different decision boundaries with a difference in their coverage areas of the input space. These features can have advantageous or disadvantageous effects on generalisation capabilities of both networks. The appropriateness of either type of decision boundary depends on the distribution of the data set of the application at hand. Therefore, the choice of a particular network is application dependent.

In terms of training, the MLP gradient descent (backpropagation) proved to produce subtle adjustments of the weights for a desired association between a network inputs and outputs. However, since such supervised training aims to perform an optimisation of the entire weights of the network; this process is also known for its slow convergence and the risk of getting stuck in local minima. On the other hand, one of the main advantages of RBFs is their fast training procedure and the possibility of training the weights of the hidden layer separately (i.e. without the need to optimise the weights of the entire network). Moreover, once the parameters of the hidden layer (the number of radial basis neurons, their centres and weights) are determined, the training of the weights of the output layer is guaranteed (as it only requires the solution of a linear system, which is also fast). However, finding the optimal parameters of radial basis neurons is not a trivial task. The initialisation of the RBF layer is also crucial because the network performance depends on the chosen values. Therefore efficient strategies have to be developed for selecting the optimal parameters of the radial basis neurons. To conclude, RBFs and MLP make two complementary approaches for the solving similar types of problems. The choice between each network is application dependent and is closely linked to the distribution of the processed data.

2.9 Applications of neural networks

Neural networks have been successfully applied in many fields such as engineering, business, medicine, telecommunication and astronomy, among others. Their ability to identify data patterns, learn their statistical distribution model and their flexible adaptation to a given problem makes them suitable for solving a variety of real world problems. They have been used in many applications such as modelling, approximation, classification, prediction and pattern recognition. There is a very large body of research on the application of neural networks and the number of publications on this topic is still increasing every year. A thorough review of the applications of neural networks is only possible if each field is considered separately as a huge number of publications are found in each field. However, in this section only a small number of these works, selected from the main fields, are cited as examples. Artificial neural networks have been used in a variety of applications such as:

- Image processing where they have been used in feature extraction, object and face recognition, compression and hand-written recognition (Hsin-Chia et al., 2000; Chaker et al., 1999; Jander et al., 1996; Godfrey et al., 1992; Jamil et al., 2001; Meng et al., 2002; Lin et al., 1997; Er et al., 2002; Kumar and Manolakos, 1997; Nasrabadi and Li, 1991; Bebis et al., 1998; Pavlidis et al., 2000; Foresti and Pellegrino, 2004).

- Medicine is another field where ANNs have been extensively used for different purposes such as diagnosis and analysis of different types of signals and images (Rachid et al., 1997; Gurgen, 1999; Akayet al., 1994; Sun et al., 1996; Nakao and Yamamoto, 1999; Cho, 2000; Li et al., 2000; Rovithakis et al., 2001).

- Telecommunications (Wang et al., 1995; Shen et al., 2004; Mozer et al., 2000; Nordstrom et al., 1995; Khoshgoftaar et al., 1997).

- Human computer interaction (HCI) (Yasdi, 2000; Beale, 1992; Stacey et al., 1992; Pazzani and Bilsus,1997),

- Speech processing and music (Fels and Hinton, 1993; Dugast et al., 1994; Trentin and Gori, 2003; Hanes et al., 1994; Yonghong, 1999; Pengyu et al., 2002; Zahorian and Nossair, 1999; Phan et al., 2000; Tillmannet al., 2000; Barnardet al., 1991),

- Data mining (Kewley et al., 2000; Fu, 1999; Konig, 2000; Lu et al., 1996; Shin et al., 2000)

- Business and financial markets forecasting (Trippi and Efraim, 1996; Chen, 1994; Tsaih, 1999; Charalambous et al., 1999; Atiya et al., 1997; Min, 2002)

- Automatic control systems (Hunt et al., 1992; Chowdhury et al, 2001; Narendra and Parthasarathy, 1990; Su and McAvoy, 1997; Kim and Lewis, 2000; Ahmed, 2000; Chowdhury, 2000)

- Astronomy (Tagliaferri et al., 2003; Andreonet al., 2000; Baccigalupi et al., 2000; Bailer-Jones et al., 2001; Borda et al., 2002 ; Brescia et al., 1996 ; Fuentes, 2001 ; Gulati and Altamirano, 2001).

2.10   On biological plausibility of conventional artificial neural networks

The different neuronal models reviewed in previous sections are based on a high abstraction of real biological neurons used as the computing unit in the brain. These simplified models use real values to encode the neuron activity and completely ignore the action potential or spike generation process which represent an important mechanism that underlies the behaviour of real biological neurons, and the means by which real neurons communicate. Consequently, they give no importance to the use of spike timing as a key feature in performing computations and learning in the nervous system. Conventional artificial neural networks proved successful in solving engineering problems, yet they are far from either capturing the learning principles of real biological neurons or reaching the incredible computing power of the brain. It is believed, in neuroscience, that neurons' firing times play a key role in modelling the surrounding environment and performing with amazing speed and accuracy different perceptual tasks. It is only through the investigation of plausible and detailed neuronal models that we can gain an insight into the nervous system computing capabilities and further our understanding of how real neurons represent, communicate and process information through these instantaneous pulses called spike. The study, implementation and comparison of these detailed neuronal models and their associated learning rules are discussed in the following chapters.

2.11   Summary

This chapter reviewed artificial networks and the new computing paradigm they have presented which is radically different from the Van Neumann machine. Instead of pre-programming a solution as a set of instructions to be executed sequentially by a computer, artificial neural networks encode the programme in their connecting weights and the whole process is performed in parallel. Besides their simplicity, their ability to learn intrinsic trends in data with complex distribution and their generalisation to new unknown data, make them powerful tools for solving engineering problems where classical sequential computers have failed.

However, although these models are inspired from the way the brain computing elements or neurons are processing information, their simplified mathematical models are still far from being a plausible model that can capture the real mechanisms by which the brain operates. This suggests that existing abstract models are far from reaching the performance and the accuracy of the real biological neurons in carrying out different computational and perceptual tasks.

In the next chapter, an overview of a new generation of artificial neural networks is presented, namely spiking neural networks (SNNs). A number of different spiking neuron models are simulated and their dynamics are studied. These networks are believed to represent plausible models of the real biological neurons and therefore may better capture their computing power, which outperforms that of classical artificial networks, which have been presented in this chapter. The focus of this work is on investigating the learning and computing capabilities based on this generation of spiking neural networks.

CHAPTER 3

Spiking neural networks

3.1 Introduction

Inspired from the biological nervous system, artificial neural networks have been used extensively in many computer applications as detailed in the previous chapter. However, in these abstract rate-based computational networks, where continuous variables are propagated from one neuron to another, the focus is more directed towards solving the problems in an optimal way and less attention is given to the biological plausibility of the employed models. Biological neurons have been well studied over the course of the previous century and much has been discovered about the details of neuron cell membrane activity and potential generation (Gerstner, 2002; Rieke, 1996; Koch, 1999; Thorpe and Imbert, 1989). In addition, alternative encoding schemes have been suggested; hypothesising that information could also be encoded in the timing of neuronal spikes or in the synchronised activity of populations of neurons (Gerstner, 2002). Real biological neurons are much more complicated, having intrinsic dynamics, which transform the inputs received through dendrites into a sequence of action potentials (also called spikes or pulses) which are then propagated forward to other neurons through the neuron axon. This spiking nature of neurons has been known since the twenties of the 20th century when Adrian and Zotterman (Adrian, 1926a,b; Adrian and Zotterman, 1926a,b) realised that, instead of producing continuous analogue output which is employed by models discussed in Chapter 2, the response of biological neurons is rather the generation of one or more action potentials called spikes.

Recent research has focused on models which exhibit more plausibility to real biological neural systems and a new generation of artificial neural networks has emerged, where more attention is given to the mathematical modelling of biophysical dynamics and the computing mechanisms of real biological neurons (Gerstner, 2002; Gerstner, 1995; Maass, 1999; Maass, 1997; Stevens and Zador, 1995, 1998). Several neural models, with different levels of details, have been created. These models describe the inherent spiking feature of biological neurons and, when simplified, retain the essence of their dynamics (Gerstner, 1999; Izhikevich, 2001).

This chapter focuses on these models of biological neurons, the different alternative schemes they use for information encoding, their dynamics and computational properties. In section 3.2, a brief overview of the physiology of the real neural cell and its biological background is presented in order to help understand the components and behaviours of a biologically inspired neural model. Section 3.3 discusses the different generations of neural models where different levels of modelling abstractions have been used. The different levels of detail used in modelling of spiking neurons are discussed in section 3.4 and the advantages and drawbacks of choosing a level of abstraction are highlighted. This discussion is followed by the presentation of simulation results of the Hodgking-Huxley, integrate-and-fire and spike response model in section 3.5, while a summary of different postsynaptic potential (PSP) shapes and a comparison between different simulated models are presented in section 3.6 and section 3.7 respectively. The rate based coding schemes and their spike-based counterparts are discussed in section 3.8. Finally, learning and learning rules in biological neurons are presented in section 3.9.

3.2 Physiology of a biological neuron

3.2.1 Elements of a biological neuron

The human brain contains approximately 10^{10}-10^{11} neurons, where a neuron is the elementary information-processing unit in the brain. In Figure 3.1, a schematic drawing of a biological neuron is shown. A neuron is a particular cell composed of a soma with a cytoplasm and a nucleus like other cells. The neuron soma integrates the different signals, which come from other neurons via the dendrites that represent extensions of the soma. There is generally one axon for each neuron and it transmits the signals to the axonal terminals, which contains neurotransmitters. An axon starts at the axon hillock and usually branches into several arbours. At the tip of such an arbour there may be a synaptic terminal, which connects to the dendrite (or sometimes to the soma) of another neuron; these connections are called *synapses*. A neuron, which sends inputs to another neuron, is called a *presynaptic neuron* and the receiving neuron is called a *postsynaptic neuron*. The interior and exterior of a neuron is separated by the *cell membrane* (see Figure 3.1). Essentially the intracellular and extracellular space of a neuron are filled with liquids, which contain a variety of ions such as K^+, N_a^+, Ca_2^+ and Cl^-. The neuron membrane, characterised by a *conductance*, contains numerous ion channels, which are permeable to only one sort of ions. The difference in the concentrations of the ions between the interior and exterior of the neuron is called the *membrane potential*; for example the K^+ concentration outside the neuron is much lower than inside the neuron.

47

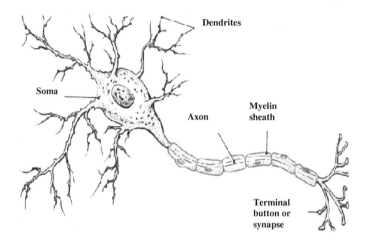

Figure 3-1 Physiology of a biological neuron. A neuron sends its spikes to other interconnected neurons (postsynaptic neurons) through its axon. The connection is made at a site called the synapse. (Carlson, 1992)

3.2.2 The action potential

Neurons function essentially on an electro-chemical basis, if there are no inputs impinging onto the neuron the membrane is at its resting potential. If the input to a cell drives the membrane potential above a certain *threshold* an *action potential* (other names are also used by neuroscientists such as *spike, neuron pulse*), a short voltage pulse of 1-2 ms duration and an amplitude of about 100 mV, is initiated (Gerstner, 2002). The generation of action potential is caused by an exchange of ions across the neuron membrane (depolarisation of the membrane potential). Such spikes are the main means of communication between neurons.

The firing of a neuron is an all or none process, i.e., the total received stimulation will either drive the neuron to fire when it exceeds a certain threshold or the neuron stays at the sub-threshold level and no spike is produced. Once a neuron fires, it enters a refractory period when it becomes less sensitive to new incoming stimulations and no further spikes can be produced. Even with very strong input, another impulse cannot be generated (because it is already in the state of having been generated). This time interval is referred to as the *absolute refractory period* which is followed by a *relative refractory period* where the generation of a new spikes is difficult, but still possible, as a strong depolarisation of the membrane potential is necessary during this period for the generation of a spike (Kandel and Jessell, 2000; Gerstner, 2002). The closer in time to the absolute refractory period, the stronger the stimulus must be (see Figure 3.2).

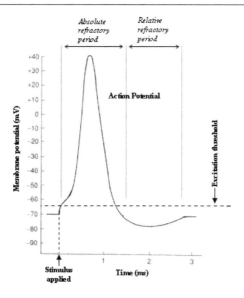

Figure 3-2 Action potential and refractoriness (resting potential at -70mV and excitation threshold at -65mV). Absolute refractory period: during this period, a second spike <u>absolutely</u> cannot be initiated. Relative refractory period: action potentials are more difficult to initiate during this period <u>relative</u> to resting potential. Figure of the spike taken from (Carlson, 1992) and annotated for illustration.

A spike is propagated down the axon and reaches a large number of synaptic terminals. At a synapse the spike is converted into a change in the membrane potential of the successor neuron, which is called a *postsynaptic potential* (PSP). A PSP, which increases the membrane potential is called an *excitatory postsynaptic potential* (EPSP) and an *inhibitory postsynaptic potential* (IPSP) if on the other hand the membrane potential decreases in response to a spike. Figure 3.3 shows a graph describing the time course of a PSP. The amplitude of a PSP depends on the efficacy of the synapse and may change over time.

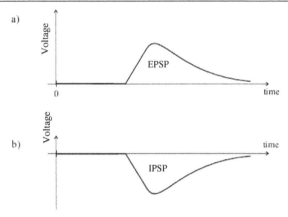

Figure 3-3 Postsynaptic potential (PSP). (a) Excitatory postsynaptic potential (EPSP) versus (b) Inhibitory postsynaptic potential (IPSP).

Most synapses are located at the dendrites of a cell and a spike is initiated and propagated through the axon hillock. It is important to understand how the PSPs generated at different synapses interact in space and time. One important fact is that PSPs do not sum linearly: the amplitude of the resulting membrane potential is lower than the sum of the individual PSPs. However, if the spatial distance between two synapses is increased this nonlinearity becomes less pronounced (Bower and Beeman, 1995). A model in which the PSPs are summed linearly is called the *integrate-and-fire neuron* (IFN). Another extension of the IFN model is considered where the membrane is assumed to be leaky due to ion channels, such that after a PSP the membrane potential approaches again the resting potential. Such a neuron is called a *leaky integrate and fire* neuron (LIFN). These two models and others are discussed and simulated in the following sections.

3.2.3 The synapse: connecting neurons

The *synapse* is the connecting site between a presynaptic neuron axon and the postsynaptic neurons. Two neurons can be connected at either the soma or the dendrite of the postsynaptic neuron. The synapse is responsible for signal transmission between interconnected neurons. Two types of synapses may connect two neurons, chemical synapses and electrical synapses also called gap junctions. The most common type of synapse in the vertebrate brain is a chemical synapse (Shepherd and Koch, 1990). Synapses are very complex components that can keep track of their history of usage over considerable time scales. "When an action potential reaches a synapse, it triggers a complex set of biochemical processes which lead to a release of neurotransmitters from the presynaptic terminal into the synaptic gap" (Gerstner, 2002)., called the *synaptic cleft* (see

Figure 3-3) . The presynaptic terminal contains several spheres (30-40 nm in diameter) called *vesicles*, which contain the *neurotransmitters*, which play a key role in signal transmission between neurons.

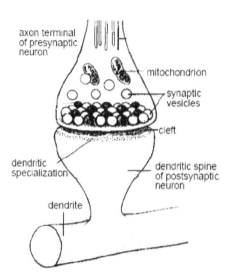

Figure 3-4 Chemical synapse. The site where the axon of a presynaptic neuron connects to the dendrite or the soma of another postsynaptic neuron. The generation of action potentials at the postsynaptic neuron is the result of neurotransmitter release at the synaptic cleft and ion flow. Synapse picture adapted from (Dayan and Abbott, 2001).

3.2.4 Synaptic strength

What is exactly meant by synaptic strength? As has been shown in the previous chapter, neural networks of the first and second generation utilise a single scalar called a weight to represent synaptic strength, usually labelled w_{ji} to indicate the synaptic efficacy between neuron i and neuron j. However, the coupling strength between two neurons is described in terms several parameters, such as the number of release sites and the probability of neurotransmitters release of a vesicle following a presynaptic spike. In real synapses, the synaptic strength is not a simple scalar, but a variable entity that changes upon the arrival of spike trains. Hence, the synaptic strength is a dynamic entity. The properties of dynamic synapses (i.e. the synaptic strength is considered as a dynamic entity that varies upon the arrival of spike trains, as opposed to a static synapses where the synaptic strength is a static value or a weight represented by simple scalar) and their transmission mechanisms will be the focus of Chapter 6, where experiments on computing and training of dynamic synapse-based networks are presented.

3.3 Three generations of neural networks

Artificial neural networks have been classified into three different generations as described by Maass (1997). The first generation is based on McCulloch-Pitts neurons as computational units, also called TLUs or threshold gates units. The feature, which characterise this generation is that these networks give only digital outputs, and they can compute any Boolean function. Typical examples for networks of this generation are Hopfield and Boltzmann machines.

The second generation is based on neurons that apply an activation function with a continuous set of possible outputs to a linear combination of the inputs. Most used activations are the sigmoid and piecewise-linear function. Sample networks from this generation are multilayer feedforward neural networks (MLPs), recurrent sigmoidal networks, and radial basis functions (RBFs). These networks have been proved to be universal approximators as any continuous function with a compact domain and range can be approximated to an arbitrarily desired accuracy. Besides, the networks of this generation support learning algorithms that are based on the gradient descent such as the famous backpropagation algorithm. The neural models of the first and second generation of artificial neural networks and the learning paradigms applied with different architectures have been the focus of Chapter 1 of this book.

In this second generation, the output of a neuron is biologically interpreted as a representation of the current firing rate of biological neurons. Since biological neurons are known to fire at various frequencies, the neurons in this generation are more plausible than the neurons in the first generation, which consider only the firing or not of a neuron. However, the firing rate, as a means of information encoding, has become questionable, as it will be shown in the next sections by the different models of spiking neurons. The third generation is based on these spiking neurons, which are now considered as more plausible models than the previous two generations. In particular they describe much better the actual output of a biological neuron and thus allow an investigation of the possibilities of using *time*, which has been deemphasised in the previous generations, as a resource of computation and communication.

3.4 Modelling neurons at different levels of abstraction

In neuroscience, two major trends have been followed in modelling biological neurons depending on the level of detail taken into account. On one hand, detailed neural models, where neurons are studied at the low level (cell and synapse level), are considered in order to gain a thorough understanding of the functioning principles of biological neurons, and consequently the computing capabilities of the brain. Using this level of abstraction, however, is time consuming and would limit the feasibility of simulating and training large scale spiking networks as more resources would be needed. On the other hand, less detailed neurons (higher abstraction), where the complex neural models are simplified yet capturing the essential neural behaviours, are considered in order to facilitate the study of computational and adaptation principles of neuron populations while reducing the computational complexity of more detailed models.

3.4.1 Detailed neural models

It is argued by neurobiologists that it is essential to take into account anatomical details of biological neurons as it allows a full understanding of the neural properties and the nervous system (Arbib'87; Bower and Beeman, 1998). These models describe the chemical processes occurring at the sub-cellular and synaptic level, including the mechanisms of ionic exchanges and biophysics of dendrites, the neurotransmitter transmissions at excitatory and inhibitory synapses, and the voltage/current-dependent processes (Destexhe et al., 1998; Mainen and Sejnowski, 1998). The model created by Hodgkin and Huxley (1952) represents a clear example of a detailed modelling of the neuron biophysical dynamics involved in the process of spike production and offers a quantitatively accurate modelling of the physiological data obtained from experiments on the giant squid axon. This model is simulated using Matlab and tested with different input amplitudes in the following sections. Despite the low level quantitative accuracy offered by this model, the construction and analysis of networks of such neurons is rather difficult. Their computational complexity, due to the need to numerically solve a large number of differential equations, can however make it difficult to understand the relevant features responsible for a particular phenomenon (Koch and Segev, 1998).

3.4.2 Compartmental models: more detailed models

The detailed models discussed in the previous section are called point neurons (Gerstner, 2000), i.e., they do not take into account the spatial structure of a real neuron. However, the morphology and electrical properties of dendritic trees, described by compartmental models (Gerstner, 2000), have an important influence on the nonlinearity of neurons (Mel, 1994; Vetter et al., 2001). Each compartment is represented by a capacitor/resistor based circuit and modelled using a system of ordinary differential equations, which represent somatic, dendritic or axonal membranes and contain a variety of synaptic inputs (Segev and Burke, 1998). These compartmental models are implemented by powerful, biologically realistic simulators, such as Genesis (Bower and Beeman, 1998) and Neuron (Hines, 1993, 1998; Hines and Carnevale, 2000). Yet, network simulations based on compartmental models are computationally intensive, both in terms of computation time and memory usage, due to their complexity. Also, they have the following drawbacks (Gerstner, 2002):
- They are not easily tractable.

- They do not scale up.

- They offer a quantitative description of the neural behaviour, thus they can restrict a full understanding of the important computation features of the nervous system.

However, despite their computational complexity, they are better suited for the investigation of the dynamics of single neural cells or small scale networks.

3.4.3 Phenomenological models: less detailed neuron models

In order to overcome the computational complexity of detailed models and facilitate the construction and analysis of the activity of neural systems (Koch and Segev, 1998; Koch, 1999), the second trend of research efforts in neuroscience focused on the spiking phenomenon of biological neurons. Within this framework, the neuron essential behaviour is retained while trying to simplify the underlying mathematical description, hence reducing their computational complexity (Gerstner, 1995; Gerstner, 2000; Gerstner and Kistler, 2002; Maass, 1995, 1997, 1999; Rieke et al., 1996).

In these (less detailed) models, the neural spatial structure, i.e dentritic trees, has been simplified (Gerstner and Kistler, 2002). Also, the number of variables (whose dynamics are expressed by differential equations) describing the behaviour of biological neurons has been reduced. For example, the four dimensional Hodgkin and Huxley model is reduced to a two dimensional model such as FitzhughNagumo (FitzHugh, 1961; Nagumo et al., 1962), Morris-Lecar (Morris and Lecar, 1981) and Izhikevich (2001) model, or to a single dimensional model such as the Integrate-and-fire model and spike response model (SRM) (Gerstner and Kistler, 2002). In the integrate-and-fire model, the spike generation process is approximated by a threshold process. Matlab simulations of Integrate-and-fire have been carried out and the resulting responses to different input forms and different frequencies are presented in the following sections. The spike response model (SRM) has also been simulated and studied in this chapter, and has been used in this work as processing elements for the feed-forward spiking network simulations which will be presented in Chapter 5, where an evolutionary strategy (ES) based supervised training algorithm has been devised and successfully tested on a pattern classification task using different benchmark data sets. While the aim of this section was to summarise the main trends in neural modelling, their advantages and drawbacks, the following sections presents a more detailed description of these models, their Matlab simulations, their behaviour and their responses to different inputs.

3.5 Matlab simulations of spiking neuron models

3.5.1 Hodgkin-Huxley neuron model

In 1952, A.L. Hodgkin and A.F. Huxley (1952) published a landmark work where they studied the electrical stimulus flow through the neuron membrane of the giant squid. They have developed a mathematical model that describes the underlying behaviour of the neuron membrane potential by modelling the different ionic channels of the cell membrane. The model was named after these two researchers and it became the basis for describing other ionic current models of excitable tissues (Feng et al., 2001b). In the squid giant axon, the membrane potential V is determined besides its passive ion channels, which result in a voltage-independent leak conductance g_l, by active K^+ and Na^+ channels. These channels have voltage-dependent conductance g_K and g_{Na}.

Hodgkin and Huxley conceived an equivalent electrical circuit diagram to represent the different ionic current flows in the mathematical model they developed, see Figure 3-5. The current is mathematically modelled by a summation of currents flowing through the capacitor and resistors.

$$I_m = C_m \, dV/dt \; + \; I_{Na} \; + \; I_{leak} + I_k \hspace{3cm} \textbf{Equation 3-1}$$

This global model is described in detail in the following:

The capacitor current $I_C = C_m \, dV/dt$ is expressed using the Ohm's law, where C_m and V represent the neuron membrane capacitor potential, respectively.

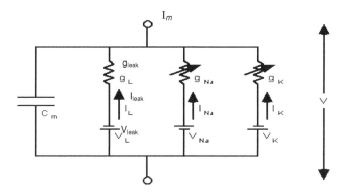

Figure 3-5 Equivalent circuit representing the Hodgkin-Huxley model. A capacitor and variable conductance elements are used to represent the ionic channels and the potential across the neuron membrane.

The conducatnces representing the reciprocals of the resistances are denoted by (g_{leak}, g_{Na}, g_K), and the currents depend on both the membrane potential and the ionic reversal potentials denoted by (V_{leak}, V_{Na}, V_K). The influx at the ionic channels is driven by the electrical variation resulting form the ionic concentration difference on both sides of the neuron cell membrane. The general equation defining an ionic current I_{ion} with a reversal potential V_{ion} and an ionic conductance g_{ion} is given by:

$$I_{ion} = g_{ion} (V - V_{ion}) \hspace{3cm} \textbf{Equation 3-2}$$

Three ionic currents (V_{leak}, V_{Na}, V_K) are shown in Figure 3-5 and are defined by:

$$I_{leak} = (V - V_{leak}) g_{leak} \qquad\qquad \textbf{Equation 3-3}$$

$$I_{Na} = (V - V_{Na}) g_{Na} \qquad\qquad \textbf{Equation 3-4}$$

$$I_K = (V - V_K) g_K \qquad\qquad \textbf{Equation 3-5}$$

where I_{leak} is for leakage current, and I_{Na} represents sodium channel current and I_K the potassium channel current. The conductance of the sodium (g_{Na}) and the potassium g_K are time varying quantities while other ionic conductances are considered constant. When the neuron membrane is depolarised, an increase in both the sodium and potassium conductance is observed. The first increase is fast and transient while the latter is gradual and sustained. The ionic time varying conductance g_{ion} is expressed in terms of the probability of the channel being opened (x) and its maximum conductance value ($g_{ion,max}$).

$$g_{ion} = g_{ion,max} \cdot x \qquad\qquad \textbf{Equation 3-6}$$

where x is represented by the following the differential equation :

$$\frac{dx}{dt} = \alpha_x(1-x) - \beta_x x \qquad\qquad \textbf{Equation 3-7}$$

α_x and β_x are non-linear functions of voltage with units of $time^{-1}$. If in one ion channel, several gates are found, its activation coefficient can then be raised to the power of the number of these gates. The ionic current is given by following equation:

$$I_{ion} = g_{ion,max} \cdot x.y.(V - V_{ion}) \qquad\qquad \textbf{Equation 3-8}$$

where x and y are the activation/ inactivation variables respectively. It has been observed that the activation rate coefficient is faster than inactivation coefficient rate. This rate difference applies, for example, to the fast sodium channel whose ion influx causes a depolarisation of the neuron membrane and possibly the production of an action.

3.5.1.1 Sodium conductance

The sodium channel conductance is governed by $g_{Na} = \bar{g}_{Na} m^3 h$ where m and h represent the activation and inactivation coefficients, while $\bar{g}_{Na}$ represents the channel maximum conductance whose dynamics are described by the following first order differential equations:

$$\frac{dm}{dt} = \alpha_m (1-m) - \beta_m m \qquad\qquad \text{Equation 3-9}$$

$$\frac{dh}{dt} = \alpha_h (1-h) - \beta_h h \qquad\qquad \text{Equation 3-10}$$

where α and β denote the rate constants which are voltage dependent. These are denoted by:

$$\alpha_m = 0.1 \frac{v+25}{e^{(\frac{v+25}{10})} - 1}, \qquad \beta_m = 4e^{(\frac{v}{18})}, \qquad \alpha_h = 0.07e^{(\frac{v}{20})}, \qquad \beta_h = \frac{1}{1 + e^{(\frac{v+30}{10})}}$$

The following equation denotes current flowing through the sodium channel

$$\begin{aligned} I_{Na} &= (V - V_{Na}) g_{Na} \qquad\qquad \text{Equation 3-11} \\ &= (V - V_{Na}) \bar{g}_{Na} m^3 h \end{aligned}$$

where V_{Na} represent the sodium channel reversal potential.

3.5.1.2 Potassium conductance

Only activation type channels are used to model the potassium channel. Its conductance is given by $g_K = \bar{g}_K n^4$ where $\bar{g}_K$ represent the maximum conductance and n is the activation coefficient for the K^+ and is given by

$$\frac{dn}{dt} = \alpha_n (1-n) - \beta_n n \qquad\qquad \text{Equation 3-12}$$

where α_n and β_n are the rate constants which are functions of the membrane voltage and are given by:

$$\alpha_n = 0.01 \frac{v+10}{e^{(\frac{v+10}{10})} - 1}, \qquad \beta_n = 0.125 e^{(\frac{v}{80})}$$

Therefore the resulting potassium channel current is given by the following expression:

$I_K = (V - V_K) \; g_K = (V - V_K) \; \overline{g}_K n^4$; where V_K is the potassium channel reversal voltage.

3.5.1.3 Leakage current

In the absence of any stimulus increasing the depolarisation of the neuron cell , the membrane potential is reset to its resting potential; the Hodgkin-Huxley model includes a leakage current to meet this neuron feature.

$$I_{leak} = (V - V_{leak}) g_{leak}$$

Equation 3-13

where V_{leak} is the leakage current reversal voltage.

3.5.1.4 Putting it all together

The global and detailed equations for the different ion channel conductance are combined into the membrane potential dynamics as according to the the Hodgkin-Huxley model. This combination is illustrated in Figure 3-6.

$$I_m = C_m \; dV \, / \, dt + I_{Na} + I_{leak}$$
$$= C_m \; dV \, / \, dt + (V - V_{Na}) \; g_{Na} + (V - V_K) \; g_K + (V - V_{leak}) g_{leak}$$

Equation 3-14

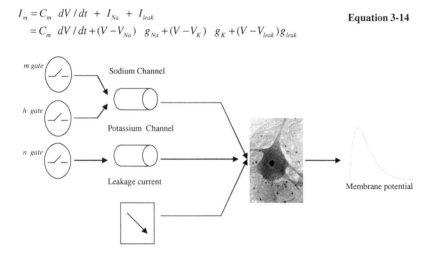

Figure 3-6 Schema of different ionic channels that drive the membrane potential in HH model. This illustrates the models equations when put together.

By replacing g_{Na} and g_K in Euqation 3-14, I_m becomes :

$$I_m = C_m \; dV \, / \, dt + (V - V_{Na}) \; \overline{g}_{Na} m^3 h + (V - V_K) \overline{g}_K n^4 + (V - V_{leak}) g_{leak}$$

Equation 3-15

With:

$$\frac{dm}{dt} = \alpha_m(1-m) - \beta_m m \; ; \; \frac{dh}{dt} = \alpha_h(1-h) - \beta_h h \; ; \; \frac{dn}{dt} = \alpha_n(1-n) - \beta_n n \; ;$$

and

$$\alpha_m = 0.1\frac{v+25}{e^{(\frac{v+25}{10})}-1} \; ; \; \beta_m = 4e^{(\frac{v}{18})} \; ; \; \alpha_h = 0.07e^{(\frac{v}{20})} \; ; \; \beta_h = \frac{1}{1+e^{(\frac{v+30}{10})}} \; ; \alpha_n = 0.01\frac{v+10}{e^{(\frac{v+10}{10})}-1},$$

$$\beta_n = 0.125e^{(\frac{v}{80})}$$

The table below (Table 3.1) summarises the values used with different variables of the Hodgkin-Husxley model (Gerstner and Kistler, 2002; Hodgkin and Huxley, 1952).

Constant	Units	Value
C_m	$\mu F/cm^2$	1.0
V_{Rest}	mV	-75.0
V_{Na}	mV	V_{Rest} + 115.0
V_K	mV	V_{Rest} - 12.0
V_L	mV	V_{Rest}+ 10.613
$g_{Na,max}$	ms/ cm^2	120.0
$g_{K,max}$	ms/ cm^2	36.0
g_L	ms/ cm^2	0.3

Table 3.1. Standard membrane parameter values for the Hodgkin-Huxley model of a nerve cell, obtained from fitting the data from experimental work on the giant squid axon.

Hence the computation of membrane voltage V requires numerical integration of its underlying the differential equations. In addition the current conductances have to be computed, which makes the simulation of a Hodgkin-Huxley model computationally consuming. In this work, the Euler method was employed and differential equations are replaced by difference equations, which are solved in discrete time intervals or time steps. The MATLAB tool was used to carry out the simulations because of its simplicity and its usefulness for rapid prototyping and particularly its powerful visualisation capabilities. More accuracy can be achieved by choosing a smaller time interval, but at the cost of intensive computations. Hence a proper choice of the time step is crucial in simulating the membrane potential dynamics. Figure 3-7 shows the firing of an action potential when the neuron is stimulated with a strong input (see Figure 3-7-(b)), however no spike is fired when a weak stimulus is applied (Figure 3-7-(a) or Figure 3-7-(c)). It is clear from the Figure 3-7-(b) that the spike generation process is inherent in the model dynamics and the so is the action potential shape.

Unlike the Hodgkin-Huxley model, in the following simplified models or so-called integrate and fire models (such as leaky integrate and fire (LIAF) and spike response model (SRM)), the spike generation is explicitly incorporated in the model through a thresholding process, and the action potential or spike is produced 'manually'. That is, it is inherent in the neuron model. That is why sometimes they are '*preferably*' called by some researchers (Izhikevich, 2000, 2001) 'integrate and fire' neuron models instead of 'spiking models'.

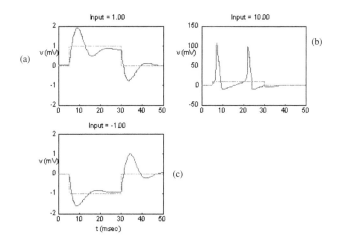

Figure 3-7 Response of a Hodgkin-Huxley model based neuron to different constant stimuli amplitudes for a period of 25ms. The stimulus is applied at time (5ms) and held for a period of 25 ms. The x-axis represents time (*ms*) and the y-axis represents membrane potential (*mV*)

3.5.2 Integrate and fire neuron model

The integrate and fire neuron (IAF) model is a simplified form of the Hodgkin-Huxley model. This simplification is based on the dynamics of action potential generation process. The membrane excitation is modelled by a thresholding process while the sub-threshold dynamics are reduced to the integration of incoming currents by a capacitor. Despite the simplicity of this model, it retains two important aspects of neuronal firing, a sub-threshold domain where the input is passively integrated and a voltage threshold, which once exceeded, leads to the generation of stereotypical spikes. However the form of the action potential is not implicit in the model equations, it is rather generated 'by hand'. In this model, no importance is given to the shape of action potentials or spikes as they are all similar. Hence, no information is conveyed in the time course of spikes and the focus is rather put on their timing.

The simplest version of an integrate-and-fire neuron, called the *perfect integrate-and- fire-neuron* model, consists of a single capacitor followed by a fixed threshold V*th* as depicted in Figure 3-8. In this case the firing frequency is directly proportional to the injected current. The model dynamics are described by the following equation:

$$C_m \cdot \frac{dV_m}{dt} = I(t) \qquad\qquad \text{Equation 3-16}$$

where C_m is the membrane capacitance, and   I(t) is the time varying input current injected to stimulate the neuron at time *t*.

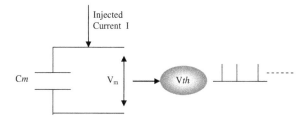

Figure 3-8 Perfect integrate and fire neuron model. This simple model is represented by a single capacitor. The voltage across the capacitor is compared to a threshold for spike generation.

The model is a physiologically inaccurate abstraction of real biological neurons but it is often used for reason of tractability. Other researchers go even further and prefer not to call them 'spiking models' but merely integrators, as they do not have a built-in mechanism to produce a spike but this latter is generated manually! (Izhikevich, 2000 2001, 2004). When the membrane voltage reaches V*th* , an action potential is then generated and the voltage is reset to its resting value. Neurons typically do not respond to their inputs instantaneously following an action potential. Due to biophysical considerations there is a certain time interval following the generation of a spike during which another spike cannot be generated, irrespectively of the strength of the injected current.

This is called a refractory period denoted by *tref*. In the integrate and fire model, the effect of a refractory period can be replicated by holding the membrane potential at rest for a fixed duration t_{ref} immediately after a spike. For a constant input current, the *f-I* is linear, f=I/C.V*th,* where *f* denote the firing rate of the model in units of HZ. This curve *I-f* is affected by introduction of a refractory period which induce a non-linear saturation

$$f = \frac{I}{CV_{th} + t_{ref}I}$$

Equation 3-17

The output of the perfect integrate-and-fire neuron is a regular spike train with an inter-spike interval ISI of *(1/f)*. However, real neurons seldom respond to a constant current input with a regular sequence of action potentials. In fact, there is substantial variability in the exact timing of the spikes, which is particularly pronounced in recordings in vivo (Gerstner and Kistler, 2002; Markram et al., 1997; Maass, 1997). A simple modification that allows the IAF model to respond with irregular spike trains in response to a constant current is to consider the voltage threshold as a random variable drawn from an arbitrary probability distribution P(V*th*). The perfect integrate-and-fire model is however an idealisation of biological neurons as the leakage current is completely neglected. The introduction of such current led to the definition of a different model called the *leaky integrate-and-fire* or LIAF model which is discussed and simulated in the following section.

3.5.3 Leaky integrate and fire neuron model

Real biological neurons are not perfect integrators; in fact they present a current leakage, which makes the neuron returning to its resting potential in the absence of a stimulus. This leakage is represented in the leaky integrate and fire model by a resistance R_m as depicted in Figure 3-9. The new model equation is as follow

$$C_m \cdot \frac{dV_m}{dt} + \frac{V_m}{R_m} = I(t)$$

Equation 3-18

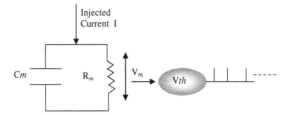

Figure 3-9 Equivalent circuit for the leaky integrate and fire neuron LIAF. A resistor is introduced to represent the leak in current which allow the voltage to return to its resting potential when no input is applied.

As in the perfect integrate and fire model, this equation is combined with the threshold crossing equation in order to define the firing times t_f of the neuron defined by $V(t^f) = V_{th}$; where Vth is the voltage threshold. If we consider a constant current I(t) as a stimulus, the differential equations can be solved explicitly.

$$V_m(t) = R_m I_0 - (R_m I_0 - V_0)e^{\frac{-(t-t_0)}{R_m C_m}}$$ **Equation 3-19**

where t_0 is initial time, V_0 is the resting membrane potential and I_0 is representing constant current. The time taken by V_m to reach the threshold voltage is:

$$t_f = t_0 + R_m C_m \ln(\frac{R_m I_0 - V_0}{R_m I_0 - Vth})$$ **Equation 3-20**

If the input stimulus is a continuous function of time, the neuron firing times are then determined by integrating the differential equation describing the sub-threshold neuron dynamics using a numerical method by choosing a proper time step, which leads to a better accuracy. The following Matlab simulations (see Figure 3-10, Figure 3-11 and Figure 3-12) of the integrate and fire neuron model show the membrane potential variability and different spiking patterns when the neuron is stimulated with different input stimuli that differ in amplitude, shape and duration.

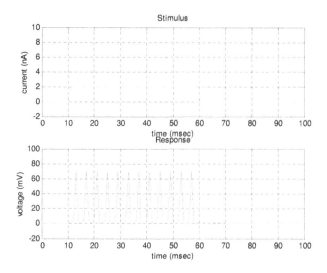

Figure 3-10 Response of LIAF neuron to a constant stimulus. The neuron fires regularly as long is the input is applied. The input is applied at time 10 ms for a period of 50 ms.

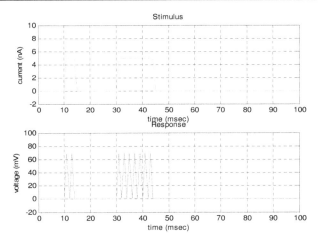

Figure 3-11 Response of LIAF neuron to a stronger stimulus with different onset times. Onset times are 10ms and 30 ms and the input is held for 5ms and 15ms respectively.

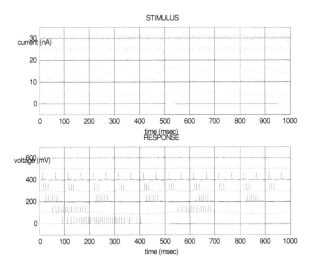

Figure 3-12 LIAF neuron response to different frequencies of a sinusoidal input. Input signals with different frequencies are superimposed in the same graph (STIMULUS graph), and the neuron response to the presented inputs are also superimposed in the same graph below (RESPONSE), such that each response (row) in the RESPONSE graph corresponds to the input at the same row in the STIMULUS graph.

The neuron firing frequency is determined when the strength of the input stimulus is varied, and the frequency current (f-I) is shown in Figure 3-13.

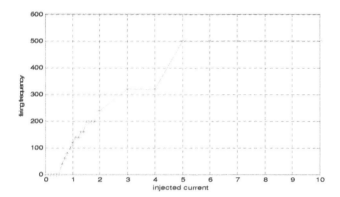

Figure 3-13 Graph showing the variation of the firing frequency with the stimulus strength. It is observed from the current frequency curve that the firing frequency stays constant when the input strength reaches a certain threshold. This is because the neuron gets *saturated* at a certain frequency value above which no more spikes can be fired.

3.5.4 Spike Response Model (SRM)

The Spike Response Model (SRM) (Gerstner, 1995) is another nonlinear model of spiking neurons. It represents a generalization of the leaky integrate-and-fire model. The direction of the generalization is, however, somewhat different. In the nonlinear integrate-and-fire model, parameters are made voltage dependent whereas in the SRM they depend on the time since the last output spike (Gerstner and Kistler, 2002; Kistler et al., 1997). Another difference between integrate-and-fire models and the SRM concerns the formulation of the equations. While integrate-and-fire models are usually defined in terms of differential equations, the SRM expresses the membrane potential at time t as integration over the past output spikes. Mathematically, the dynamics of the spike response model are modelled by the following equation:

$$u_i(t) = \sum_{t_i^{(f)} \in F_i} \eta_i(t - t_i^{(f)}) + \sum_{j \in \Gamma_i} \sum_{t_j^{(f)} \in F_j} w_{ij} \varepsilon_{ij}(t - t_i^{(f)}) \qquad \text{Equation 3-21}$$

$\eta_i(s)$: Models the refractory behaviour. It is used to reset the neuron and it decays to zero afterwards; $\eta_i(s) = 0$ for s<0.

$\varepsilon_{ij}(s)$: Represents the PSP (Post-Syanaptic Potential) form, which models the influence of spikes from pre-synaptic neurons. $\varepsilon_{ij}(s) = 0$ for s<0.

w_{ij}: Represents the connection strength (weights), which modulates the amplitude of a PSP.

F_j: represents the set of firing times of neuron j; and Γ_i is set of pre-synaptic neurons to neuron i.

The membrane potential of a neuron i, is described by a single variable $\underline{u}_i$. In the absence of spikes, the variable $\underline{u}_i$ is at its resting value, $u_{rest} = 0$. Each incoming spike will inflict a change on the postsynaptic potential $\underline{u}_i$ as illustrated in Figure 3-14. The function ε_{ij} describes the time course of the response to an incoming spike. If, after the summation of the effects of several incoming spikes, u_i reaches the threshold an output spike is triggered and the neuron state is reset to its resting potential by adding the amount $\eta_i(s)$, which make the neuron reluctant to new incoming spikes during certain period, called the refractory period.

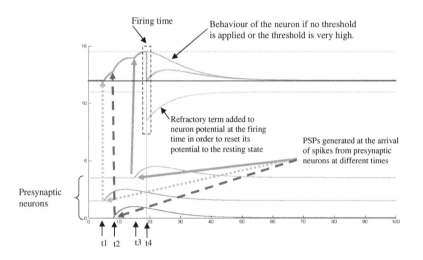

Figure 3-14 Temporal integration of postsynaptic potentials. Different PSPs are triggered at different arrival times (indicated by t1, t2 and t3). The membrane potential is compared to a certain threshold and a spike is generated when the threshold is reached from below (at time t4). At the firing time (t4) a refractory term is added to the neuron potential and the neuron is reset to its resting potential and integration of input is started again. Also shown (top) the potential of the neuron if no threshold is applied or if the threshold is considered too high to allow excitation and firing. The curves (at the bottom) represent the PSPs generated at the arrival of each spike. The x-axis represents the time and the y-axis represent the neuron potential.

In the equation modelling the SRM model, the second term where the incoming spikes are summed up, the summation runs over all the previous firing times and over all the presynaptic neurons j connected to neuron i. Also in the refractory period term, the summation runs over the previous firing times, but in a simplified model, only the last firing time can be considered. The delays representing the time between onset of a spike and the time at which it reaches the postsynaptic neuron is ignored in the above equation. The dynamics represented by the SRM framework are shown in Figure 3-14. In the bottom, three presynaptic neurons generate three spikes at different times (t1, t2 and t3), which cause an increase in the postsynaptic potential, represented at the top of

66

the figure. When the postsynaptic neuron reaches a threshold (this time is depicted by t4 in Figure 3-14.), a spike is triggered and the neuron enters a refractory period. This is achieved by adding a refractory term $\eta_i(s)$ which has negative amplitude. The addition of such a term resets the neuron potential to its resting potential and makes it reluctant to fire again within a short period after the firing time (Figure 3-14. shows a relative refractory period, as a new firing of the neuron depends on the strength of the summed PSPs).

3.5.5 FitzHugh-Nagumo model

Unlike the original Hodgkin-Huxley system, which incorporates four variables (the membrane potential u, m and h for the sodium ion channel and n for the potassium ion channel), FH-N model is a simplification of the HH model (Feng and Zhang, 2001; Feng et al., 2001). It only has two variables - one fast and one slow. The fast variable u (the transmembrane potential), whose behaviour is determined by a cubic polynomial, is called the excitation variable and the slow variable w is the recovery variable. This model is less used for simulating spiking networks.

$$\frac{du}{dt} = \varepsilon u(u - \lambda)(1 - u) - w + I \qquad \text{Equation 3-22}$$

$$\frac{dw}{dt} = u - aw \qquad \text{Equation 3-23}$$

where $0<\lambda<1$ and $a,\varepsilon>0$.

3.6 Different forms of a PSP

In the currently used models, different shapes are used to model the postsynaptic potentials (PSP), see Figure 3-15. However, it is always associated with each synapse to modulate the amplitude of the PSP. These weights are considered to be plastic, and the process of learning is associated with the method of their alterations. As illustrated in Figure 3-15 (a), this form of a PSP is described by an instant jump followed by an exponential decay which is defined by

$$psp(t,t_i) = e^{(\frac{t-t_i}{\tau})} \qquad \text{Equation 3-24}$$

where τ represents the membrane time constant and t_i denotes the synaptic delay, i.e. the time it takes a spike to reach the postsynaptic neuron once fired. More realistic models include an exponential rise and a decay of the PSP which is represented by an alpha function defined by

$$psp(t,t_i) = \frac{t-t_i}{\tau} \cdot e^{(\frac{-t-t_i}{\tau})} \qquad \text{Equation 3-25}$$

or a double exponential function with different rise and decay time constants defined as follows:

$$psp(t,t_i) = \frac{\tau_r \tau_f}{\tau_r - \tau_f} \cdot \left[e^{(-\frac{t-t_i}{\tau_r})} - e^{(-\frac{t-t_i}{\tau_f})} \right]$$ **Equation 3-26**

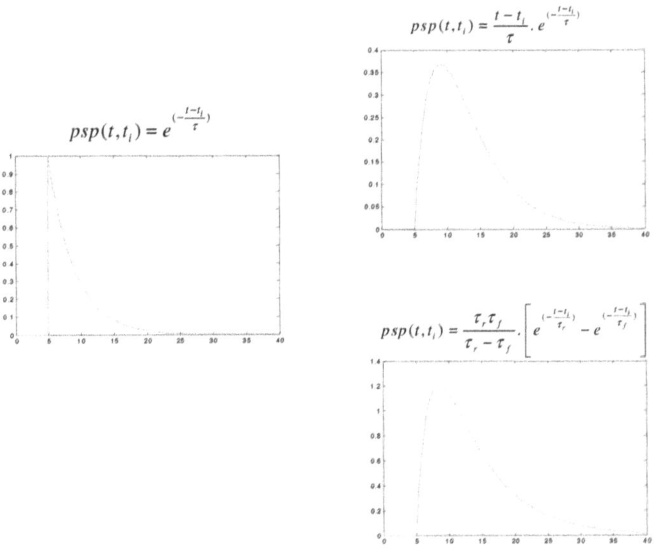

$$psp(t,t_i) = \frac{t-t_i}{\tau} \cdot e^{(-\frac{t-t_i}{\tau})}$$

$$psp(t,t_i) = e^{(-\frac{t-t_i}{\tau})}$$

$$psp(t,t_i) = \frac{\tau_r \tau_f}{\tau_r - \tau_f} \cdot \left[e^{(-\frac{t-t_i}{\tau_r})} - e^{(-\frac{t-t_i}{\tau_f})} \right]$$

Figure 3-15 Different shapes of Post Synaptic Potential (PSP). (a) The PSP is modelled by a sudden jump followed by an exponential decay. (b) and (c) The PSP is modelled by an exponential rise and decay.

3.7 Comparison between different models

The Hodgkin-Huxley model is considered as a more detailed description of the membrane cell response to an input current presented above it is a four dimensional variable system which make it a computationally intensive model. On the other hand, the FHN model is a simplification of HH model, as it reduces the dimensionality of the Hodgkin-Huxley dynamic system down to two variables and therefore reducing the computation overhead. The integrate and fire neuron model in its perfect form, despite its simple implementation (Tikovic and Durackova, 2000; Tikovic et al., 2001), is biologically implausible because of the lack of representation of the leakage feature of real neurons. However the leaky integrate and fire neuron model combined with the refractoriness, represents a more tractable model in comparison with the detailed model of the Hodgkin-Huxley model. On the other hand, the formulation of the SRM model has greatly facilitated the investigation of computations in networks of spiking neurons (Maass, 1999). It offers an analytical formulation of the integrate and fire model initially described by a differential equation. Although this model has a mathematically much simpler formulation, it is able to capture the dynamics of Hodgkin-Huxley neurons quite well (Kistler et al., 1997).

3.8 Spike-based encoding schemes

Neurons communicate through propagation of sequences of spikes (called spike trains) or action potentials. As quoted in (Rieke et al., 1996):

"Spike sequences are the language for which the brain is listening, the language the brain uses for its internal musings, and the language it speaks as it talks to the outside world"

But how do neurons encode information using these spikes? This is one of fundamental questions discussed in neuroscience. How the brain represents the external world and how it stores and processes its stimuli? Two main trends can be found in the literature, which differ from the trivial assumptions employed in classical neural networks where only a binary or a real value output has been considered. It is hypothesised in the first scheme that neural information is conveyed in the firing rate while in the second scheme, it is believed that information is encoded in the precise timings of generated spikes. These hypotheses are reviewed and discussed in the following sections.

3.8.1 Rate coding vs. temporal coding

The principle of rate coding has been introduced and widely used in computational neuroscience (Recce, 1999). While the binary neurons did not use the rate concept, as only a zero or one output is used to indicate the firing or non firing of a neuron, the perceptron-based neurons used the concept of a neuron rate in the form of a real scalar, representing the neural average activity. The rate encoding scheme was used to describe the properties of several types of neurons of the nervous system, where the firing of such neurons is maximal when certain stimuli are applied (Kandel et al., 2000). However, the use of rate for stimuli encoding and processing was strongly apposed by different researchers. Observations on the speed of visual pattern analysis and recognition by cortical visual neurons suggested that the firing rate cannot be considered as the only form of spike-based information encoding (Abeles et al., 1993; Abeles and Gat, 2001; Thorpe et al., 1996, 1989; Perret et al., 1982). Consequently, the use of precise timing of action potentials for information encoding and processing becomes the focus of neuroscientists' experimental studies (Abeles, 1993; Arsten, 1993; Arbib, 1995; Bialek and Rieke, 1992; Hopfiels, 1995; Rieke et al., 1996; Senowski, 1995; Thorpe and Imbert, 1989; Gerstner and Kistler, 2002). In the context of temporal coding, neurons can encode information through synchronization which is based on spike latencies (Cariani,

1997) , inter-spike intervals (time difference between individual spikes) of different neurons (Hopfield, 1995; Gawne et al., 1996; Maass, 1997; Thorpe and Gautrais, 1998), time-to-first spike (Van Rullen and Thorpe, 2001) where the most strongly stimulated neurons fire early, while neurons that fire later may indicate a weak stimulus. These different encoding hypotheses are reviewed and discussed in the following sections (see Figure 3-16 for a list of suggested schemes, which are classified based on spike rate or spike time).

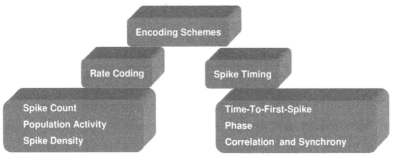

Figure 3-16 Spike-based information encoding schemes classified into two categories, rate-based and spike timing-based coding.

3.8.2 Firing Rate-based coding

The essential information is coded in the firing rates, which are averaged over time or over several repetitions of the experiment (Gerstner and Kistler, 2002). Sometimes spatial rate is considered, when an average over a population of neurons is taken into account.

3.8.2.1 Rate as a spike count

The firing rate is usually defined by a temporal average. The experimentalists set a time window and count the number of spikes that occur in this time window, see Figure 3-17. Division by the length of the time window give the mean firing rate $r = \dfrac{NumberOfSpikes}{T}$.

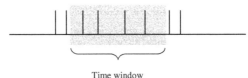

Time window

Figure 3-17 Rate encoding viewed as a spike count within a certain time period. Rate here is the firing frequency.

3.8.2.2 Rate as a spike density

The same stimulation process is repeated several times (n) (see Figure 3-18) and the neuron rate is determined by considering the average of its responses over the number of times the stimulation is repeated. It is given by $r = \dfrac{1}{N}\dfrac{NumberOfSpikes}{\Delta T}$.

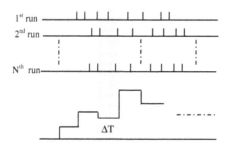

Figure 3-18 Rate as a spike density. The firing frequency considered over several runs.

3.8.2.3 Rate as population activity

Formally, a population activity is defined by the following equation: $A(t) = \dfrac{1}{\Delta T}\dfrac{n(t,t+\Delta T)}{N}$; where N is the population size, Δ is a small time interval and $n(t,t+\Delta)$ the number of spikes generated by neurons in the population. The spatiotemporal property of this code makes it able to reflect changes in the stimulus nearly instantaneously Figure 3-19. Therefore the drawbacks of temporal average at the neuron level only are avoided when population activity is used instead (Brunel et al., 2001; Gerstner, 2000).

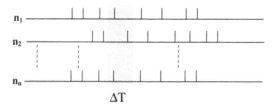

Figure 3-19 Rate as a population activity. In this case several neurons are considered and the rate is their average activity as a populating.

3.8.3 Firing time-based coding

3.8.3.1 Time-to-first-spike coding

A neuron that fires first can signal the detection or recognition of a particular object and also can signal a strong stimulation while neurons that fire at a later time may signal a weak stimulus, see Figure 3-20..

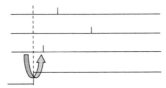

Figure 3-20 Time-to-first-spike could convey information about the input stimulus. For example the neuron firing first could indicate the presence of a particular input pattern or the strength of the stimulus.

3.8.3.2 Correlation and Synchrony

Information can be distinguished by the activity of different pools of neurons, where a neuron may participate at several pools. In this case the synchrony in a population of neurons can also be considered for representing a temporal pattern, see Figure 3-21 shown below.

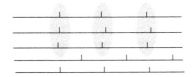

Figure 3-21 Synchronisation-based coding. The synchronised firing of a population of neurons could indicate the detection of a particular object and therefore could explain the binding problem where an the features of an object are distributed (encoded) through several neurons and the neurons and the neuron synchronisation is a means by which the neurons (populations) involved are identified.

3.8.3.3 Phase coding

Oscillations of population activity can be found in different area of the brain such as the hippocampus and the olfactory system. These oscillations can be used as a reference signal against which the timings of other neurons' spikes are compared. Information is then encoded in the phase of action potential with respect to the reference signal; see Figure 3-21 for an illustration

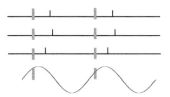

Figure 3-21 Phase coding. the firing times are compared to a background signal which serve as an internal reference to account for synchronisation/desynchronisation.

3.9 Learning in spiking neural networks

Learning is one of the important features of neural systems. It is related to the evolution of synaptic efficacies and the way they are adapted when exposed to different stimuli or experiences. It is believed that synapses play a key role in neural adaptation, memory and learning process. Consequently, it is often referred to as synaptic plasticity. Learning refers to the methods by which connection strengths change and evolve to learn the specific task or to memorise input patterns. As the learning rules related to classical neural networks (i.e. non-spiking neurons) have been reviewed in the previous chapter, the focus in this section is directed towards learning mechanisms applied to biological neurons, particularly temporal learning.

3.9.1 Hebbian learning and long term potentiation

Neuroscientist research efforts focussed on the investigation of synaptic plasticity are mostly inspired by the psychologist Hebb's postulate stated below:

"When an axon of a cell A is near enough to excite cell B or repeatedly or persistently takes part in firing it, some growth or metabolic change takes place in both cells such that A's efficiency, as one of the cells firing B, is increased".

This learning rule belongs to the class of of unsupervised learning. It is also a local rule, i.e. it affects individual neurons independently of the network performance as it is only expressed as a function of the inputs and outputs of the individual neurons. Hebb's postulate suggests that weight alteration is influenced by the activity correlation between two interconnected neurons, i.e, both pre and postsynaptic neurons have to be coactive. As a result of Hebb's work, correlation-based learning is referred to as Hebbian learning (Gerstner and Kistler, 2002). Results from biophysical experiments (Bliss and Gardner-Medwin, 1973) were found to be consistent with Hebb's theory. In the experiments by Bliss and Gardner-Medwin (1973), a neuron membrane potential is recorded using an intracellular electrode while an extra-cellular electrode is used to stimulate presynaptic

73

fibres. The neuron membrane potential is observed when stimulation is applied (see Figure 3-22). first, a weak stimulation is applied so that only a PSP is produced and no spike is triggered. Then the neuron is forced to fire by the application of a high frequency stimulus. It was observed that there was an increase in the postsynaptic response to small pulses when stimulated again. This change persists over many hours and so is called Long Term Potentiation (LTP). These changes, induced by correlated activity in post-pre synaptic units, seem to be consistent with Hebb's postulate.

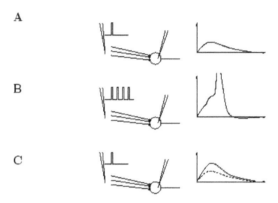

Figure 3-22 Long term potentiation (LTP) from experiments by Bliss and Collingridge (A). A weak stimulation produce the postsynaptic response shown on the right-hand side of the figure, no spike is fired. (B). A sequence of stimulations triggers postsynaptic neuron spikes. (C). A test stimulus produce a larger postsynaptic potential than what was initially obtained. Figure taken from (Gerstner and Kistler, 2002)

Another experiment was carried out to confirm that the synaptic strengthening was in the previous experiment was independent of the input stimulation, i.e. it was not only caused by the continuous firing of the postsynaptic neuron. In this experiment, two pathways S (strong) and W (weak) are introduced (see Figure 3-23). Stimulation of S causes the postsynaptic neuron to fire and stimulation of W alone does not evoke firing. A strengthening of W synapses was observed when both pathways are stimulated simultaneously. Which is consistent with Hebb's theory, i.e. synaptic efficiency is altered when both pre and postsynaptic neurons are active.

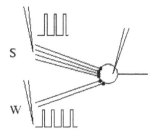

Figure 3-23 Bliss and Collingridge's Intracellular Experiment. The synapses of pathway W are strengthened when both pathways (S and W) are stimulated and firing occurs at the postsynaptic neuron. Figure taken from (Gerstner and Kistler, 2002)

Although Hebb's postulate suggests that the activity of both postsynaptic and presynaptic neurons influences the alteration of the synapse efficacy, it does not take into account temporal requirements for this adjustment, i.e., it does not clearly indicate the time resolution during which the weight alteration occurs. However, advances in the experimental techniques allowed the intracellular stimulation and recording from synaptically connected neurons and therefore the investigation of synaptic plasticity at better temporal resolution (Bi and Poo, 1998, 2001; Zhang et al., 1998), which led to the derivation of the spike-time dependent synaptic plasticity rule (STDP).

3.9.2 Spike-time dependent synaptic plasticity (STDP)

Spike-time dependent synaptic plasticity is a temporal learning rule based on the timing of individual spikes. Using cultured hippocampal neurons, pairing experiments performed by by Bi and Poo (Bi and Poo, 1998) proved that the alteration of synaptic weights is rather a function of the difference between the presynaptic and postsynaptic individual spike times (see Figure 3-24) and an estimate of the timing conditions for synaptic plasticity was obtained.

Based on the time difference (Δt) between postsynaptic and presynaptic spikes, the change in synaptic strength is modelled by the function F(Δt) given by :

$$F(\Delta t) = \begin{cases} A_+ \, exp(\Delta t / \tau_+), & if \ \Delta t \geq 0 \ (\, Potentiation \,) \\ -A_- \, exp(\Delta t / \tau_-), & if \ \Delta t < 0 \ (\, Depression \,) \end{cases}$$

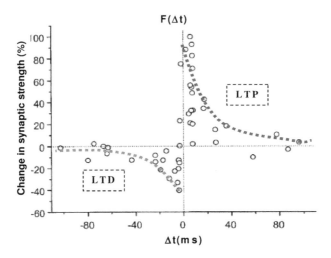

Figure 3-24 Change in synaptic efficacy based on the time difference between post- and presynaptic spikes. Long term potentiation (LTP) occurs when a presynaptic spike is followed by a postsynaptic spike, while a long term depression (LTD) occurs in the inverse case. Figure adapted from Bi an Poo (1998).

The synaptic strengthening/weakening based on the difference between post and presynaptic firing times is illustrated in Figure 3-25. The parameters τ_+ and τ_- determine the time window between pre- and postsynaptic spikes over which synaptic alteration (potentiation or depression) occur. A_+ and A_- are two positive scalars which determine the maximum change in synaptic strength. The maximum change occurs when the presynaptic and postsynaptic spikes occur close to each other, i.e. $\Delta t \sim 0$. This temporal learning rule has been implemented by Song and Abott and its convergence is studied with different network connectivity and input signals (Song et al., 2000). Other variations and adaptation of spike time dependent plasticity have been investigated by other researchers such as (Gerstner and Kistler, 2002; Panchev et al., 2002; Panchev and Wermter, 2004; Yao and Dan, 2001).

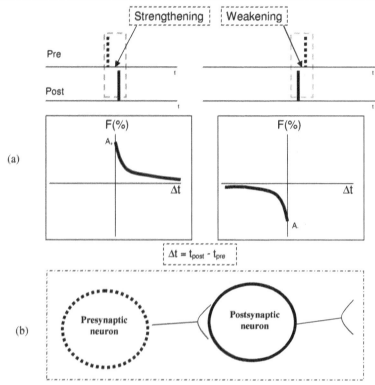

Figure 3-25 Spike-Time Dependent Plasticity (STDP). (a) Synaptic strengthening versus weakening based on the difference between the post and presynaptic spike times. Spike represented with dashed line refers to the presynaptic action potential, while the spike represented with continuous line refers to postsynaptic action potential. (b) two neurons connected through a synapse.

3.9.3 Supervised learning

The learning approaches mentioned above are all unsupervised, i.e. no a priori knowledge or desirable output signal is made available before the synaptic connections start evolving. The only supervised algorithm was developed by Bohte (2000) where the classical backpropagation used with the multilayer perceptrons (MLPs) is adapted to spiking neural networks based on the spike response model (SRM). However this algorithm suffers from numerous drawbacks such as scale, convergence and initial parameters setting. Further details about this supervised algorithm will be included in chapter 5. As this algorithm was the only supervised training found in the literature, it has been used for comparison of the newly supervised training developed in this work and presented in detail in chapter 5.

3.10   Summary

This chapter reviewed the biological foundation of spiking neurons and their modelling trends in computational neuroscience which allowed us to outline the advantages and disadvantages of each modelling direction. It was shown that different levels of details could be used for different tasks and goals. On one hand, more detailed models are better suited for simulating and studying of the behaviour of single neurons or small scale networks. On the other hand, less detailed neural models allow the simulation of larger scale networks and the study of learning and computation principles underlying the computational performance of the nervous systems. MATLAB Simulations of some of these neural models have also been presented and discussed. This chapter has also discussed the different encoding schemes and their classification into two main categories, i.e. rate-based and spike-based encoding schemes. The existing unsupervised and supervised learning paradigms were also reviewed and it was shown how the synapse plays a key role in learning and memory processes.

More attention has been given in the literature to unsupervised learning paradigms, either in the form of correlation based (or Hebbian-based) or in the form spike-time dependent plasticity, and less effort has been made to derive supervised learning algorithms, which are more suitable for solving problems when information about the desired system outputs is known a priori. As stated in the introductory chapter, one of the aims of this research work is to investigate supervised learning with spiking neurons and devise new approaches with applications to classification tasks. To this end, an investigation of the applicability of optimisation techniques, with particular focus on evolutionary computing (another biologically inspired paradigm), to the supervised training of spiking has been carried out, and an evolutionary strategy (ES) based supervised learning approach was devised and presented in chapter 2 and 3. Before this newly developed supervised learning method is fully described, evolutionary algorithms and optimisation techniques are first introduced and discussed in the following chapter.

CHAPTER 4

Evolutionary computing

4.1 Introduction

This chapter discusses the concepts of evolutionary computation and its applications in problem optimisation. The objective of this discussion is two-fold. The first aim is to define the class of optimisation algorithms to which evolutionary strategies (ES) belong, as the latter forms the basis of the supervised learning approach, developed in this work and presented in chapters 5 and 6 respectively, for training spiking neural networks and computing with dynamic synapse based networks. The second objective is to highlight the elements and the fundamental concepts of evolutionary algorithms as well as the key points related to the design of such optimisers. Although only a real time encoding scheme is used in this work, the binary representation is presented in this chapter due to its importance in the history and development of evolutionary algorithms. This chapter is organised as follows:

The theory of evolution and the different variants of evolutionary algorithms are introduced in section 4.2, while the key components of evolutionary algorithms are discussed in section 4.3. Then the various implementations are discussed in section 4.4. Finally, the combination of evolutionary algorithms and neural networks is introduced in section 4.5.

4.2 Evolutionary algorithms

Evolutionary algorithms (EAs) are stochastic search/optimisation techniques that are inspired from the Darwinian paradigm of evolution. According to Darwin's theory of evolution published in his work "On the Origin of Species" (Darwin, 1959), only individuals that are best adapted to their environment will be able to compete and therefore will survive the natural selection process and reproduce. This selection process, repeated through different generations, where best adapted individuals are favoured, is called "survival of the fittest". In addition, variation is considered as an important driving force of the evolution process. For an individual, specific combination of its features (traits) can affect its fitness to survive and create new offspring. If the new traits, resulting from feature combination, enhance the individual adaptability (i.e. result in a higher fitness), the

79

individual is most likely to survive and will then pass them to the next generation. Otherwise, the individual will fail to survive and hence the new obtained traits are stopped from being spread to new offspring. New traits can also result from small random changes, called mutation, in the individual features during its evolution through different generations. Again, these new characteristics are put through the selection process, where beneficial ones are carried over to the next generation and the less useful are discarded. This iterative process will evolve a given population such that only individuals which are best adapted to their environment are maintained.

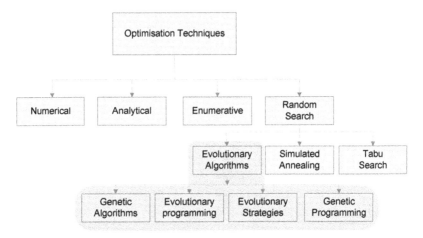

Figure 4-1 Classification of Evolutionary Algorithms with other optimisation techniques. The drawbacks and/or limitations of numerical, analytical and enumerative techniques led to the development of random based search techniques which are able to search for optimal or sub-optimal solutions for a given problem that is hard to solve using other methods.

Although most terminology used in EAs is derived from biology, EAs are only a simplification of the evolutionary process found in nature. There is no rigorous definition given to EAs, however this term is generally employed to denote any stochastic optimisation technique where the search for optimal/sub-optimal solutions is population-based. The diagram shown in Figure 4-1 illustrates the classification of optimisation techniques and highlights EAs and their different variants as a random search method among other methods. The history of EAs can be traced back to the mid-twentieth century where they were first suggested (Fogel, 1998). Then and since the late 1960s, four different variations of evolutionary algorithms have been introduced; evolutionary programming (EP) by Lawrence Fogel (Fogel et al., 1966), evolutionary strategies (ES) by Ingo Rechenberg and Hans-Paul Schwefel (Bäck et al., 1991; Schwefel, 1995; Bäck et al., 1997), genetic algorithms (GA) by John Holland (Holland, 1975; Goldberg, 1989) and genetic programming (GP) (Koza, 1990, 1992; Koza et al., 1999). Although different evolutionary paradigms exist with different historical backgrounds and different implementations, the terms Evolutionary Algorithms (EAs) and

Evolutionary Computation (EC) are exchangeably used to denote the whole family of optimisation techniques that are inspired from the Darwinism paradigm of natural evolution. These different categories of evolutionary algorithms share some common features such as:

- All EAs variants are based on a population of candidate solutions that is evolved during the search for optimal or near optimal solution.

- All EAs include a selection approach to choose the candidate solutions that are passed to new generations. The selection approach is based on the fitness evaluation such that a candidate solution with a good fitness (higher for maximisation or lower for minimisation) will be more likely selected and its elements spread to new generations.

- Inheritance: elements of new solutions are inherited from successfully selected candidate solutions using some variation operators.

Evolutionary paradigms share the abovementioned similarities, yet they still differ in the implementation of the basic elements of Darwinian evolution theory, such as the encoding scheme, variation operators, and selection schemes. They also differ in their suitability for application to different real world problems. The following diagram illustrates the iterative evolutionary algorithm and its basic elements shared between different evolutionary paradigms (Figure 4-2).

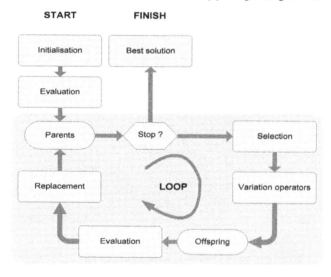

Figure 4-2 The iterative evolutionary algorithm. The process begins by initialising a starting population, the candidate solutions then repeatedly undergo a selection procedure and variation operators to create new potential solutions which are evaluated at each iteration until a stopping criterion is met and an optimal/sub-optimal solution is obtained.

Before discussing the elements of an evolutionary algorithm, the following sub-sections first describe the different versions of evolutionary algorithms (i.e. EP, ES, GA and GP) and highlight their features, history and differences.

4.2.1 Evolutionary Programming

Evolutionary programming (EP), initially proposed by L. J Fogel (Fogel, 1966) in the mid sixties, is based on the evolution of a population of finite state machines (FSMs) and is used for solving prediction problems. The FSM transition table is changed, within the corresponding finite alphabet discrete space, using random mutation and the evaluation of candidate solutions' performance corresponds to the number of symbols that are correctly predicted. Using mutation (no recombination is used), each automata from the parent population generate one new offspring and the best solutions between the parent and the offspring survive and therefore will be passed on to later generations. A mutation, applied with a uniform probability, was implemented as a random change of the description of the FSM (an example is shown in Figure 4-3) and included a change of a state transition or an output symbol, addition/deletion of a state (Bäck and Schwefel, 1996).

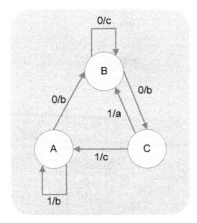

Figure 4-3 A three state finite state machine (FSM). The three nodes indicate the FSM states which form a set S={A,B,C} with a set of input alphabets I={0,1} and a set of output alphabet O={a,b,c}. A transition between two states s_i and s_j is represented by an oriented labelled edge i/o and is expressed by a function δ defined by $\delta((s_i, i)= (s_j, j)$, i.e. when the machine is in state s_i and an input $i \in I$ is encountered, the state s_j is reached and the output $o \in O$ is produced.

Evolutionary programming were originally suggested to work on finite state automata, however they were later further developed by D.B Fogel. Their encoding schemes were extended to real numbers (Fogel, 1992) and tournament selection used for selection. With the use of real valued individuals, EPs became similar to evolutionary strategies (discussed in section 4.2.3) which were developed independently particularly in terms of individual representation and the use of mutation as a variation operator (Bäck and Schwefel, 1993; Bäck et al., 1997).

4.2.2 Genetic Algorithms

Genetic Algorithms (GAs) were first proposed and developed by John Holland (Holland, 1962, 1975) and his students between the mid sixties and the mid seventies. They were used for adaptive search and optimisation. They represent the most known and used form of evolutionary algorithms. They use binary strings (also referred to as chromosomes) to represent individuals such as each bit set to one or zero denotes, respectively, the presence or absence of a particular feature (e.g numbers or symbols) of a candidate solution. An initial population of such bit strings is evolved through the simulation of Darwinian evolution, i.e by putting it through a selection process based on fitness evaluation, recombination and mutation procedure for reproduction. Genetic algorithms emphasize the role of recombination (crossover) as a search operator and mutation is only used as a background operator (Yao, 2002). Genetic algorithms as proposed by John Holland are referred as Simple Genetic Algorithm (SGA) and its application potential and adaptive capabilities were further investigated by De Jong (1975, 1991, 1992) and Goldberg (1989a,b; Goldberg et al., 1991).

4.2.3 Evolutionary Strategies

Evolutionary strategies are more suited for multidimensional continuous problem optimisations as they use real value encoding scheme to represent the parameters that could make up the solution. They were first developed by Rechenberg and Schwefel in the late sixties and early seventies (Schwefel, 1965; Rechenberg, 1973) and were originally used for experimental optimisation of hydrodynamic problems. They differ from simple genetic algorithms by using real values instead of bit-strings to encode the problem parameters. In the early proposed versions, only one n-dimensional real valued individual was used in a population and the algorithm was called a two-member ES and denoted by $(1+1)$ ES. In this type of ES, an individual v is represented by a pair of real value vectors x and σ and is denoted by $v=(x, \sigma)$ such as x represents the problem parameters to be optimised and σ is its corresponding standard deviation vector. A new individual is created by applying a Gaussian mutation with zero expectation and standard deviation σ. Both individuals undergo a selection process such as the fittest will survive and therefore will form a new generation, while the less fit individual will die out. The selection process will form the new generation.

In addition to $(1+1)$ ES, two different variants referred to as $(\mu+\lambda)$ES and (μ,λ)ES were later introduced (Schwefel, 1995). In these two variants, called multimember ES, a population contains μ individuals as opposed to their counterparts, the two-member ESs, where only one individual is used. In a $(\mu+\lambda)$ES, the application of Gaussian mutation to the population's μ individuals results in

λ new individuals being generated, but only the best μ individuals are selected among the total $\mu+\lambda$ individuals and will form the population of the next generation. Similarly in a (μ,λ)ES, λ offspring are created through Gaussian mutation, but the μ best individuals are chosen from the newly created λ individuals only (i.e. the current μ individuals are excluded this time) to form the new population. λ and μ are generally chosen such as $\mu \in [1, \lambda]$.

Due to the importance and robustness of evolutionary strategies when used for optimising continuous problems, an adaptation of this variant of evolutionary algorithms is investigated in this work in order to devise supervised training algorithms for spiking neural networks. The use of ES for supervised training of spiking neural networks based on the spike response model (SRM) and more biologically plausible dynamic synapses will form the bulk of the next two chapters, where ES are described in more detail and their self-adaptation capabilities and suitability for training such biological networks are demonstrated.

4.2.4 Genetic Programming

Although the previous forms of evolutionary algorithms proved successful in numerical optimisation problems, they are however less suitable for symbolic or structural processing which needs a more flexible tree based representation instead of array representation (bit strings or real valued vectors). Using a tree structure to represent individuals allows the encoding of computer programmes, networks, equations, molecule structures and consequently makes the extension of evolutionary paradigm to new search spaces (e.g. computer programmes space) possible. The adoption of such representation led to the definition of genetic programming (GP) by Koza (Koza, 1990, 1992; Koza et al., 1992, Koza et al., 1999) as a new evolutionary algorithm, where the individuals of a population do not consist of arrays of bits or values with fixed length which represent possible solutions to the problem being optimised. Rather these consist of candidate programmes (represented by parse trees) that can solve the problem when executed.

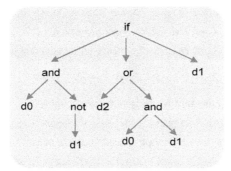

Figure 4-4 Example of a LISP programme represented by a tree structure. When two such trees (individuals) are altered, a new programme is created using a mutation which consist of extracting branches from one tree and inserting it in another tree so that the validity of the new programme is guaranteed. New obtained programs are evaluated and a fitness based selection is performed. The process of producing and selecting new programmes is iterated until a programme that best solves the problem is obtained.

The initial aim of genetic programming was to evolve programmes written in LISP (see Figure 4-4), and their use was later extended to other programming languages (Kinnear, 1994) and solving several types of problems whose representation can be expressed using tree structures (Ryan et al., 1998; Kinnear, 1994).

4.3   Elements of evolutionary algorithms

The various forms of evolutionary algorithms discussed in the previous section, although slightly differ from each other, share common elements that generally characterise an evolutionary approach. This section discusses these main components, their roles and related terminology on a generic level while the details of their implementation will be described in section 4.4.

For a complete definition of a particular evolutionary algorithm, the following elements, procedures or operators need to be clearly specified:

- A *representation* scheme, where individual parameters are defined
- An *evaluation function* or *fitness function* which define an individual quality and how likely it is to spread its features to next generations.
- A *population*, which contains a set of evolved individuals.
- *Variation operators*, used to produce new individuals through recombination and mutation based on the chosen representation.
- A *parent selection* or *mating selection* procedure by which the parents of the next generation are determined.

- A *survivor selection* procedure or *replacement* mechanism by which individuals from offspring and previous population are selected to form a new population.

Beside the definition of each of the above elements, an initialisation procedure and a stopping criterion must also be defined.

4.3.1 Parameter representation: phenotype versus genotype

The definition of an EA starts with mapping the space of the problem to be solved into a space manipulated by the EA. The term *phenotype* is used to denote objects forming possible solutions within the original problem context, while the term *genotype* refers to individuals, which encode the phenotype, that are directly handled by the evolutionary algorithm operators. Therefore, a genotype represents an encoding instance which contains all parameters of a potential solution. The adoption of a particular encoding scheme (data structure) and the mapping between a phenotype space and its corresponding genotype space is referred to as *genetic representation.* For example, given an optimisation problem where the minimum of a one dimensional function defined in the space of integral numbers is required, the function definition space of integers would form the set of phenotypes. A possible encoding scheme is to use bit strings to represent them. In this case, the number 10 is seen as a phenotype and the encoding bit string 1010 would be its corresponding genotype. The set of all different genotypes that could be obtained by a particular representation will form the genotype space. The mapping between a phenotype and its genotype is straightforward for the given illustration example, however it could be relatively complex for other problems and different representations. It is important to note that the two spaces may differ and that the EA searching process is performed in the genotype space. Another example, which will be described in detail in the next two chapters, is the mapping a spiking neural network (SNN), one using neurons based on the spike response model (SRM) and the other based on the integrate-and-fire neurons with dynamic synapses, into an arranged array of real values. Clearly in this case, the two spaces are completely different, as an SNN representing the phenotype belongs to the space of spiking neural networks (with different underlying neural models/synapses), while the genotype is a point in the space of multi-dimensional real valued vectors where the EA search is performed. Since the potential optimal solution is obtained by decoding the optimal genotype obtained after convergence, it is crucial to ensure that the searched optimal solution, not known in advance, can be represented by a valid genotype. Different terminologies, adopted from biology, are used in the literature to describe the genetic representation of a given problem. A summary of these terms and their meaning in the EA context is given in the following table (Table 4-1):

Biological Context	EA Context
Population	Also used in EA and denotes a set of encoded individuals (string of bits, real numbers, etc)
Chromosome	Individual, encoded form of a candidate solution
Gene	A feature, variable, parameter
Allele	Feature value, parameter value
Locus	Position of a feature or variable
Genotype	A representation of candidate solution in the original problem. The structure used for its representation. It is a point in the space where the EA search is performed
Phenotype	A point in the space of possible solutions, i.e. a decoded genotype

Table 4-1 summary of the common terms borrowed from biology and used in an evolutionary algorithm context

4.3.2 Fitness function

As described before, EAs are used as an optimisation technique which searches for a candidate optimal solution of a given problem. To this aim, a fitness function (also called evaluation function) must be defined so that the quality of candidate solutions is assessed and the selection of best solutions in each cycle can be performed. It defines a quality measure of an individual and therefore indicates its likelihood of survival and improvement (Eiben and Smith, 2003). In fact, it is this function that needs to be optimised by the EA in order to solve the problem at hand. One has to choose a fitness function such that small improvements in an individual quality are rewarded with an increase in its fitness, while worse genotypes should be assigned a smaller fitness value.

For example, if the function $f(x)=x^2$ is to be maximised and bit strings are used for genetic representation, the fitness of the genotype 101 could be defined as the square of its corresponding phenotype $5^2=25$. In the case of supervised training of spiking neural networks with fixed structure which will be described in the following two chapters, the fitness of a genotype (e.g. array of weights, delays, neuron time constants) could be defined as the summed squared error (SSE) between the actual and the desired firing times of neurons at the output layer. Also the sum of the absolute error between the desired and actual firing times can be chosen as an alternative fitness function for the same problem. It is clear that in order to evaluate the above mentioned fitness functions, a genotype has to first be decoded into its corresponding phenotype (mapping between the bit string 101 and the value 5 in the first example, and mapping between a real valued vector/array and a spiking neural network in the second example).

The optimisation of a given problem does not necessarily mean the maximisation of its objective function. It is rather the minimisation of objective functions that is required for some problems. However, it is a trivial task to transform maximisation into minimisation and vice versa. The term *objective function* is used by researchers (field of operational research) in the context of the original problem, and the fitness function/evaluation function is used in the context of EAs and can be identical to, or a transformation of the given objective function (Eiben and Smith, 2003). It is important to note that the choice of a fitness function is task dependent and the formulation of a function that provides an efficient measure of the quality of a potential solution is not always straight-forward.

4.3.3 Population

Working on a population of candidate solutions is a characteristic that distinguishes EAs from traditional optimisation techniques where a single individual is used. It consists of a multi-set (a set that might contain copies of an element) of candidate solutions representations (genotypes) and it forms the unit of evolution (Eiben and Smith, 2003). That is, it is the population that is evolved in an EA and not the individual, the latter forms units of selection instead.

Three important factors need to be carefully considered when defining a population, namely the population size, its diversity and its initialisation. The size of the population plays an important role in the quality of the obtained individuals and the convergence to a global optimum. A small size may not suffice to cover the best individuals in the search space and may lead to premature convergence to a local optimum. A bigger size, however, may increase the time needed for the EA to converge to an optimal solution; particularly when the evaluation of the individuals' fitness function is time consuming. The diversity of a population is a measure of the number of *different* candidate solutions present. There is, however, not a unique measure for diversity as it could for example be defined as the number of different fitness values present, the number of different phenotypes present, the number of different genotypes present (using a similarity/dissimilarity measure) or even could be expressed using statistical measures such as entropy (Eiben and Smith, 2003). Population diversity is preferred as because it helps prevent premature convergence to a local optimum, and also to allow identification of several optima when optimising a multi-modal objective function. Several approaches have been used to maintain population diversity, such as fitness sharing (Goldberg and Richardson, 1987; Deb and Goldberg, 1989; Yin and Germay, 1993), crowding (De Jong, 1975) and the elitist clearing method (Petrowski, 1996). The use of such approaches has proven to offer a beneficial extension to the basic EA; however they also add extra parameters which need to be carefully tuned. A detailed discussion of these methods cannot be given in this chapter; however for more details the reader is referred to the original works published in the above mentioned references.

4.3.4 Variation operators

Evolutionary algorithms are also classified as a '*generate-and-test*' optimisation technique. The search for optimal solutions is performed by generating new individuals from their parents through the application of variation operators. That is, variation operators are used to explore the genotype space for points representing optimal or near optimal solutions. Variation operators should adequately be chosen in accordance with the adopted representation scheme so the EA iterative search process converges to an optimal solution within a reasonable number of generations. Two types of variation operators are used in the literature, a binary operator called *recombination* or *cross-over* and a unary operator called *mutation*.

4.3.4.1 Recombination

Using recombination operators, the exploration of new points in the genotype space is performed by merging of genes of two different individuals (parents) to produce one or two new individuals (offspring). This merging is achieved by splitting the parent individuals into two or more parts, the latter are then exchanged to form new individuals. The implementation, as well as the importance of the recombination operator, may vary from an EA variant to another. While in some variants, recombination is considered as the only variation operators (e.g. genetic algorithms), it is applied probabilistically in others (with a chance of not being applied during the search progress) and never used in other variants such as evolutionary strategies and evolutionary programming. However, there are some research investigations into the efficiency of employing recombination with ES and EP.

The concept of recombination is inspired from the biological process called *meiosis*, which involve cross-over between living organism chromosomes. Recombination has also been successfully used by breeders of plants and livestock to produce new species with desirable characteristics. In an EA context, although it is not always beneficial, recombination is applied with the aim of producing new better individuals by mating two parents with different but desirable features. Due to the stochastic nature of recombination operators, the newly produced offspring may contain some undesirable individuals, others with equal or worse quality than their parents and obviously some desirable improved individuals. The efficiency of a recombination implementation can be determined by evaluating its probability of producing new individuals with similar or better quality than their parents. This probability can be increased if the adopted encoding scheme and the problem nature are taken into account when designing recombination operators.

Depending on the chosen encoding scheme, various recombination operators can be designed. For example, when bit-strings are used to represent individuals: single point, multi-point, uniform and arithmetic recombination are used. Whereas, discrete and intermediate (arithmetic) recombination are used when real valued encoding is used (Eiben and Smith, 2003; Bäck and Schwefel, 1993). Different implementations of recombination operators are described and discussed in section 4.4.2.

4.3.4.2 Mutation

In contrast to recombination, mutation is a unary operator. It is applied to a single individual to produce a modified version of it, i.e. a new offspring, and is intended to cause an unbiased random change (Eiben and Smith, 2003). It alters an individual gene separately through the application of a random change to its value. The generation of an individual allele through mutation can also be seen as a jump to a different point in the genotype search space. Similar to recombination operators, mutation is applied with certain probability and its role differs from an EA variant to another. While it represents the only variation operator used in evolutionary strategies (EAs) and evolutionary programming (EP), it is only seen as a '*background operator*' in genetic algorithms (GAs) (Holland, 1975) where recombination operators are more emphasised, whereas in genetic programming it is often never used.

It is worth noting that mutation has a vital importance in improving the convergence of searching the genotype space as it helps maintain the population diversity, a desired feature of evolutionary algorithms that is reduced by the selection process each time different genes present in less fit individuals are discarded (Rudolph, 1996; Rudolph, 1996). However a carefully adjusted mutation, in terms of both frequency and magnitude, is required to avoid the destruction of advantageous features obtained through recombination. This is often a trade-off that needs to be considered when tuning mutation parameters.

Finally, the implementation of mutation operators depends on the chosen genetic representation (Spears, 1998; Bäck and Schwefel, 1993; Eiben and Smith, 2003). For example in the case of binary representation, mutation acts on a single bit by toggling its value (from 0 to 1 and vice versa), while a Gaussian perturbation (other distributions can also be used) is added to the individual alleles (i.e. values) when real valued encoding is employed. These implementations are discussed and illustrated in the following section.

4.3.5 Parent selection (or mating selection)

The goal of parent selection, also referred to as mating selection, is to identify individuals of the current population that will take part in creating new offspring, i.e. becoming parents of the next generation. It is based on the value of the fitness function and the selected individuals will be modified by the variation operators. It is usually probabilistic where individuals with higher fitness are favoured and those with lower fitness are given a slim chance to become parents. While parent selection is, together with survivor selection, responsible for pushing quality improvement (Eiben and Smith, 2003), population diversity is on the other hand responsible for better exploration of the search space. Indeed, even individuals with a small fitness value may contain good alleles that could benefit the optimisation of the problem. Consequently, for better performance of an evolutionary algorithm, it is preferred to maintain diversity when designing a selection scheme in case the search process risks getting caught in a local minimum.

4.3.6 Survivor selection (or replacement strategy)

Survivor selection, also called replacement strategy, is applied once the offspring of the selected parents have been obtained and their fitness values determined. The purpose is to choose those individuals among the parents and the newly created individuals that will be allowed in the next generation. Besides the fitness values of individuals, their ages may also be considered when forming the population of the new generation, e.g. preferring offspring and discarding parents. For example, genetic algorithms use parent selection with an age-biased survivor selection where the old population is completely replaced by the new offspring (De Jong, 1975; Goldberg, 1989: Bäck and Schwefel, 1993). Evolutionary strategies on the other hand, use a deterministic selection approach where the μ best individuals are chosen among the λ newly obtained offspring ((μ,λ)ES form) to form the new generation (i.e. age-biased selection). However, in the ($\mu+\lambda$)ES form, the total of parents and offspring is considered and (i.e. $\mu+\lambda$ individuals) and the best μ individuals are then selected to form the new generation (both age and fitness are used) (Bäck and Schwefel, 1993; Eiben and Smith, 2003). An overview of these selection approaches and their implementation is given in section 4.4.3.

4.4 Implementation of evolutionary algorithm components

The various and most frequently employed implementations of the elements of evolutionary algorithms are discussed and illustrated in this section. However, this discussion does not include the fitness function as its design depends on the particular problem and there is no rule of thumb in defining such a function. Moreover, the discussion of representation schemes and different variation operators is limited to those related to parameter optimisation problems and excludes those that are specific to genetic programming, as this field is not directly related to this work and the description of related representations and operators is beyond the scope of this book. The reader interested in more details about GPs is referred to the publications mentioned in section 4.2.4 of this chapter where this EA variant was introduced.

4.4.1 Parameter encoding schemes

The choice of a particular representation of the system to be optimised is an important and critical aspect in implementing an evolutionary algorithm. The chosen representation must include all necessary details about the searched optimal solution, as the optimisation process will only use information contained within the encoded genotypes. Therefore, the encoding scheme should be based on a clear understanding of what could constitute an optimal solution. The chosen representation scheme also affects the type of variation operators that can be applied. Various applications of evolutionary algorithms led to the creation of several encoding schemes and variation operators. Binary encoding is certainly the most popular scheme, particularly used with GAs, but other representations, such as integer and real valued encoding, permutation encoding and parse trees representation, have also been used and proved to outperform binary encoding. However, only binary and real value encoding schemes are discussed here, as they represent the most relevant representations to the work presented in this book. As will be shown in the next two chapters, real value encoding scheme is used to represent the free parameters of spiking neural networks. In the case where the spike response model is used, the synaptic weights and delays are encoded and arranged in a real valued one dimensional array, whereas in the case where dynamic synapses are employed, their time constants are encoded using an array of real values ordered according to the spiking network layers.

4.4.1.1 Binary representation

Binary representation is the traditional scheme for representing the parameters of an evolutionary algorithm. It was historically used by GAs and was suggested by Holland (1975) to represent all solutions. It is clear that bit-strings are the most suitable choice for representing Boolean features. However, they are also used to represent integer (discrete) and real (continuous) valued parameters, and in permutation and combinatorial problems. For Boolean attributes, where a single bit suffices for encoding each of them (see Figure 4-5.a), an N-bit array is used, which allows the representation of 2^N different solutions. No decoding procedure is required, as a bit value '1' indicate the presence of the encoded attribute, and a bit value '0' indicates its absence. However, when encoding real values, more bits are needed to encode each parameter (see Figure 4-5.b), and a decoding procedure must be defined in order to convert the binary representation to a real valued number. For example, given a real valued parameter x that is encoded using N-bits, the corresponding allele (gene value) $value_x$ is given by the following transform function:

$$value_x = x_{min} + \frac{x_{max} - x_{min}}{2^N - 1} \left(\sum_{i=o}^{N-1} x_i \, 2^{N-1-i} \right)$$

Equation 4-1

where, $x \in [x_{min}, x_{max}]$, x_i represents bit value at the ith location in the N-bits structure.

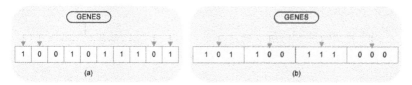

Figure 4-5 Binary encoding using single (a) and multiple bits to represent the different attributes of a given problem.

Another binary encoding scheme is called Gray code. It ensures that adjacent points in the integer space are represented by bit strings that differ in only one bit, i.e. the Hamming distance between their binary codes is 1. Therefore, adjacency is maintained between points in the problem space (phenotype) and their corresponding points in the search space (genotype), a feature that is not always provided when standard binary encoding is used (Michalewicz, 1996; Whitley and Rana, 1997; Rana and Whitley, 1999).

Binary encoding is not without problems. One of its drawbacks is the uncontrollable jumps in the search space that occur when the bits of a genotype are altered. Also the application of variation operators (crossover or mutation) to individual bits on a multi-bit gene may result in illegal combinations being produced. To avoid such problems, the standard binary encoding has to be customised to suit such specific constraints and such customisation will therefore add another computational overhead as a result of encoding and decoding procedures. For continuous problems, however, choosing a binary representation may not be advisable. More appropriate real valued encoding schemes should be employed instead with corresponding variation operators.

4.4.1.2 Real value representation

In this encoding scheme, real values are used to represent the genes of an individual. They offer a natural and straightforward representation of continuous optimisation problems, as floating-point numbers are used to encode the problem parameters and no decoding is required. In contrast to binary representation, the integrity of each gene is maintained when undergoing recombination. In addition, mutation operators act on the entirety of the gene (change the whole number), instead of altering single bits of its lower level binary representation. The gene forms the basic unbreakable unit of the genotype. Another feature of real value representations is the number of possible alleles (values of a gene). Contrary to binary coding where the set of gene values depends on the length of the bit-string, it is infinite with real value schemes and only the machine floating-point precision is the limit. Since a particular representation affects the type of variation operators that can be used, different mutation and crossover operators are adopted by real-coded EAs. These operators will be illustrated in the following sections.

4.4.2 Recombination operators

Recombination is used by evolutionary algorithms to improve the quality of the features of a candidate solution. It is a distinguishing characteristic of EAs, as other optimisation techniques do not use such operators. Recombination treats good features as building blocks scattered throughout the population and tries to recombine them into new and improved individuals (Eshelman, 2000). It is possible to obtain individuals with undesirable features as a result of combing two individuals, however these are expected to die out when put through a selection process. Based on the encoding scheme, several implementations of recombination operators have been created; these operators related to parameter optimisation problems are reviewed in the following sections.

4.4.2.1 Single crossover

This form of combining two parents is widely used with binary representation and represents the simplest crossover operator. It consists of merging information of two parent genotypes into new offspring by randomly choosing a crossover (cutting) position and exchanging the segments of the two parents after the cutting position to form two new offspring (see Figure 4-6). Mathematically, a single-point crossover can be formulated as follows:

Given two parent genotypes pg^a and pg^b of size n such as :

$$pg^a = pg^a_{n-1} \; pg^a_{n-2} \; \cdots\cdots pg^a_1 \; pg^a_0 \quad \text{and} \quad pg^b = pg^b_{n-1} \; pg^b_{n-2} \; \cdots\cdots pg^b_1 \; pg^b_0 .$$

A crossover position denoted by xp is randomly chosen in the set $\{0,1,\ldots,\ n-1\}$ and two new offspring genotypes og^a and og^b with the same size n are then created according to the following equations (Equation 4-2):

$$og^a_i = \begin{cases} pg^a_i & i \le xp \\ pg^b_i & i > xp \end{cases} \quad \text{and} \quad og^b_i = \begin{cases} pg^b_i & i \le xp \\ pg^a_i & i > xp \end{cases} \quad \forall\, i \in [0, n-1] \qquad \textbf{Equation 4-2}$$

The new offspring are a complementary recombination of the information contained in their mating parent.

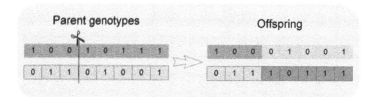

Figure 4-6 Single-point crossover. The vertical dashed line indicate the crossover point which randomly selected. All the genetic information contained in the parent genotypes is still present in the offspring. However resulting sequences may yield a higher fitness and therefore improved individuals.

4.4.2.2 Multi-point crossover (n-point crossover)

Multi-point crossover represents a generalisation of single-point crossover where n crossover points are used instead. The cut points on the parent genotypes are randomly generated and the resulting segments are taken alternatively to form the new offspring. Like single-point crossover, multi-point crossover is applied on two parent individuals and two new individuals are produced. The special case where $n=2$ *is* referred to as *double point crossover*. It has the benefit of preserving advantageous combinations of genes that are interrelated and arranged closely to each other. This referred to as positional bias (Eshelmann et al., 1989) where the arrangement of individual genes is based on their functional dependencies. It should also be realised that using double point crossover, as illustrated in Figure 4-7, the genotype end points are rarely manipulated.

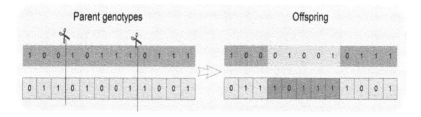

Figure 4-7 Double-point crossover. Two random points (vertical dashed lines) are generated and the parts between them are exchanged to form new offspring.

4.4.2.3 Uniform and discrete crossover

Each offspring gene is created by randomly, usually uniformly, choosing a gene from one of the parent genotypes. Only a single offspring can be created using this process, however a complementary selection of genes can be used to produce a second offspring, as illustrated in Figure 4-8. The offspring created by uniform crossover usually contain equal information from both parents and, in contrast to multi-point crossover, no positional bias is caused (Eshelmann et al., 1989). For continuous problems where real valued encoding is used, uniform crossover is equivalent to discrete crossover where whole values are exchanged instead of bits (Bäck and Schwefel, 1993).

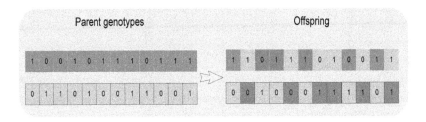

Figure 4-8 Uniform crossover. Each gene is chosen separately from either parents in a random way. The second genotype is obtained by inverting the selection performed to generate the first one.

Although it has been suggested that in some cases uniform crossover outperforms the single and multi-point crossover (Spears and De Jong, 1991; Syswerda, 1989; Caruna et al., 1989; Schaffer, 1989; Eshelmann et al., 1989), there is actually neither theoretical nor empirical evidence as to which operator is most appropriate. Moreover, when dependencies between optimised parameters (genes) are considered, crossover operators with positional bias are rather preferred (Bäck and Schwefel, 1993).

4.4.2.4 Intermediate (arithmetic) crossover

This type of crossover is applied to real coded representations where the genes of parent genotypes are linearly combined to create new offspring. Only one offspring is created using this crossover. Given two real valued parent genotypes pg^1 and pg^2 of size n and a weighting scalar w randomly drawn from a uniform distribution $U(0,1)$, a new offspring genotype og is created according to Equation 4-3 described below:

$$og = w\ pg^1 + (1-w)\ pg^2 \qquad\qquad \textbf{Equation 4-3}$$

In a two dimensional space ($\mathfrak{R}^2$), the newly created offspring (point) *og* will lie between its two parent points as shown in Figure 4-9. A special case of the above transform, choosing w=0.5 will produce an offspring genotype that is an arithmetic mean of it parents. In this variant, the same weight is applied to all genes of individuals.

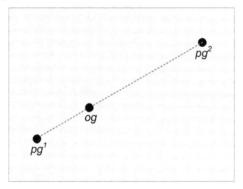

Figure 4-9 Intermediate crossover with one weight applied to all genes of an individual. In a two dimensional space (genotypes are represented by a 2-dimensional real valued vector), the resulting offspring lies between the two parents.

Another variant can be obtained by applying a different weight to each gene. Mathematically, this is described as follows:

Given two parent genotypes pg^1 and pg^2 defined in an *n*-dimensional space ($\mathfrak{R}^n$) by:

$pg^1 = (pg^1_{n-1}, pg^1_{n-2}, ..., pg^1_1, pg^1_0)$ and $pg^2 = (pg^2_{n-1}, pg^2_{n-2}, ... pg^2_1, pg^2_0)$, and a weight vector $w = (w_{n-1}, w_{n-2}, ... w_1, w_0)$, the new genes of the offpring genotype are defined by Equation 4-4:

$$og_i = w\, pg^1_i + (1-w)\, pg^2_i$$

Equation 4-4

Consequently, in a two dimensional space ($\mathfrak{R}^2$), the new offspring is located within the hypercube delimited by the two parents as shown in Figure 4-10.

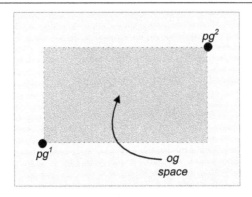

Figure 4-10 Intermediate crossover with n different weights. The possible offspring points generated from two parent genotypes are highlighted.

A third variant of intermediate crossover is obtained by increasing the arity (i.e the number of arguments) of the abovementioned first variant, i.e. using more than two parent genotypes to generate a new offspring. Given k parent genotypes, $pg_1,...pg_k$, a new offspring genotype og is obtained as follows:

$$og = \sum_{i=1}^{k} w_i pg_i \quad \text{where } w_i \in [0,1] \text{ and } \sum_{i=1}^{k} w_i = 1 \qquad \textbf{Equation 4-5}$$

In a two dimensional space ($\Re^2$), the resulting offspring is located inside the convex hull defined by the parent genotypes as shown in Figure 4-11

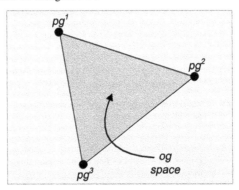

Figure 4-11 Intermediate crossover where more than two parents are combined. The possible offspring points generated from three parent genotypes are highlighted.

98

It should be noted that real valued crossover is not always used with evolutionary strategies (ES) and evolutionary programming (EP), where mutation is the only variation operator used to evolve a population.

4.4.3 Mutation operators

4.4.3.1 Bit-flip mutation

This type of mutation is used with binary representations where a genotype is encoded by a bit-string. Bit-flip mutation is the most widespread operator which consists of randomly modifying (toggling a gene value as shown in Figure 4-12) a small percentage of the genes within a given population.

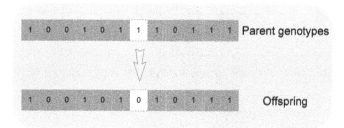

Figure 4-12 Bit-flip mutation. A bit value is occasionally toggled (changing a value 1 to 0 and vice versa). This operator helps explore the search space and improve the quality of individuals, as the resulting genotype may evaluate to a better fitness.

A reasonable mutation rate needs to be defined as a rate that is too high may cause an excessive change of the genes and therefore the deterioration of good ones. There is no rule of thumb for choosing an appropriate mutation rate; it is rather ruled by pure randomness (Bäck and Schwefel, 1993). A good mutation rate helps maintain the population diversity which helps the searching process avoid being caught in a local optimum.

4.4.3.2 Uniform mutation

This type of mutation is less often used with real valued genotypes. It consists of replacing the alleles (real values) of an individual by a new value that is randomly drawn within the range of possible alleles. It is uniform as each allele has an equal chance of being replaced, i.e. the probability of being changed is uniformly distributed.

4.4.3.3 Non-uniform mutation

In this form of mutation, a random value is added to the individual allele instead of replacing it. The added random value is usually drawn from a non-uniform distribution; generally with mean zero and more likely resulting in small values being generated instead of larger ones. Indeed, adding small values will help exploiting the obtained candidate solution by limiting the searching process to its local proximity. Large values, however, are also needed to help explore the whole search space and maintain population diversity.

Given a real valued encoded genotype $x=(x_1,x_2,...,x_n)$ defined in $[min_x, max_x]^n$ and a randomly sampled vector $m=(m_1, m_2, ..., m_n)$, a new offspring x' is created by:

$$x' = x + m;$$

Equation 4-6

Where m is most commonly generated using a Gaussian distribution defined by $N(0, \sigma)$, i.e. a normal distribution with mean zero and a certain standard deviation σ. As a Gaussian distribution function is defined on the whole space of real value, i.e. $\Re$, the resulting alleles outwith the range of values are usually reset to the search space boundary values (min_x and max_x). There are, however, other distributions (e.g. Cauchy) which proved to be successful in search of continuous optimal solutions.

4.4.3.4 A note on mutation tuning

It is important to note that beside the adjustment of mutation rate, the probability distribution standard deviation must be carefully tuned in order to control the effect of mutation on the quality of the generated offspring and its exploration/exploitation capabilities. Assigning σ a too high value makes the fine-tuning of the searched solution difficult (poor exploitation), whereas a too low value may risk getting the search process stuck in a local optimum. Several methods have been proposed for automatically adjusting mutation parameters. The most interesting approach is the self-adaptation technique used in evolutionary strategies (ES) where the standard deviation, called *strategy parameter*, is embedded with the genotype, i.e. encoded with the problem parameters, and also changed by variation operators; i.e. coevolved (Bäack et al., 1991; Bäack and Schwefel, 1993; Eiben and Smith, 2003).

The adaptation of self-adaptable evolutionary strategies (ES) to supervised training of spiking neural networks will be discussed in detail in the next two chapters. The strategy parameters are coevolved with spiking neural network parameters and no recombination is used. The suitability of self-adaptable ESs for training biologically plausible neural networks and the obtained performance, demonstrated on a classification task, will also be presented.

4.4.4   Selection techniques

The update of the population during the evolution process is defined by the chosen selection method. It is important for improving the quality of candidate solutions and removing those with low fitness values. The main approaches to realise this competition between population individuals throughout different generations are: Generational algorithms where the entire population is replaced and steady-state approaches where only a fraction of it is changed. However, the selection of both approaches is based on the individual fitness value. It is crucial for the chosen selection method to maintain a balance between the selection pressure, which controls the survival rate of individuals, and the population diversity. These two aspects are inversely related to each other as increasing the selection pressure will decrease the population diversity and vice versa. A too high selection pressure may limit the search to a small subset of the search space and therefore lead to a premature convergence to a local optimum. On the other hand, a too low selection pressure may slow down the convergence of the evolutionary algorithm.

4.4.4.1   Tournament selection

For each individual of the new generation, a tournament is held between n individuals that are randomly chosen from the current population and the fittest individual is finally selected as a member of the new population. The selection pressure is controlled through the tournament size; usually two individuals are selected to form a tournament as a larger number will cause a strong selection pressure and therefore result in a premature convergence. Tournament selection is widely used due to its simple implementation, smaller number of adjustable parameters, and its speed. This selection scheme is illustrated by the pseudo-code shown in Figure 4-13.

```
Tournament Selection{
    for ( i=1; i<= Population Size; i++){
    Randomly select two individuals Indiv1 and Indiv2 from currunt population ;
    Compare their fitness values;
    Insert the best individual in the new population
    }
}
```

Figure 4-13 Pseudo-code for tournament selection (tournament size=2). Two individuals are selected for competition.

4.4.4.2 Fitness proportional selection (biased roulette wheel)

In this probabilistic selection scheme, each individual is assigned a survival probability based on its fitness value. The survival probability of a given individual p_i is calculated as a ratio between its fitness value and the total summed fitness of the population, and formulated by the following equations:

$$p_i = \frac{f_i}{\sum_{j=1}^{n} f_i}, \quad i \in [1,n]$$

Equation 4-7

Where, n is the size of population and i is the index of a given individual. These probabilities satisfy the sum condition:

$$\sum_{i=1}^{n} p_i = 1$$

Equation 4-8

This selection scheme is modelled as a roulette wheel where each individual is assigned a slot according to its survival probability p_i, i.e. the size of an individual slot is proportional to its fitness value (see Figure 4-14 for an illustration). Selection is performed by spinning the roulette wheel (i.e. generating a random number) and the individual corresponding to the winning slot is inserted in the population of the next generation.

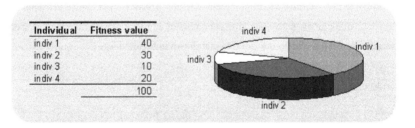

Individual	Fitness value
indiv 1	40
indiv 2	30
indiv 3	10
indiv 4	20
	100

Figure 4-14 Fitness proportional selection scheme represented by a biased roulette wheel whose four individuals are assigned four slots according to their fitness values (example simulated using Microsoft Excel).

A major drawback of this method is the difficulty of controlling the selection pressure. Unlike the tournament selection where it is simply controlled by a single parameter (i.e. tournament size), in the fitness proportional scheme the selection pressure depends on the relative fitness values of each population of individuals. As the roulette wheel is largely covered by individuals with high fitness value, they tend to quickly dominate the whole population which results in premature convergence.

4.4.4.3 Rank selection

Rank selection was proposed by Baker (1985) in order to overcome the uncontrolled selection pressure problem inherent in the fitness proportional selection scheme (Baker, 1987). In this method, the survival probability of a given individual is based on its fitness rank rather that its fitness value. Using individual ranks will allow better control of the selection pressure and therefore prevents individuals with higher fitness from quickly dominating the whole population. It has been suggested that rank based selection outperforms the fitness proportional selection and can also be employed to speed up the evolutionary algorithm search process (Whitley, 1989). Ranking population individuals can be seen as assigning each individual a new fitness value according to its first calculated fitness. The individual survival probability is determined using linear and non-linear transforms. Using linear transforms, rank selection can be formulated as follows:

Given a population of n individuals sorted according to their fitness value such that the best and the worst individuals are given ranks n and 1 respectively. The individual survival probability is then determined using a linear function given by:

$$p_i = \frac{1}{n}\left(P_{worst} + (P_{best} - P_{worst})\frac{i-1}{n-1} \right), \quad i \in [1,n] \qquad \textbf{Equation 4-9}$$

where:

i represents the individual rank;

The quantities (P_{best}/n) and (P_{worst}/n) represent the survival probability of the best and the worst fit individuals, respectively (Blickle and Thiele, 1995). In order to satisfy the probability condition (Equation 4-8), it is a requirement that $P_{worst} \geq 0$ and $P_{best}=2-P_{worst}$. An example of using such a linear transform is shown below in Table 4-2:

Individual rank	Survival probability p_i
12	0.13
11	0.12
10	0.11
9	0.10
8	0.09
7	0.09
6	0.08
5	0.07
4	0.06
3	0.06
2	0.05
1	0.04
	1.00

Table 4-2 Linear ranking selection applied on a population of twelve individuals

In order to allow better control of the selection pressure, another non-linear transform is used, where the survival probabilities are calculated using the exponential function defined by:

$$pi = \frac{c^{n-1}}{\sum_{j=1}^{n} c^{n-j}}, \quad i \in [1,n]$$

Equation 4-10

Where $c \in [0,1]$ is a tuneable parameter used for adjusting the selection pressure. While larger values of c (i.e. $c \approx 1$) result in a weak selection pressure as survival probabilities converge to the same value, smaller values (i.e. $c \approx 0$) strengthens the selection pressure and the highly ranked individuals are more favoured.

4.4.4.4 Elitism

The role of elitism is to keep track of the best candidate solutions of a given problem by copying the best individuals from the population of the previous generation to the subsequent generation. This helps maintain the information contained within the best individuals and ensures it is not lost due to the application of variation operators. It is important to retain a reasonable number of best individuals in order to maintain a good level of population diversity.

4.5 Neural networks and evolutionary computing

It has been shown in the previous sections that evolutionary algorithms are capable of optimising multimodal problems and offer a promising model-free optimisation technique. In contrast to analytical methods such as gradient methods, EAs can be used to optimise objective functions that are not necessarily differentiable. Because of these interesting features, EAs have been adopted for training different types of artificial neural networks, where classical training approaches are either not feasible or they may experience difficulties in adjusting the network free parameters. Evolutionary algorithms have been used for optimising artificial neural networks (ANNs) at three levels: connection weights; architectures; and learning rules (Yao, 1999).

In terms of weight evolution, evolutionary algorithms offer an alternative global training approach where the space of network free parameters (i.e. weights) is searched globally rather than locally as it is the case of gradient based training techniques. Both binary (Whitley et al., 1990; Srinivas and Patnaik, 1991; de Garis, 1991; Janson and Frenzel, 1993) and real valued (Montana and Davis, 1989; Fogel et al., 1990; Porto et al., 1995; Yao et al., 1996; Berlich and Kunze, 1997; Fogel et al., 1997; Fogel et al., 1995; Schultz and Wechsler, 1994; Sarkar and Yegnanarayana, 1997; Angeline, 1997) encoding schemes have been used to represent network weights. They are also used to train recurrent networks where it is difficult to use other training techniques (Greenwood, 1997; Hutchins, 1994; Lei and Jiang, 1997; Saravanan and Fogel, 1994; Torreele, 1991; Mandischer, 1995). The use of EAs is also extended to the optimisation of network architectures, as it allows the automatic adaptation of their topologies to various tasks (Koza and Rice, 1991; Bornholdt and Graudenz, 1992; Tang et al., 1995; Perez and Holzmann, 1997; Ragg and Gutjahr, 1997; Likothanassis and Georgopoulos, 1992). Hence, EAs provides an approach to automate ANN design as both ANN connection weights and structures can be evolved (Yao, 1999). Besides, EAs are also combined with ANNs to evolve the learning rules (Bengio and Bengio, 1990; Bengio et al., 1992; Fontanari and Meir, 1991; Baxter, 1992; Chalmers, 1990). This can be seen as a process of "learning to learn" in ANNs (Yao, 1999). Furthermore, EAs have also been used to evolve the neuron activation functions by evolving their adjustable parameters.

This work is partly concerned with supervised training of spiking neural networks (chapters 5 and 6) where network architectures are fixed manually (trial and error) and only synaptic parameters (i.e. weights, delays or time constants of neuron membrane) are learned. Therefore the use of evolutionary algorithms (precisely evolutionary strategies) with spiking neural networks has been investigated only at the level of network free parameters, and not at the architecture level.

4.6 Summary

This chapter identified evolutionary algorithms (EAs) as a robust optimisation technique for both discrete and continuous problems. It has also discussed their ability to cope with complex and multimodal objective functions where traditional optimisation approaches proved less efficient and sometimes not feasible. Different varieties of evolutionary algorithms have been identified and compared with respect to their historical background, their customised implementations of different components of EAs and their suitability for optimising different categories of problems. Also different implementations of the key elements of an evolutionary algorithm were identified, and their advantages and disadvantages were highlighted. This chapter has also identified evolutionary algorithms as an effective tool for optimising different aspects of artificial neural networks. It has been shown that evolutionary algorithms offer a robust alternative to gradient based techniques where the ANN error function is globally minimised and its differentiability is not required. Furthermore, they offer a natural alternative for training recurrent ANNs where classical training techniques are not feasible. Due to these interesting features, evolutionary algorithms have been adopted in this work for training biologically plausible neural networks, with particular focus on a different variant of evolutionary strategies, called self-adaptable evolutionary strategies, where strategy parameters are automatically adjusted and no human intervention is required. Their suitability for continuous problem optimisation and their appealing self-adaptability feature make them a natural choice for searching the optimal parameters that underlie the learning process in spiking neurons and therefore the creation of evolutionary spiking neural networks (ESNN). The introduction of evolutionary algorithms into spiking neural networks is presented in detail in the following two chapters. In chapter 5 EAs form the basis of supervised training of spiking neural networks based on a variant of integrate-and-fire neurons, called the spike response model (SRM) neurons, and in chapter 6 EAs are used for supervised learning of the optimal parameters of a more detailed model of synapses called dynamic synapses.

CHAPTER 5

Towards evolutionary spiking neural networks

5.1 Introduction

While the previous chapter discussed the efficiency of evolutionary algorithms and their widespread use in different types of optimisation problems, this chapter presents in detail how one of EA variants, namely evolutionary strategies (ES), can be successfully applied for supervised training of spiking neural networks based on the spike response model (SRM) (which was reviewed in Chapter 3). The problem of learning the free parameters of spiking neural networks for performing a particular task is approached as a continuous optimisation problem, where an evolutionary strategy is adopted as a natural way for searching the spiking network parameters. However, before presenting the devised approach, the existing supervised approach is briefly presented and its drawbacks are discussed. The content of this chapter is organised as follows:

Section 5.2 highlights the abundance of research on unsupervised training algorithms for spiking neural networks and the lack of efficient supervised approaches. It also discusses the importance of supervised approaches when a priori knowledge about the task to be learned is available. Section 5.3 discusses the neuron model chosen for this approach and the possibility of extending the approach to other neural models. Spikeprop is then briefly presented in section 5.4 and its drawbacks are highlighted in section 5.5. Section 5.6 presents in detail the proposed approach where the network architecture, its genetic representation, the use of evolutionary strategies and the proposed simple alternative encoding scheme are elaborated. A demonstration of the proposed approach on classification of nonlinearly separable problems, where benchmark data sets are used, is presented in Section 5.7. Finally, a discussion of the performance obtained, limitations and possible areas of improvements are presented in section 5.8.

5.2 To supervise or not to supervise?

Most existing training algorithms for spiking neural networks are unsupervised and/or competitive learning methods that are based on the famous Hebbian or STDP (Spike Timing Dependent Plasticity) paradigms. A number of research works have been carried out in this direction, such as

(Song et al., 2000; Ruf and Schmitt, 1997; Panchev and Wermter, 2004; Panchev et al., 2002; Hopfield, 1995; Gerstner, 1995; Gerstner et al., 1996; Gerstner and Kistler, 2002; Bi and Poo, 1998, 2001; Kistler and Hemmen, 1999, 200; Kistler, 2002; Kepecs and Rossum, 2002; Froemke and Dan, 2002; Karmarkar and Buonomano, 2002; Kobayashi and Poo, 2004; Suri and Sejnowski, 2002; Yao and Dan, 2001; Bofill-i-Petit and Murray, 2004; Oster and Liu, 2004; Izhikevich, 2003; Saudargiene, 2004; Burkitt et al., 2004; Tegner and Kepecs, 2002). In these methods, correlation between pre- and post-synaptic firing times/activity is considered as a basis for local modification of the synaptic strengths as spike trains get transferred from nerve cell to another. However, a priori knowledge about the available data is not exploited when adjusting (learning) the synaptic free parameters that underlie the learning of a specific task or the mapping between a set of input and output patterns. Unsupervised learning is undoubtedly important for discovering existing relations between the processed data samples (clustering). An example of such a learning paradigm, particularly competitive learning, is investigated in Chapter 7 of this book where a different neuronal model, called *neural oscillators*, is used for a colour image segmentation application. However, supervised training is more suitable and often outperforms its unsupervised counterpart when knowledge about the processed data is available upfront (e.g. classifying labelled data).

This chapter discusses a devised supervised learning approach for spiking neural networks where an evolutionary strategy is used to evolve the spiking network free parameters, i.e. synaptic weights and delays. The application of this supervised approach is applied to static synapse-based networks in this chapter, while its application to dynamic synapse-based networks is discussed in the next chapter (Chapter 6). The neural model (Spike Response Model) that underlies the spiking network processing elements is first presented. Then, before elaborating the design and implementation of the newly developed learning approach, the existing supervised learning algorithm found in the literature is presented and its drawbacks and limitations are discussed.

5.3 Neuron model

The neuron model chosen for this work is the spike response model (SRM) which has been already described in Chapter 3. This model is chosen due to its tractability and the fact that it represents a mathematical generalisation of the leaky integrate-and-fire model which is defined by a set of differential equations. This model has also been used in the existing gradient-based supervised training, called Spikeprop (Bohte et al., 2002), which offer a benchmark for performance comparison. Static synapses, as opposed to dynamic synapses, are used to connect neurons to input sources of spikes and to other neurons in subsequent layers. This type of connection is characterised by an efficacy (weight) represented by a real valued scalar and a delay represented by a positive number which represents the time required by a spike generated at a presynaptic neuron before its starts affecting the postsynaptic neuron. This type of synapse is called *static* because the synaptic strength does not depend on the temporal structure of the incoming spikes. On the other hand, dynamic synapses, a more biologically plausible model, are *weightless* and their efficacy varies upon the arrival of spike trains (more details about this type of synapse in Chapter 6). The use of this type of synapse will form the bulk of the next chapter and the application of the proposed supervised training to dynamic synapse-based spiking networks will be presented.

However, it is important to note that the application of the proposed training approach is not limited to the spike response model (SRM). The proposed training algorithm can also be applied to other forms of integrate and fire model such as leaky integrate and fire, and conductance-based models. An extension of the proposed approach to a spiking neural network based on the leaky integrate-and-fire model and its hardware implementation on Field Programmable Gate Arrays (FPGAs) has presented in (Johnston et al., 2004).

5.4 Existing gradient based supervised training (Spikeprop)

This section briefly reviews the existing supervised training approach, called Spikeprop, presented in (Bohte et al., 2002). This algorithm is based on the gradient descent method and is inspired by the famous error backpropgation (BP) algorithm used with classical artificial neural networks. It therefore represents an adaptation of BP to spiking neural networks. The following subsections describe briefly the network architecture used in this algorithm, the adaptation of BP to spiking networks and the adopted receptive fields-based temporal encoding.

5.4.1 Network architecture

A feedforward spiking network architecture is adopted in Spikeprop where each connection between two neurons is subdivided into multiple synaptic sub-connections. Each sub-connection is characterised by a fixed delay (i.e. not trained) and an adjustable weight (see Figure 5-1 for an illustration). A synaptic delay (d^k in Figure 5-1) is considered as the time difference between the firing time of the presynaptic neuron (t_i in Figure 5-1) and the time it starts affecting the postsynaptic neuron membrane potential, i.e. the time the postsynaptic potential starts to rise. The authors used 16 sub-connections and assigned a different delay value for each sub-connection (sub-connections 1 to 16 have been assigned delays from 1 to 16 milliseconds respectively). No indication is, however, given as to how the individual synaptic delays are initialised nor what could be the optimal number of such sub-connections and how they affect the convergence of the derived error backpropagation training algorithm.

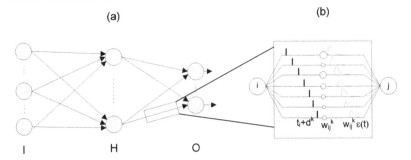

Figure 5-1 Spiking network architecture adopted in Spikeprop (Bohte et al., 2002). (a) Feedforward network with input (I), hidden (H) and output (O) layers where (b) multiple sub-connections are used to connect two neurons, such that each synaptic connection is characterised by a fixed delay and a weight.

The spike response model (SRM) is adopted in this algorithm where an alpha function is used to model the shape of postsynaptic potentials. The state of a neuron j which receives inputs from all its predecessor neurons is determined by the integration of the weighted contributions of all spikes generated at all sub-connections from all predecessor neurons. It is given by the following equation:

$$x_j(t) = \sum_{i \in \Gamma_j} \sum_{k=1}^{m} w_{ij}^k y_i^k(t)$$

Equation 5-1

Where w_{ij}^k denotes the weights of each sub-connection k and m represents the total number of these sub-connections. Γ_j is the set of predecessor neurons of neuron j and $y_i^k(t)$ is the delayed unweighted contribution of a spike generated at a sub-connection k. This unweighted contribution is given by

$$y_i^k(t) = \varepsilon(t - t_i - d^k)$$

Equation 5-2

Where $\varepsilon(t)$ is an alpha function modelling the shape of a PSP and given by

$$\varepsilon(t) = \frac{t}{\tau} e^{1-\frac{t}{\tau}}$$

Equation 5-3

The parameter τ represents the neuron membrane time constant which determines the rising and decaying time of the postsynaptic potential.

5.4.2 Error backpropagation-based Training

In order to minimise the error between the desired firing times of the output neurons and their actual firing times, the authors (Bohte et al., 2002) derived an error backpropagation algorithm, called Spikeprop, similar to the derivation of the classical backpropagation rule used with conventional multilayer perceptrons (MLPs). Although the error function is not differentiable with respect to the connecting weights, its derivation was made possible through the assumption of the linearity of the neuron state variable $x_i(t)$ (a nonlinear function as indicated in Equation 5-1) around a small neighbourhood of the neuron firing time. This has led to the derivation of the output firing time function t_j (considered as a nonlinear function of the neuron state variable x_j) with respect to x_j:

$$\frac{\partial t_j}{\partial x_j(t)}(t_j^a) = \frac{\partial t_{j(x_j)}}{\partial x_j(t)}\bigg|_{x_j=\theta} = \frac{-1}{\dfrac{\partial x_j(t)}{\partial t}(t_j^a)} = \frac{-1}{\sum_{i,l} w_{ij}^l \dfrac{\partial y_j^l(t)}{\partial t}(t_j^a)} \qquad \text{Equation 5-4}$$

where θ is the threshold and $y_j^l(t)$ is the potential response from synapse l for output neuron j. The learning rule for the synaptic weight modification between the output neuron j and its presynaptic neuron i (in the hidden layer) is given by :

$$\Delta w_{ij}^k(t_j^a) = -\eta \frac{y_i^k(t_j^a)(t_j^d - t_j^a)}{\sum_{i\in\Gamma_j}\sum_l w_{ij}^k \dfrac{\partial y_j^l(t_j^a)}{\partial t_j^a}} \qquad \text{Equation 5-5}$$

Where t_j^d and t_j^a represent the desired firing time and actual firing time respectively.
The learning rule for modifying the connecting weights between neurons in the hidden layer (denoted by index i) and the neurons in the input layer (denoted by index h) is given by:

$$\Delta w_{hi}^k = -\eta\, y_h^k(t_i^a)\delta_i = -\eta \frac{y_h^k(t_i^a)\sum_j\{\,\delta_j\sum_k w_{ij}^k \dfrac{\partial y_i^k(t_j^a)}{\partial t_i^a}\}}{\sum_{n\in\Gamma_i}\sum_l w_{ni}^l \dfrac{\partial y_n^l(t_i^a)}{\partial t_i^a}} \qquad \text{Equation 5-6}$$

Where

$$\delta_i = \frac{\sum_{j\in\Gamma^i}\delta_j\{\ \sum_k w_{ij}^k \dfrac{\partial y_i^k(t_i^a)}{\partial t_i^a}\ \}}{\sum_{h\in\Gamma_i}\sum_l w_{hi}^l \dfrac{\partial y_h^l(t_i^a)}{\partial t_i^a}} \qquad \text{Equation 5-7}$$

and Γ_i is a set of afferent neurons for neuron i.

For more details about the derivation steps and the algorithm itself, the reader is referred to (Bohte et al., 2002). As spiking neurons can only handle information in the form of spikes, the following section will briefly review the receptive fields encoding scheme used in Spikeprop and also applied in the proposed approach for comparison reasons.

5.4.3 Receptive fields-based temporal encoding

The inputs of spiking neural networks are temporally encoded in the form of spike trains, the only representation form a spiking neuron can handle. The multidimensional raw data, which consists of real values, are first transformed into temporal patterns before being processed by the network. A sparse coding scheme is adopted in Spikeprop, where a real value is encoded by a population of neurons based on an array of receptive fields. Gaussian receptive fields have been used in order to generate firing times from real values.

The range of the data is first calculated, and each input feature is then encoded with a population of neurons that cover the whole range of input data. For a variable with a range of *Max-Min*, a set of *m* neurons are used with Gaussian receptive fields. The centre C_i and the width σ of each neuron *i* are determined by Equation 5-8 and Equation 5-9:

$$C_i = Min + \frac{1}{m-2} \frac{(2i-3)}{(Max-Min)})$$

Equation 5-8

$$\sigma = \frac{1}{m-2} \frac{1}{\beta(Max-Min)}$$

Equation 5-9

where a value of 1.5 is used for the variable β. The authors in (Bohte et al., 2002) state that this parameter is tuned experimentally. For each n-dimensional input pattern, the encoding scheme results in a matrix of *n x m* values comprised between zero and one as shown on the vertical axis in Figure 5-2. These values are then converted to delay times, where an early time t =0 is associated with a value of one, and later times up to t =10 with lower responses, and the resulting spike times are rounded to the nearest simulation time step. An illustration of this encoding scheme is shown in Figure 5-2, where the firing times resulting from the encoding of the real value '40' using four receptive fields are shown.

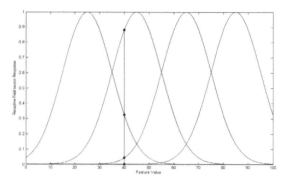

Figure 5-2 Matlab simulation of Sparse Coding of a real value, and its corresponding firing times defined by the intersection of the vertical line with the Gaussian receptive fields of each encoding neuron.

5.5 Drawbacks of gradient-based supervised training

The existing supervised training (Spikeprop) reviewed above is a gradient based approach. In order to allow the derivation of the output error function, originally a multidimensional non differentiable function, the algorithm assumes that the time course of the resulting postsynaptic potential can be approximated by a linear function and that a synapse consists of a fixed number of sub-connections (16 sub-connection were considered), each of which has a fixed delay with the restriction to use only positive weights. This algorithm suffers of the following shortcomings:

- The convergence of the algorithm is vulnerable to being caught in local minima, since it is gradient-based and the error function is a multidimensional nonlinear function with a very large set of adjustable parameters.

- The convergence of the algorithm is not guaranteed as it depends on fine tuning of several parameters before the start of the algorithm. The effect of setting the initial weights, the learning rate and the neuron time constants is not clear, and the author stated that the algorithm fails to converge when these parameters are not carefully chosen.

- The structure of the synapse which consists of a fixed number of sub-connections, each of which has a fixed synaptic delay, 16 sub-connections are considered in (Bohte et al., 2002), leads to a drastic increase in the number of connecting synapses and therefore the number of adjustable weights. Consequently, the implementation of such an algorithm requires more memory and the complexity of the error surface is increased since a large set of weights needs to be tuned.

- The huge number of synaptic connections makes it difficult for such algorithms to scale up when processing high-dimensional datasets is considered.

- Also having a fixed number of sub-connections with fixed delay values is not a necessity and yields a lot of redundant connections.

- The algorithm entails the problem of 'silent neurons'; i.e. if the output do not fire then the algorithm halts, since no error can be calculated.

In this work, a new alternative derivative-free approach is devised and its implementation details are described in the following sections. The approach has been demonstrated on classification tasks where benchmark datasets are used. Its performance and limitations are also compared to existing supervised training of spiking neural networks as well as classical artificial neural networks.

5.6   Proposed evolutionary spiking neural network (ESNN)

In order to overcome the drawbacks of gradient-based training of spiking neurons and the shortcomings of Spikeprop mentioned in the previous section, and since evolutionary strategies offer a natural way for global optimisation of continuous problems as highlighted in the previous chapter, a new spiking neural network architecture with an evolutionary-based supervised training is devised and presented in detail in this section. The use of evolutionary strategies (ES) allows global optimisation of synaptic delays and weights and therefore the problem of getting stuck in a local optimum is avoided. Also, the differentiability of the network error function is no longer a requirement, hence several forms of error functions can be chosen.

The important self-adaptability feature of ESs, where both optimised parameters and strategy parameters are co-evolved according to the individual performance, offers more flexibility in terms of the initialisation of the network free parameters as the less fit individuals are automatically discarded and prevented from being carried over to next generations. On the other hand, no careful tuning of the learning rate is required, as the parameter itself is not required in the proposed approach. Also the problem of silent output neurons is solved in this approach. If an output neuron stays silent, a very late 'virtual' firing time is assigned to it, which results in a big error being generated and therefore the whole candidate solution (spiking network) is automatically discarded by the evolutionary strategy because of its poor performance (generating a big error). The following sections describe the adopted network architecture, the genetic representation of a network and the process of mapping a phenotype (network) to its corresponding genotype and vice versa. Other aspects are also elaborated such as the proposed temporal coding, the ES-based supervised training, and finally a demonstration of the proposed approach on a classification task, where some selected benchmark datasets are used.

5.6.1 Network architecture

A feed-forward fully connected spiking network is implemented, where the different layers are labelled I, H, O for the input, hidden and output layer respectively as shown in Figure 5-3. The spiking neurons are based on the spike response model (SRM), and are connected via static synapses which are featured by a real valued weight representing the synaptic strength and a delay representing the time required for a spike, generated at the presynaptic neuron, to reach the postsynaptic neuron (see highlighted connections between an output neuron and its predecessor neurons which are illustrated in Figure 5-3).

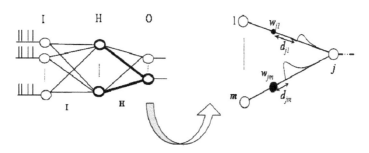

Figure 5-3 Network architecture with connections between a neuron j and its predecessors highlighted. A connecting synapse is characterized by a weight w reflecting its strength and a delay d that a spike generated at presynaptic neuron needs to reach the postsynaptic neuron

Unlike the network structure adopted in the work of Bohte et al. (2002) where several sub-connections are used between each pair of neurons, the proposed structure considers only one synaptic connection between two neurons, each of which is characterized by a weight and a delay value. As a result, the number of free parameters is considerably reduced, particularly when a large scale network is required, which has the advantage of reducing the time required for the training convergence, the memory required for software simulation and also the resources needed for possible hardware implementation, e.g. Field Programmable Gate Array (FPGA), of such networks. Moreover, no restriction on the sign of synaptic weights is imposed, both positive and negative weights are allowed.

As illustrated in Figure 5-3, a neuron j is connected to a set Γ_j of immediate predecessors referred to as pre-synaptic neurons from which it receives a set of spikes with firing times denoted by t_i, where $i \in \Gamma_j$. Although biologically implausible, it is assumed that a neuron generates one spike at most during the simulation time, i.e. more importance is given to the first spike in a spike train. Neurons fire when their state variable, i.e. their membrane potential, reaches a certain threshold θ from below. The internal state of a neuron, $x_j(t)$, is determined by the integration of the received spike responses modulated by the synaptic strengths and is expressed in Equation 5-10 as follows:

$$x_j(t) = \sum_{i \in \Gamma_j} w_{ji} y_i(t)$$
Equation 5-10

Where $y_i(t)$ is the unweighted post-synaptic potential (PSP) generated by a single spike coming from the presynaptic neuron i and impinging on neuron j. The amplitude of the PSP is modulated by the synaptic static efficacy w_{ji} to obtain the actual height of the post-synaptic potential. The quantity $y_i(t)$ represents the unweighted impact of a synaptic connection on the membrane potential of the postsynaptic neuron j and is given by Equation 5-11

$$y_i(t) = \varepsilon(t - t_i - d_{ji})$$
Equation 5-11

where d_{ji} is the time delay associated with the synaptic connection as shown in Figure 5-3, t_i is the firing time of the presynaptic neuron i, and $\varepsilon(t)$ defines the function of a response to an incoming spike and describing a standard form of a PSP (as shown in Figure 5-4). The function $\varepsilon(t)$ is modelled by an α-function as described in Equation 5-12 below:

$$\begin{cases} \varepsilon(t) = \dfrac{t}{\tau} e^{1-\frac{t}{\tau}} & \text{if } t > 0 \\ \varepsilon(t) = 0 & \text{if } t \le 0 \end{cases}$$
Equation 5-12

where τ is the membrane potential time constant defining the PSP rising and decaying times. The firing time t_j is defined as the first time the membrane potential of the neuron j reaches the threshold from below as shown in Figure 5-4. Thus, the firing time t_j is a non-linear function of the state-variable x_j. Similarly to the work of Bohte et al. (2002), the threshold θ is set to a constant value and the same value is used with all neurons in the network.

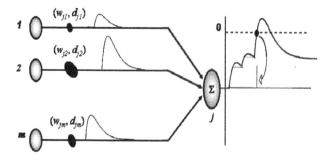

Figure 5-4 Integration of the responses to spikes, coming from predecessor neurons, (delayed and modulated by the synaptic weights) at the receiving neuron. The resulting membrane potential is compared to a certain threshold and a spike is produced when the threshold is reached from below.

5.6.2 Genetic representation of an SNN: from phenotype to genotype

Before an ES can be applied to evolve the free parameters of a spiking network, it is necessary to map the latter (phenotype) into its genetic representation (genotype), i.e. a vector (or other representation forms) which contains the adjustable parameters of a given spiking neural network (weights and delays). As the ES is adopted for evolving the network parameter and real value encoding is chosen, therefore the synaptic weights and delays do not undergo a binary encoding-decoding process. It is however necessary to decide about the order in which the synaptic weights and delays from different layers are concatenated in a genotype. As both weights and delays are assigned to different synapses and distributed over different layers, there are clearly several possibilities for arranging the spiking network parameters in an array of contiguous real values. In this work, the synaptic weights from different layers are concatenated together and form the first half of the genotype, where the weights of the input-to-hidden layer are inserted before the weights of the hidden-to-output layer. Similarly, the synaptic delays from different layers are grouped together and form the second half of the genotype where the delays of the input-to-hidden layer are inserted before the delays of the hidden-to-output layer (and after the weights of the hidden-to-output layer) as illustrated in Figure 5-5.

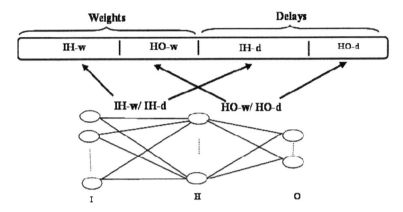

Figure 5-5 Mapping between a spiking neural network (phenotype) and its genetic representation (genotype). IH-w/ IH-d: Input to Hidden layer weights/delays. HO-w/ HO-d: Hidden to Output layer weights/delays.

Once evolved, a genotype is decoded such that a corresponding spiking network is built using the newly obtained weights and delays which are mapped to the same connections and layers as being used during the encoding phase. An example of mapping a given spiking network to its genotype and vice versa is shown in Figure 5-6 (where only integer numbers are used in this example for the sake of simplicity). It is important to note that other forms of genotypes can also be used within this framework where other recombination operators can be easily applied and tested. For example, instead of using an array of network parameters, a matrix can be used to hold the spiking network free parameters.

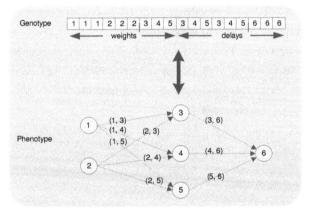

Figure 5-6 Mapping between an SNN (phenotype) and its genetic representation (genotype). Weights from each layer are concatenated together and are inserted before delay values from different layers.

5.6.3 Evolutionary strategy-based supervised training

While genetic algorithms (GAs) focus primarily on recombination which creates new candidate solutions by combining features of promising solutions, the primary variation operator in evolution strategies (ES), on the other hand, is mutation (Yao, 1999; Beyer, 1996; Goldberg et al., 1991). New candidate solutions are created by adding a random perturbation to individual genes of parent solutions. The power of an evolutionary strategy is mainly based upon its ability to perform a 'second order' evolutionary process. This process adapts the internal strategy parameters especially the mutation strength, in such a way that the whole algorithm exhibits near optimal performance, i.e. an ES drives itself into an optimal working regime (Beyer, 1996).

The training algorithm is aimed to learn a set of target firing times at the output layer, for a given set of temporal input patterns fed to the input layer. We define a set of temporal input patterns denoted by $\{P(t_1,...,t_m)\}$, where $P(t_1,...,t_m)$ represents a single input pattern such that the components $t_1,...,t_m$ define the firing times of each input neuron $i \in I$. For these input patterns a set of target firing times is assigned, denoted by $\{t^t_o\}$, at the output neurons $o \in O$. In order to learn the set of target firing times corresponding to the set of input patterns presented to the input neurons, an evolutionary strategy ES (derivative-free) is used to search for the optimum weights and delays that minimize the total error between actual and target output firing times. The objective function to be minimized is given by Equation 5-13:

$$E = \sum_{t}^{T} \sum_{o \in O} (t^a_o(t) - t^t_o(t))^2 \qquad \textbf{Equation 5-13}$$

where $t^a_o(t)$ and $t^t_o(t)$ are, respectively, actual and target output firing times of node i for pattern t, and T is the total number of patterns in the training set. Other error functions such as the sum of absolute differences can also be used within this framework.

An evolutionary strategy is chosen due to its ability to work on real numbers without the overhead of complex binary encoding schemes. As was emphasized in the previous chapter, ES have been proved to be well suited for treating continuous optimization problems. A number of different mutation operators have been developed. The traditional mutation operator adds to the alleles of the genes some random values selected from a Gaussian normal distribution. Other mutation operators include the use of a Cauchy distribution.

In this work a modified ES is used to train the spiking network in a supervised way, where a combination of both the Cauchy and Gaussian mutation is used. The use of the Cauchy distribution allows the exploration of the search space by making large mutations and helping to prevent premature convergence. On the other hand the use of the Gaussian mutation allows the exploitation of the best solutions found as it performs a local search. The spiking network is first mapped to a vector of real values as shown in Figure 5-5, which consists of the weights and delays of the synapses. A set of such vectors (individuals) will form the population to be evolved by the ES, which converge to a global optimum network that is tuned to the input patterns. The Evolutionary Strategy is implemented as follows:

Each population member of the ES consists of n-dimensional vectors, where n is the total number of existing weights and delays of different connections within input, hidden and output layer. The search for optimal parameters is performed in both spaces of weights and delay. While positive and negative weights are used, only positive delay values are allowed as they represent synaptic time delays in real neurons. The population at any given generation g is denoted by $P(g)$.

The implementation of the self-adaptive evolutionary strategy is described below (see Figure 5-7 for a diagrammatic illustration of the evolutionary process):

1. Generate the initial population of μ individuals (spiking networks), and set generation g=1. Each individual is taken as a pair of real-valued vectors, (x_i, η_i), $\forall\ i \in \{1,\ldots, \mu\}$, where the x_i's are objective variables representing the synaptic free parameters, and the η_i's are standard deviations for mutations. The vector x_i is the phenotype representation of a spiking neural network obtained by applying the mapping process mentioned above.

2. Evaluate the fitness score for each individual (x_i, η_i), $i=1,\ldots,\mu$, of the population based on the error function defined by Equation 5-13. Each individual is decoded into a network and run with the training patterns to determine its fitness value.

3. Each parent (x_i, η_i) generates a single offspring (x_i', η_i') such as:

for j=1,…, n, where n is the total number of existing weights and delays,

$$x_i'(j) = x_i(j) + \eta_i(j)N_j(0,1) \quad or \quad x_i'(j) = x_i(j) + \eta_i(j)\delta_j \qquad \textbf{Equation 5-14}$$

$$\eta_i'(j) = \eta_i(j)\,e^{(\tau'N(0,1)+\tau N_j(0,1))} \qquad \textbf{Equation 5-15}$$

where $x_i(j)$, $x_i'(j)$, $\eta_i(j)$ and $\eta_i'(j)$ denote the j-th component of the vectors x_i, x_i', η_i and η_i' respectively. $N(0,1)$ denotes a normally distributed one dimensional random number with mean 0 and standard deviation 1. $N_j(0,1)$ indicates that the random number is generated anew for each value of j. The factors τ and τ' are set to $\dfrac{1}{\sqrt{2\sqrt{n}}}$ and $\dfrac{1}{\sqrt{2n}}$.

δ_j is a Cauchy random variable with a scale of one, and is generated anew for each value of j. The functions in Equation 5-14 implement alternative mutation functions, such as at any particular run either Gaussian or Cauchy mutation is randomly used.

4. Calculate the fitness of each offspring (x_i', η_i'), $i=1,...,\mu$.

5. Generate a new population $P(g)$ using tournament selection (as previously described in Chapter 4) with elitism to keep track of the best individual at each generation.

6. Stop if a maximum number of generations is reached ($g=g_{max}$) or a target error is met; otherwise, $g=g+1$ and go to step 3.

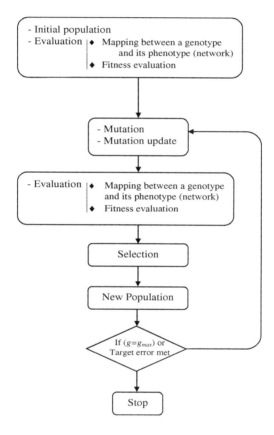

Figure 5-7 Supervised training of spiking neural networks based evolutionary strategy-based. An important feature of this approach is that both the spiking network free parameters and the evolutionary strategy parameters are automatically coevolved. Before evaluating a given genotype, it must be first mapped into its corresponding SNN (phenotype).

The one dimensional Cauchy density function centred at the origin is defined by

$$f_t(x) = \frac{1}{\pi}\frac{t}{t^2 + x^2} \; ; -\infty < x < \infty \qquad\qquad \textbf{Equation 5-16}$$

where $t>0$ is a scale parameter. The corresponding distribution function is given by the following equation:

$$F(x) = \frac{1}{2} + \frac{1}{\pi} \arctan(\frac{x}{t})$$

Equation 5-17

The shape of the Cauchy density function resembles that of Gaussian density function but approaches the axis so slowly that an expectation does not exist. As a result, the variance of a Cauchy distribution is infinite. Figure 5-8 shows the difference between the two distributions by plotting them on the same axis. It is obvious that the Cauchy function is more likely to generate a random number far away from the origin because of its long tail. This implies that the use of Cauchy mutation is more likely to escape from local minimum due to big jumps in the search space resulting from the application of such random distributions.

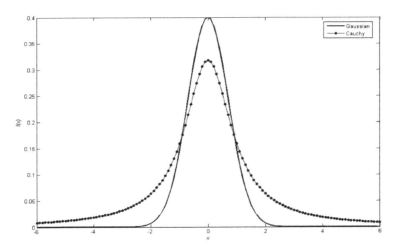

Figure 5-8 Gaussian and Cauchy distribution functions. The difference in standard deviation is made clear as well as its effect on the probability of generating large random values.

5.6.4 Temporal encoding

5.6.4.1 Drawbacks of receptive fields encoding scheme

The receptive field-based encoding scheme uses a population of neurons for encoding a given feature of a certain object from the real world. That is, every single value is distributed over a set of neurons that lie spatially within a certain neighbourhood where the neuron at the centre of a receptive field shows the strongest response and therefore will first generate a spike indicating its association with a particular feature. The receptive fields encoding scheme in its form used in (Bohte et al., 2002) can be categorised as a firing time-based coding as discussed in Chapter 3 (Section 3.8.3). However, the use of such encoding scheme is not without pitfalls. As a result, the dimensionality of the obtained temporal data, which is processed by the spiking network, is increased. Hence, the newly obtained temporal feature vectors are very long which yields a drastic increase in the number of free parameters to be trained. Therefore more synaptic connections are required to process such high-dimensional data because the dimensionality of the processed data imposes the size of the spiking network input layer. Also one needs to carefully tune the parameters of receptive fields, such as the optimal number of receptive fields as well as their widths and centres. In order to overcome such drawbacks, particularly the increase in the input data dimensionality, a simple encoding scheme called '1-D encoding scheme' is adopted and presented in the following sub-section. The sparse encoding scheme is also used for comparison reasons.

5.6.4.2 Linear or 1-D encoding scheme

This work uses another alternative encoding scheme, where each real value only generates one temporal value or firing time, hence maintaining the original data dimensionality and allowing the use of an optimal number of spiking neurons at the input layer. This encoding scheme is referred to as "1-D coding" (see illustration in Figure 5-9). The mapping between real feature values and temporal values is performed through a simple linear function, which converts a given real valued feature into a neuron firing time within a bound time interval called "encoding interval". The range of the original data is first calculated and the following linear function Equation 5-18 is applied:

$$y(f) = \frac{(b-a)}{range} . f + \frac{(a.Max - b.Min)}{range} \qquad \textbf{Equation 5-18}$$

where f represents the original raw feature values, $[a, b]$ represents the temporal coding interval, $range = Max - Min$ is the range of the original data and (Min, Max) represents the minimum and the maximum bounds of the original data respectively. The function y can only generate positive values as it represents the firing times of the input neurons.

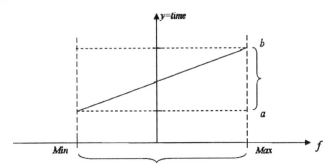

Figure 5-9 '1-D' encoding scheme. Feature values are mapped into firing times using a linear function which are bound within a temporal coding interval.

5.6.5 Introducing a framework for evolutionary SNNs (ESNNs)

The proposed approach offers a framework for training spiking neural networks in a supervised way using a self-adaptable evolutionary strategy. An illustration of this framework, called evolutionary spiking neural networks or ESNNs., is shown in Figure 5-10.

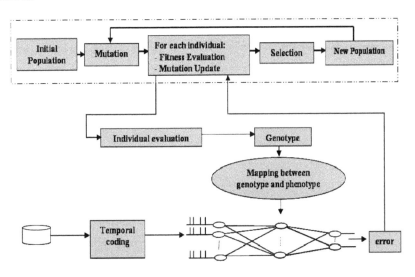

Figure 5-10 A framework for Evolutionary Spiking neural networks.

First of all, the data to be learned is temporally encoded so that information encoding real world objects (features) is expressed in the form of spikes, the only form spiking neurons can process and the means by which these neurons communicate. Obviously the encoding scheme is not limited to the sparse coding or the 1-D encoding schemes; the use of other encoding techniques is also possible as well as the use of temporal data when it is readily available. The choice of a particular encoding scheme is driven by its effect on the network size and its reliability in performing a particular task.

In parallel to temporal encoding procedure, a decoding of the genotype into a phenotype (a spiking network) is performed. Again, different mapping techniques can be envisaged within this framework. The temporally encoded data is then fed to the obtained network whose performance is evaluated based on an error measure. The use of evolutionary strategies allows multiple choices for the error function regardless of their differentiability. The performance of a network reflects its fitness value and contributes to its survival chance. The evolution of several networks, which can be parallelised for performance improvement, results in an optimal or near optimal solution that is able to learn the model of the processed temporal data. During the evolution process, the selection can be extended to other techniques as well as other variation operators, i.e. the combination of the mutation operator, the only variation operator used in this approach, with a crossover operator and/or the combination of other distributions for mutation.

5.7 Demonstration on classification tasks

A discrete time simulation was carried out using Matlab with a time step of 0.1 ms, where a number of routines are designed to implement the dynamics of spike response model of spiking neurons, as well as the evolutionary strategy operations. The training algorithm has been applied successfully to learn non-linearly separable problems, namely the XOR problem, the IRIS benchmark data set and the Breast Cancer data set.

5.7.1 Nonlinearly separable problems: the XOR problem

Before applying this approach to standard benchmark data sets, its ability to learn non-linearly separable patterns is first demonstrated with the famous XOR problem. Binary values are first transformed to a temporal code, where for output values a zero logic value is assigned a late firing time (20ms) and a logic value of one is assigned an early firing time (10ms). While for input values, a logic value of zero is assigned an early input firing time (0 ms) and a logic value of zero is assigned a later input firing time (6 ms). It is however possible to use different combinations with respect to inputs and outputs. The temporal values shown in Table 5-1 are in milliseconds. In order to demonstrate the learning of this nonlinear problem, a network structure of 2x5x1 is used (as shown in Figure 5-11), and a sum squared error (SSE) of 0.01 is set as an early stopping criterion of the training procedure. The nonlinear XOR problem is perfectly learned within 450 generations, although a clear discrimination between both classes is reached earlier at generation 180, as can be seen from Figure 5-12.

Digital inputs			Temporal codes		
Input 1	Input 2	Output	Input 1	Input 2	Output
0	0	0	0	0	20
0	1	1	0	6	10
1	0	1	6	0	10
1	1	0	6	6	20

Table 5-1 Temporal encoding of the XOR problem. Inputs: a logic value '0' is assigned an early input firing time (0ms) while a logic value '1' is assigned a late firing time (6ms). Output: an output logic value '0' is assigned a late firing time (20ms) while an output logic value '1' is assigned an early firing time (10ms). It is obviously possible to use other combinations.

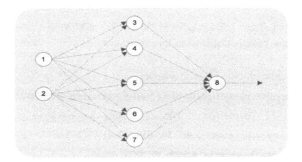

Figure 5-11 Spiking network for the XOR problem. Each synaptic connection is characterised by a weight (representing the synaptic strength) and a positive value (representing synaptic delay).

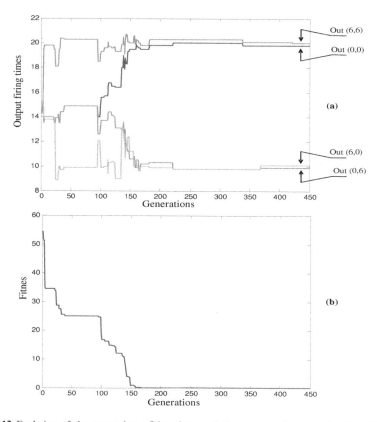

Figure 5-12 Evolution of the output layer firing times and the corresponding error function (a) XOR problem Convergence of the output firing times which correspond to different input firing times {(0,0), (0,6), (6,0), (6,6)}. <u>Before</u> weights and delays are trained: the output neuron produce spikes at irregular times. <u>After</u> the weights and delays are trained: the output neuron produce spikes at desired times for each class of the input, i.e. ~20ms for inputs {(0,0),(6,6)} and ~10ms for inputs {(0,6) and (6,0)}. (b) Convergence of the ES best error through different generations. It is shown that weight convergence is obtained around generation 200.

5.7.2 Classification of the IRIS benchmark dataset

After demonstrating the capability of the training approach to learn nonlinearly separable problems using the XOR test, its performance is further demonstrated with the IRIS benchmark data set, which consists of three classes of which two are non-linearly separable. A data set contains 150 random samples of flowers from the iris species setosa, versicolor, and virginica, each sample consists of 4 features (four-dimensional problem). From each species there are 50 observations for sepal length, sepal width, petal length, and petal width measured in centimeters. This dataset was used by Fisher (1936) in his initiation of the linear discriminant function technique.

127

The real values were temporally encoded using sparse coding, for comparison reasons, and the proposed 1-D encoding methods. With the sparse coding method, four receptive fields are used (m=4) with a network of 16x10x1, while a network of 4x10x1 is used with 1-D encoding scheme. The data set is split into a training and test set, each of which has 75 samples, and the target firing times of 6, 10, 14 ms are chosen to define the first, second and third class respectively.

A comparison of the performances obtained for the training and test sets, with respect to different settings and other types of classical artificial neural networks, Matlab ANN with backpropagation and LM (Levenberg-Marquardt) learning procedures, are summarized in Table 5-2. The convergence of the error function which corresponds to the best obtained solution at each generation is illustrated in Figure 5-13. The figure shows that an acceptable solution is obtained within less than 500 generations. Table 5-2 show that comparable performances are obtained with the use of both encoding schemes. Besides, the use of 1-D encoding schemes allows an even smaller scale network to perfectly learn the same problem, i.e. with less neuron resources.

	Maximum classification accuracy		
	Network	Training set	Test set
ES approach (sparse coding)	16x10x1	98.67 %	96.00 %
ES approach (1-D coding)	4x10x1	98.67 %	97.33%
Spike-Prop	50x10x3	97.5 %	96.2 %
Matlab BP	50x10x3	97.33 %	94.67 %
Matlab LM	50x10x3	98.67 %	96.00 %

Table 5-2 Comparison of performances for the IRIS data. The classification accuracy (during training and test) and the network size are compared between the proposed approach (ES with sparse coding and ES with 1-D encoding) and Spikeprop, Matlab BP and matlab LM.

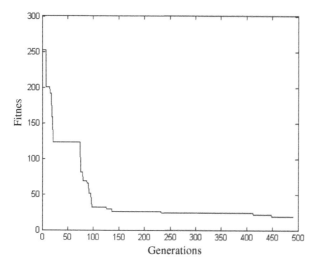

Figure 5-13 IRIS benchmark data set. Convergence of the error function for the best population network at each generation during the evolution process.

5.7.3 Classification of the Breast Cancer benchmark dataset

The breast cancer data set is obtained from the University of Wisconsin Hospitals[1], which is used for breast cancer diagnosis problem (Woldberg and Mangasarian, 1990; Mangasarian and Wolberg, 1990). The data set contains 699 samples, and is divided into benign and malignant classes. Each sample is described with nine attributes, represented by an integer ranging from one to ten with larger numbers indicating a greater likelihood of malignancy. There are, however, 16 samples that contain missing data. The data is split into two parts, training and test data sets with 341 and (342+16) samples in each set respectively. The samples with missing data are used for test and both the mean and mode were used to replace the missing data. However, comparable results are obtained for both pre-processing approaches. The 1-D linear temporal encoding is used to transform the real features into input neuron firing times and the performances obtained are shown in Table 5-3. Despite the use of a smaller network size, the performance of the proposed training approach is still comparable to existing approaches in terms of classification accuracy. Better generalisation is obtained when testing the network with new unseen data. The error convergence of the best population individual of each generation is shown in Figure 5-14.

---

[1] ftp://ftp.ics.uci.edu/pub/machine-learning-databases/breast-cancer-wisconsin/

	Maximum classification accuracy		
	Network	Training set	Test set
ES approach (1-D coding)	9x6x1	97.2 %	98.24%
Spike-Prop	64x15x2	97.8 %	97.6 %
Matlab BP	64x15x3	98.5 %	96.9 %
Matlab LM	64x15x3	98.00 %	97.30 %

Table 5-3 Comparison of obtained network performance on the Breast Cancer dataset. Only the 1-D encoding scheme is used in this test, as the use of sparse encoding increase drastically the number of input neurons and therefore the evaluation of each phenotype (SNN) becomes time consuming. While a smaller network size is used, a comparable accuracy and good generalisation are obtained

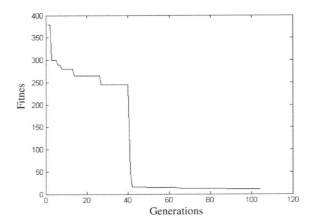

Figure 5-14 Cancer benchmark data set. Error convergence or the evolution of the error of the best network obtained at each generation.

5.8 Discussions

An alternative approach for supervised learning with spiking neural networks is proposed where individual spike times are used for information representation and processing. A simple architecture is presented, whose complexity is not affected when large-scale networks are considered. Unlike sparse coding, a simple linear temporal encoding scheme is used, which retains the dimensionality of the analyzed data sets rather than increasing it and consequently increase the size of the network. The training algorithm is based on a derivative-free approach using a self-adaptive evolutionary strategy with real value encoding of the spiking neural network free parameters, namely the synaptic strengths and delays.

The experimental evaluation with different nonlinearly separable problems demonstrates that the proposed approach proved successful in performing temporal learning and good performances are obtained when compared to previous works reported in the literature. However the training algorithm was time consuming for some problems. The simulations were run on a sequential machine (PC Pentium 4). While the testing phase takes only few seconds to decide about the class of the input sample, the training phase takes hours for a small scale problem such as the XOR problem and couple of days for larger scale problems such as the Breast Cancer data set. Being time consuming is generally an inherent feature of evolutionary based approaches, particularly when the evaluation of the fitness function is time consuming which is the case with spiking neural networks. Also the number of individuals that form a population affects the simulation time as all these individuals need to be evaluated in each generation, which involve processing the whole training samples each time an individual is evaluated. Obviously, further optimization could be introduced in order to speed up the simulation process. For example, an event-driven approach could be used to simulate the dynamics of spiking neurons and to calculate the output firing times, since no effort has been made within this work as a synchronous step by step (discrete) simulation is adopted. The simulation time in an event driven approach depends on the activity of the network (i.e. the firing frequency) and its application to the networks in this work may dramatically reduce the simulation time due to their low activity. Also the parallelisation of the evolutionary strategy would also reduce the time required for obtaining an optimal network. Moreover, as only the mutation operator is used for the ES approach, the effect of other recombination operators on the quality of the final solution as well as the speed of the convergence could be further investigated.

5.9 Summary

A devised derivative-free approach for supervised training of spiking neural network has been presented. The approach uses self-adaptable evolutionary strategies for automatic tuning of the free parameters, weights and delays in this case, of spiking networks that underlie the learning of a particular task. More flexibility is offered with respect to the choice of error functions, temporal encoding schemes and the setting of the network initial parameters. Also, an alternative simple encoding scheme is used which offers the advantage of maintaining the initial problem dimensionality instead of increasing it, as it is the case in other transforms. The demonstration of the proposed approach on benchmark classification tasks has shown that the spiking networks obtained are capable of perfectly learning nonlinearly separable problems using temporal coding. Comparable accuracies and good generalisation are obtained even when smaller network sizes are used. The proposed approach proved time consuming when larger networks are trained; this is due to the time required for evaluating a single network, as it needs to process all the available training samples before an error performance is obtained. However, some areas of improvements are suggested such as the use of an event-based approach and the parallelisation of the evolutionary strategy or even better a hardware implementation of the training approach on reconfigurable devices such as FPGAs (Field Programmable Gate Arrays).

While the neuron model used in this chapter is based on the spike response model (SRM) where neurons are interconnected through synapses (characterised by a weight and a delay, i.e. static synapses), the next chapter will explore the use of a more biologically plausible synapse model called 'dynamic synapses' (weightless synapses). An important feature of such models is that the efficacy (strength) of a synapse varies upon the structure of the received spike trains. The simulation and training of dynamic synapse-based spiking networks will form the bulk of the next chapter, where the performance of the spike-timing dependent plasticity (STDP) rule will be evaluated against the evolutionary strategy-based approach proposed in this chapter.

CHAPTER 6

Computing with dynamic synapses

6.1 Introduction

The previous chapter presented an evolutionary supervised training algorithm applied to feed-forward spiking neural networks with static synapses based neuron interconnection. The strengths of these synapses are represented by fixed scalars, called weights, and are independent of the structure of the incoming spike trains. In this chapter, however, a different synaptic model, called the dynamic synapse, is used and the investigation of training and computation capabilities of spiking networks with such biologically motivated synapses is presented. Unlike the conventional (static) synapse adopted in artificial neural networks, which is assumed as a static entity with a fixed weight, the dynamic synapse efficacy changes upon the arrival of input spikes, and depends on their temporal structure. Therefore a dynamic synapse is weightless and is represented by a dynamic entity whose value is spike-dependent. In this chapter the author uses this synaptic model in spiking neural networks for multidimensional data classification. The neurons are based on the integrate-and-fire model and both supervised and unsupervised training approaches are investigated. The unsupervised training is based on the biologically plausible spike-time-dependent plasticity rule (STDP) while the supervised training consists of extending the evolutionary strategy approach developed in chapter 5 (applied to spiking networks with static synapses and spike response model-based neurons) to this type of connecting synapses. The aim of the training in this case is to tune the parameters (time constants) of dynamic synapses so as the response of the output neurons is adapted to the pattern presented at the input layer in the form of spike impulses.

This chapter is organised as follows: Section 6.2 introduces the concept of dynamic synapses and highlights their differences with traditionally assumed static synapses. The biological dynamics of dynamic synapses are presented in section 6.3. Section 6.4 discusses the network architecture, the adopted neuron model, the temporal encoding of inputs and the decoding of the outputs. Section 6.5 outlines the STDP-based unsupervised training approach and discusses its suitability while section 6.6 presents the extension of the evolutionary strategy-based supervised training approach to spiking networks with dynamic synapses. The demonstration of the supervised training approach on classification tasks of selected benchmark datasets is described in section 6.7 with a discussion of the performances obtained given in section 6.8. The question of choosing between abstract or detailed models of synapses and neurons is addressed in section 6.9. Finally, section 6.10 summarises and concludes the chapter.

6.2 Dynamic synapses: what is different?

Most simulations of artificial neural networks share the assumption that synaptic efficacy is considered to be static during the reception of afferent spike trains. However recent experimental studies of real biological neural cells show that the synaptic efficacy generating the postsynaptic potential is a variable (dynamic) quantity which depends on the presynaptic activity, i.e. the temporal structure of the presynaptic spike train. It has also been shown from various experimental data that the post synaptic responses (PSR) produced by a synapse undergo systematic changes on a time scale of milliseconds and second, a time scale which is much shorter than the assumed time scale for learning, i.e. long term potentiation and long term depression (Fuhrmann et al., 2002; Markram and Tsodyks, 1996; Tsodyks et al., 1998; Maass, 1999; Bibitchkov et al., 2002; Bressloff, 1999; Abbot and Nelson, 2000; Zador and Dobrunz, 1997). These findings give rise to questions about the effects and the role of these rapid changes in information representation and processing in a neural system. Synapses are the specialised connections that allow signals to propagate from one nerve cell to the next. They play an important role in learning, memory and computations in neural circuits. They are not merely passive relays that faithfully transmit the signal they receive. They are, rather, gatekeepers that actively govern and modulate the flow of information in neuronal circuits (Zador and Dobrunz, 1997). A marked characteristic of these synapses is that they are dynamic, i.e. their transmission between neocortical neurons depends on the activity and frequency of the presynaptic spike trains and, when repeatedly stimulated, they can affect the postsynaptic response by either increasing (in case of facilitating synapses) or decreasing (in case of depressing synapses) it. It has been reported that dynamic synapses affect single neurons and network behaviour and that their transmission dynamics are variable among different classes of neurons (Thomson and Deuchars, 1994; Tsodyks and Markram, 1996, 1997).

The role of dynamic synapses on neurons and network behaviours has been recently researched where both feedforward and recurrent networks were considered. Natschläger et al. (2001) have shown that using dynamic synapses in a single layer feedforward network can approximate nonlinear filters. In other research by Liaw et al. and George et al. (1996, 1997), it has been shown that it is possible to extract significant features from unprocessed noisy speech signals and that the cross-correlation of the network output can selectively be increased for certain speech waveforms representing single words spoken by multiple speakers. Neural networks based on dynamic synapses have also been combined with wavelet feature for speech applications (George et al., 2003). Using recurrent networks, some researchers have shown that complex regimes of activity and synchrony can be obtained by a large population of excitatory neurons with depressing synapses. The behaviour of such recurrent networks has shown the emergence of synchronous, asynchronous and rhythmic activities similar to those observed throughout the cortex (Bressloff, 1999; Kistler and Hemmen, 1999; Senn et al., 1996; Tsodyks et al., 1998, 2000). Bibitchkov et al. (2002) studied the effect of synaptic depression on the attractors' fixed points and showed that both the stability of the stored patterns and the storage capacity are affected. This work has been extended by Pantic et al. (2002) where the role of noise and synaptic recovery in pattern retrieval was explored. They reported that recurrent spiking networks with depressing synapses are noise sensitive and show rapid switching between stored patterns (both overlapping and non-overlapping). The properties of coincidence detection in dynamic synapse-based networks were studied in (Pantic et al., 2003); it was reported that dynamic synapses, when threshold values are carefully chosen, can detect coincidence of afferent temporal patterns with larger frequencies than static synapses. These findings were proved for both Hodgkin-Huxley as well as integrate-and-fire neural models (Pantic et al., 2003).

This chapter presents a study of the feasibility and performance of evolutionary strategies in supervised training of spiking networks based on activity dependent synapses, i.e. dynamic synapses. Evolutionary strategies are used to search for the optimal parameters (time constants) of dynamic synapses which allow a feed-forward spiking network adapt the postsynaptic response of its output neuron/neurons according to different temporal patterns presented at the input layer. The ES-based supervised training is demonstrated on classification tasks and the performance obtained is compared with static synapses-based networks. The suitability of the spike-time-dependent plasticity (STDP) rule is also explored.

6.3 Biological dynamics of synapses

As already been introduced in section 3.2.3 (Chapter 3), synapses are elementary units for building neural circuits and represent communication channels responsible for fast signal transmission between interconnected neurons. Pairs of neurons may be interconnected by chemical or electrical synapses (also referred to as gap junctions). Synapses of the first type are however the most common in the vertebrate brain (Shepherd and Koch, 1990) and are also the most studied. They convert a presynaptic electrical signal into a chemical signal and then back into a postsynaptic electrical signal.

Although synapses have classically been considered as simple static entities which passively transmit the incoming spikes to the postsynaptic neurons, it is now documented that they are rather very complex machines that can keep track of their usage history and that they undergo substantial activity-dependent changes in response to a presynaptic spike. For some synapses, there is an increase in the poststsynaptic response (PSR), when repeatedly stimulated, to many times the size of an isolated PSR. When this growth occurs within one second or less and decays equally rapidly, it is called synaptic facilitation. Long term potentiation (LTP) refers to potentiated responses that last for hours or even days (Abbot and Nelson, 2000; Fuhrmann et al., 2002). On the other hand, some synapses show fatigue or depression when repeatedly stimulated which leads to a progressive decrease in the postsynaptic response. However, most synapses show a mixture of these dynamics so that in response to a presynaptic activity, the postsynaptic response may briefly increase due to synaptic facilitation before it is overwhelmed by depression (Fuhrmann et al., 2002). As a result of these dynamics, the classical assumption of a simplistic static model of synapses may underestimate their important role in information processing and learning mechanisms in the brain.

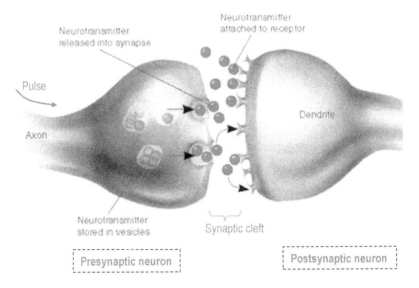

Figure 6-1. Biological dynamics of a synapse. The generation of action potentials at the postsynaptic neuron is the result of neurotransmitter release at the synaptic cleft and the resulting ion flow at the postsynaptic neuron membrane. Synapse picture taken from (Peter et al., 1992) and annotated for illustration.

As can be seen from Figure 6-1 the actual output of a neuron is the neurotransmitters which are released, upon the arrival of spike trains, at the synaptic cleft by the presynaptic terminal. Once released, neurotransmitters cross the synaptic cleft in order to bind to the postsynaptic receptors and alter the conductance of the ion channel in the postsynaptic membrane. A postsynaptic potential is then initiated as a result of this chemical process and either an EPSP (Excitatory Post Synaptic Potential) or an IPSP (Inhibitory Post Synaptic Potential) is produced. These important dynamics are completely ignored in the static model as the synapse strength is reduced to a single static weight. It has been reported that the probability of the neurotransmitter release varies significantly upon the arrival of each action potential, due to various mechanisms of different time scales, such as facilitation, potentiation and feedback modulation (Fuhrmann et al., 2002). Since the synaptic strength is partially determined by the probability of neurotransmitter release, it is dynamically adjusted by the temporal pattern of the arriving spike trains. The role of synapses can then be perceived as a translation of the sequence of spike trains received at the presynaptic terminal into another sequence of neurotransmitter release events. The spike trains generated by a presynaptic neuron are therefore transformed into a spatio-temporal pattern which is a new representation of the input patterns.

6.4 Dynamic synapse-based Network architecture

Before outlining the training algorithms (unsupervised and supervised) applied to feed-forward spiking neural networks with dynamic synapses, this section will first describe the network architecture and the chosen neural model, present simulations of the phenomenological model of dynamic synapse when connected to integrate-and-fire neurons and stimulated with different temporal patterns and also discuss the temporal encoding/decoding schemes used to encode patterns at the input layer and decode the postsynaptic response at the output layer.

6.4.1 Neuron model

The leaky integrate-and-fire neuron model is used to capture the neural dynamics of spike generation. Detailed descriptions of both ideal as well as leaky integrate-and fire models and their Matlab simulations, when stimulated with different input currents, were presented in Chapter 3, section 3.5.2 and 3.5.3 respectively. A neuron (represented by black circles in Figure 6-2) is modelled by a voltage across its cell membrane and a threshold. The status of the neuron is determined by the integration of its excitatory and inhibitory postsynaptic potential (EPSP, IPSP). When its membrane potential reaches a certain threshold, the neuron generates a spike or action potential. The neuron dynamics are modelled by the following equation:

$$\tau_m \frac{dV}{dt} = -V + R_m I_{syn}$$

Equation 6-1

where τ_m is the time constant of the neuron membrane, R_m is its resistance and I_{syn} represents the total synaptic inputs. (The following values are used during this work simulation: τ_m =40ms, R_m =100MΩ, these values are based on the range of values found in the literature).

A feed-forward fully connected spiking network is used whose different layers are labelled I, H, O for the input, hidden and output layer respectively as shown in Figure 6-2. Pairs of spiking neurons are connected using dynamic synapses (represented by white circles in Figure 6-2), the neurons at the input layer are used as sources of spike trains while other neurons at the hidden and output layer receive their inputs from the dynamic synapses to which they are connected.

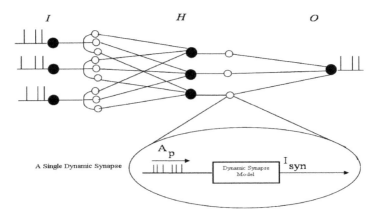

Figure 6-2. Network architecture: input neurons are sources of spike trains, connected through dynamic synapses to other postsynaptic neurons in the next layers. Each dynamic synapse causes a change in the postsynaptic potential and the receiving neuron merely integrates the different changes caused by different dynamic synapse. The input spike trains are transformed into a spatio-temporal structure to be learned by the output neuron using the time of its maximum response.

In the figure above, the outputs of neurons at the output layer are represented in the form of spike trains (vertical bars). However, in this study it is rather the time of the maximum postsynaptic response (PSR) that is considered for decoding the temporal patterns detected/learned by the spiking network. This can be likened to less excitable neurons or neurons with a very high threshold at the output layer. This convention is further described in the following section on temporal encoding/decoding schemes.

6.4.2 Phenomenological model of dynamic synapses

This study is based on the model of dynamic synapses from (Tsodyks et al., 1998; Abbot and Nelson, 2000), as it has shown to fit experimental data for various excitatory and inhibitory synapses. The model assumes that a dynamic synapse is represented by a finite amount of resources called neurotransmitters. Each pre-synaptic spike (arriving at time t_{sp}) activates a fraction (U_{SE}, utilization of synaptic efficacy) of resources, which then quickly inactivate with a time constant (τ_{in}) and recover with another time constant (τ_{rec}) (Tsodyks et al., 1998). The amount of available resources being activated, represented by U_{SE}, is analogous to the release probability of synaptic resources in the probabilistic model (Fuhrmann et al., 2002; Matveev and Wang, 2000). The mathematical model of the dynamics of depressing synapses is given by the following system of differential equations (Equation 6-2):

$$\begin{cases} \dfrac{dx}{dt} = \dfrac{z}{\tau_{rec}} - U_{SE}.x.Ap(t - t_{sp}) \\[2mm] \dfrac{dy}{dt} = -\dfrac{y}{\tau_{in}} + U_{SE}.x.Ap(t - t_{sp}) \\[2mm] \dfrac{dz}{dt} = \dfrac{y}{\tau_{in}} - \dfrac{z}{\tau_{rec}} \end{cases} \qquad \text{Equation 6-2}$$

where x, y, and z are the fractions of resources in the recovered, active, and inactive states, respectively. $Ap(t- tsp)$ is the action potential received at time t_{sp}. Variables τ_{in} and τ_{rec} represent the time constants for inactivation and recovery processes. The postsynaptic current (the input current received by the postsynaptic neuron membrane) from a synapse i is taken to be proportional to the fraction of resources in the active state and is given by Equation 6-3

$$I^i_{syn} = A_{SE}\ y_i(t) \qquad \text{Equation 6-3}$$

where A_{SE} represents the absolute synaptic strength which correspond to the maximal postsynaptic current which can be obtained when all the synaptic resources are activated at once. For a neuron that is connected to N dynamic synapses, the total synaptic current $Isyn$, as indicated in Equation 6-1, is determined by the summation of individual currents emitted by each dynamic synapse and is given by:

$$I_{syn} = \sum_{i=1}^{N} I^i_{syn} \qquad \text{Equation 6-4}$$

The synaptic model in Equation 6-2 describes the transmission characteristics of a depressing synapse and does not include a facilitating mechanism (Tsodyks et al., 1998). Short-term facilitation can be obtained through the extension of the depressing synapse model such as the amount U_{SE} (assumed fixed in the depressing synapse model) is made dynamic where its value increases at the arrival of each presynaptic spike and decays to a resting value in the absence of action potentials (Fuhrmann et al., 2002). The corresponding dynamics of the variable U_{SE} are given by the following equation:

$$\frac{dU_{SE}}{dt} = -\frac{U_{SE}}{\tau_{facil}} + U_1 (1 - U_{SE}) Ap (t - t_{sp})$$
Equation 6-5

Where U_1 determines the step increase in U_{SE} caused by each incoming spike and τ_{facil} is the relaxation time constant of facilitation.

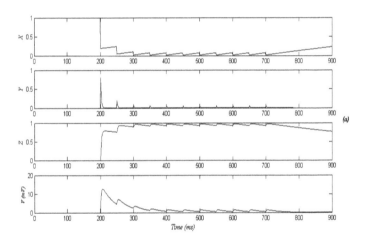

Figure 6-3. Time course of the three states of a dynamic synapse (X, Y, Z) and the response of a neuron (V) connected to this depressing synapse. This dynamic synapse is injected with a regular spike train with 20Hz (i.e. an Inter Spike Interval ISI=50ms) with first spike at time t=200ms, last spike at t=700ms.

Figure 6-3 shows the MATLAB simulations of an integrate-and-fire neuron connected to a depressing synapse. The synapse is stimulated using a regular spike train with an inter spike interval of 50ms and an onset time of 200ms. The evolution of the amount of resources in the recovered, active, and inactive states are illustrated (X, Y, Z) according to the dynamics governed by Equation 6-2. The curve Y shows the shape of the synaptic current received by the postsynaptic neuron whose potential (representing the PSR) evolution is represented by the curve V. The postsynaptic response increases at the start due to an increase of the activated resources before it starts decaying due to depression.

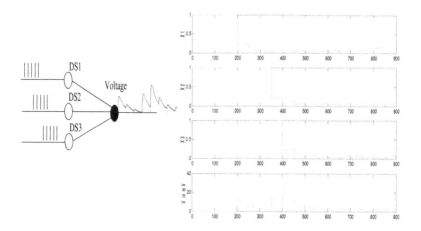

Figure 6-4. Time course of a neuron potential (V right panel) connected to three separate dynamic synapses DS1,DS2 and DS3 (left panel) represented by their states (X1, X2, X3), each DS is injected with a spike train with a frequency 20Hz and starting at different onset times (200ms, 350ms, 400ms respectively). Parameters values are: $U_{SE}=0.8$, $A_{SE}=250\ pA$, $\tau_m=40ms$, $R_m=100M\Omega$, $\tau_{rec}=800ms$ $\tau_{in}=3ms$. (These values are based on the range of values found in literatures)

Figure 6-4 on the other hand shows the changes of the postsynaptic potential of a neuron connected to three separate (but similar) dynamic synapses each of which is injected with a spike train with an ISI of 50ms. The onset times for the three synapses are however different and are set to 200ms, 350ms, 400ms respectively. The postsynaptic response reaches its maximum (peak) around t=400ms and then decays gradually to its baseline value. It is the time of the maximum postsynaptic response that is used in this work to decode the response of the neurons at the output layer. Its adaptation is obtained through the training (tuning) of the synapse parameters, namely the time constants of the inactivation process (τ_{in}).

6.4.3 Temporal encoding

It has been shown that dynamic synapses receive action potential events which are then transformed into neurotransmitters release events and eventually into a spatio-temporal pattern processed by the postsynaptic neurons. This means that only temporal data which is already available in the form of spike events can be directly processed by these synapses. This is however not the case for most of the available data that represent real world objects and the surrounding environment for which a temporal encoding strategy has to be decided. This section outlines the encoding schemes adopted for input patterns as well as the decoding strategy for the postsynaptic response at the network output layer.

6.4.4 Input encoding

Due to the time consuming nature of dynamic synapse based computations (discrete integration of three dynamic variables for each synapse), the sparse encoding scheme is discarded in this work as it tends to create more neurons at the input layer and consequently the number of required dynamic synapses which leads to an increase in the number of free parameters that needs adjusting during the training process. In order to overcome this problem, only the linear temporal encoding scheme proposed in Chapter 5 (section 5.6.4) is used. It offers a simple yet efficient approach for mapping real valued features into temporal events while maintaining the original data dimensionality. Linear temporal mapping is used when the features are defined on a space of real numbers (infinite interval). However, if the features are represented by discrete numbers and the set of possible values is reasonably small, other encoding alternatives can be used such as time to first spike or rank order encoding schemes. This is the case for the famous non-linearly separable XOR problem as will be shown in next sections. Although the XOR problem allows testing of the ability of a neural circuitry to learn non-linearly separable patterns, most realistic problems are however much more complicated than the XOR problem.

6.4.5 Output encoding

It has been observed from the dynamics of depressing synapses modelled by the system in Equation 6-2 that the variation of the time constant τ_{in} (related to the inactivation process) leads to a change in the 'time to maximum response' of the postsynaptic neuron. The neuron potential reaches its maximum response 'earlier' for smaller values of τ_{in}, while the use of bigger values causes a delay in reaching the peak of the postsynaptic response (see illustration in Figure 6-5). For a neuron at the output layer, the early/late time to maximum response could therefore be exploited to signal the presence of a particular input pattern at the input layer (classification task). It is this synaptic parameter that is adjusted during the training procedure for each connection in a spiking network. Other parameters have also been varied (e.g τ_{rec}) but no significant change in the time to maximum response was observed. Obviously it is possible to consider all the parameters of the model to be adjusted during the training but this will unnecessarily complicate the training process (e.g. adjusting many parameters will increase the length of chromosome in the case of evolutionary strategy based training and affect the training performance). The use of time to maximum response is similar to assuming that the output neurons are less excitable (i.e with very high thresholds). The application of a small threshold may not result in a useful range of firing times (of the output neurons) that can be exploited as a means of detecting specific patterns presented at the input layer. It can be seen from Figure 6-5 that using a small threshold for example will result in very close firing times even when two different values of τ_{in} are used.

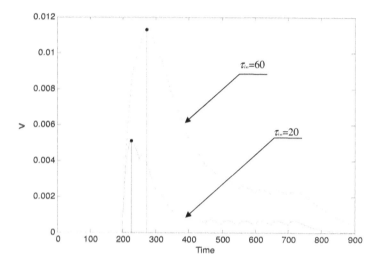

Figure 6-5. Decoding of network outputs. The time to maximum postsynaptic response is used. Different timings of the maximum response of an output neuron are obtained when two different values of the time constant τ_{in} are used.

6.5 STDP-based unsupervised training

Before the application of the ES-based supervised training approach, unsupervised training in the form of spike-time-dependent plasticity (STDP as described in section 3.9.2 of Chapter 3) has first been investigated as it represents a biologically plausible learning rule. However its application on the network used in this work proved unsuccessful as the network failed to learn the non-linearly separable XOR patterns with which it was trained and no convergence was obtained despite a reasonable number of trials. A remedy to this failure could be the addition of more extra neurons at the output layer (equal to the number of classes to be learned) as well as the addition of another layer of neurons to produce supervising signals to help pushing the times of the postsynaptic responses towards the desired values. Lateral inhibitory connections may help increase the competition between the output neurons and therefore the implementation of a winner-take-all paradigm. The addition of extra neurons and connections is, however, not without extra costs. The computation and the training convergence times will drastically increase. The combination of the STDP learning rule with a supervising layer of neurons used only during the training phase has been implemented and applied successfully in a coordinate transformation task (both 1D and 2D coordinate transforms were learned). More details on this approach can be found in the author's publication referenced at (Wu et al., 2005).

6.6 Evolutionary strategy-based supervised training

6.6.1 Tuning synaptic parameters

As supervised training (i.e. tuning the feed-forward network parameters without the need for extra neurons) is the best approach to use when a priori knowledge about the desired outputs is available (which is the case in classification tasks), the following sections will explore the suitability and efficiency of an evolutionary strategy-based supervised training of spiking neural networks with dynamic synapses. This is an extension of the evolutionary training approach developed in the previous chapter which was successfully applied to spiking networks with static synapses. Once trained, the postsynaptic response is adapted to reflect the class of the patterns presented at the input layer. This adaptation is achieved by adjusting the synaptic free parameters represented in this work by the synaptic time constants related to the inactivation process (the parameter τ_{in}). As was shown in the previous section on output encoding, changing these time constants (free parameters) will directly affect the form of the postsynaptic response and the time at which its peak is reached. However before the iterative evolutionary training begins, it is necessary to transform a spiking network (the phenotype) into a genotype representation as it is the latter that an evolutionary algorithm acts upon. The following section will briefly outline this mapping process.

6.6.2 Parameters encoding and phenotype/genotype transform

The evolutionary strategy does not directly modify a spiking network; therefore a mapping process is required. Its role is to encode a spiking network based on dynamic synapses into a genotype representation, a real valued encoded individual in this case. The latter is grouped with other individuals to form a population which undergoes iterative modification by the evolutionary strategy based supervised training. The inverse operation is also performed by the mapping process as prior to the evaluation of a genotype fitness value, it is necessary to convert the genotype back into a spiking network (phenotype) which helps calculate the error at the output layer neurons obtained by each training sample (see illustration in Figure 6-6).

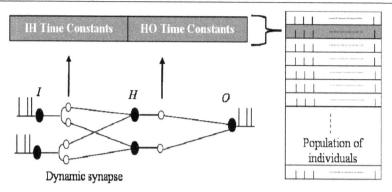

Figure 6-6 Mapping between a phenotype (dynamic synapse based spiking network) and its genotype (real valued encoded individuals). The synaptic free parameters are grouped according to the layers they are connecting together, i.e. synapse connecting the input layer to the hidden (IH) layer are grouped in the first part of the genotype and so for synapses connecting the hidden to output layer (HO). A set of such individuals will form the population which is iteratively modified by the evolutionary strategy algorithm.

The synaptic parameters are encoded using real values and no binary to real values conversion is required. Real value encoding is more tractable, more accurate as it does not depend on the binary digit resolution required in a binary encoding, and more suitable when large scale spiking networks are considered as, unlike binary encoding, the size of a genotype is not drastically increased. A dynamic synapse based network is transformed into an array of real values (genotype) which represent the time constants (τ_{in}) of each connecting synapse. The size of this array is equal to the number of existing dynamic synapses. The order of the array elements corresponds to the distribution of synapses over different layers of the spiking network. For example, in the case of a three layer spiking network (neurons at the input layer are used as a source of input spikes) a genotype consists of two parts. The first part consists of the time constants of dynamic synapses linking the neurons of the input layer to those in the hidden layer, and the second part of the genotype is formed by the time constants of synapses linking hidden layer neurons to their successors in the output layer (see illustration in Figure 6-7). This order is obviously maintained when a spiking network is reconstructed from a given genotype representation. A one dimensional array representation has been adopted in this work, however one can also choose a different genotype structures such as two dimensional matrices. Consequently different evolutionary operators which suit the genotype representation may also be required.

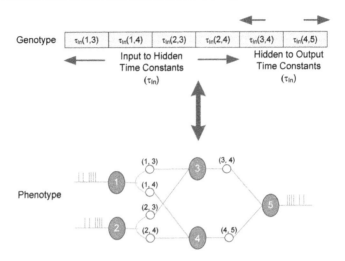

Figure 6-7 An example of mapping between the synaptic time constants of a given spiking network and its genetic counterpart according to the mapping order as shown in Figure 6-6. The size of a genotype is equal to the number of existing dynamic synapses.

6.6.3 Aim of the training algorithm

The aim of this supervised training algorithm is to make the output neuron reach its maximum response at different times for different classes of patterns. For this purpose, the evolutionary strategy based approach developed in the previous chapter is extended and applied to optimize the dynamic synapses free parameters which contribute to the learning of different patterns. The choice of evolutionary strategies is motivated by their suitability for treating continuous optimisation problems, without the complexity of binary encoding schemes. Evolutionary strategies are also suitable for optimisation tasks that are data driven and also for problems where a derivative of the objective function may not exist, which is the case for a supervised training of a spiking network based on dynamic synapse. This task is approached as an optimisation problem where the error between output neuron times and the desired ones is optimised (minimised in this case) through iterative tuning of synaptic parameters. When compared with other evolutionary algorithms, evolutionary strategies offer a distinguished characteristic of self-adaptability where the parameters of the evolutionary algorithm (strategy parameters) are co-evolved with the optimised parameters of the problem. Once the initial parameters of the evolutionary process are set and the latter is started, no user intervention is required. After the mapping between spiking networks and their genotype representation is carried out and a population is formed, the encoded synaptic parameters are continuously altered through a combination of Cauchy and Gaussian mutations. The use of Cauchy mutation allows the coarse tuning of synaptic parameters (i.e. the exploration of the space of possible solutions) while the application of Gaussian mutation aims to fine tune the solutions discovered by the Cauchy mutation (i.e. exploitation of the obtained solutions). The implementation of self-adaptable evolutionary strategies to supervised training of spiking networks with dynamic synapses is formally described in the following section.

6.6.4 Implementation

The features of the training patterns (representing the real world and originally encoded in binary, integer or real values) are first transformed into temporal patterns using the temporal encoding scheme described in section 6.4.4. A set of such temporal patterns is denoted by $\{P(t_1,...,t_m)\}$, where $P(t_1,...,t_m)$ represents a single input pattern such that the components $t_1,...,t_m$ define the firing times of each input neuron $i \in I$ at the input layer. Another set of desired times, denoted by $\{t'_o\}$, is assigned at the output neurons $o \in O$ in accordance with the input patterns at the input layer. These output time values represent the expected timings of the maximum postsynaptic response at the output layer (taking the time to maximum postsynaptic response can be compared to neuron with a high threshold, i.e. a less excitable neuron). The supervised training then consists of optimising the objective function given by the following equation:

$$E = \sum_{t}^{T} \sum_{o \in O} | t_o^a(t) - t_o^t(t) |$$

Equation 6-6

where $t_o^a(t)$ and $t_o^t(t)$ define the actual and target timings respectively, and T is the total number of patterns in the training set. This error function is used to evaluate each individual of the evolutionary strategy population and select in each iteration those to be carried over to next generations.

The iterative steps of the self-adaptive evolutionary strategy are implemented as follows:

1) Generate an initial population of μ individuals, and set g=1. Each individual consists of a pair of real-valued vectors, (x_i, η_i), $\forall i \in \{1,..., \mu\}$, where x_i's are objective variables representing the synaptic time constants, and η_i's are standard deviations used for mutations. The vector x_i is the genotype representation of a spiking neural network formed according to the mapping process described in section 6.2.2.

2) Evaluate each individual in $\{(x_i, \eta_i), i=1,...,\mu\}$ using the error function in Equation 6-6. This will entail presenting all the training samples

3) Each parent (x_i, η_i) generates a single offspring (x_i', η_i') as follows:

for $j=1,..., n$, where n is the size of x_i and η_i.

$$\begin{cases} x_i'(j) = x_i(j) + \eta_i(j)N_j(0,1) & or \quad x_i'(j) = x_i(j) + \eta_i(j)\delta_j \\ \eta_i'(j) = \eta_i(j)e^{(\tau' N(0,1)+\tau N_j(0,1))} \end{cases}$$

Equation 6-7

where $x_i(j)$, $x_i'(j)$, $\eta_i(j)$ and $\eta_i'(j)$ denote the j-th component of the vectors x_i, x_i', η_i and η_i' respectively. $N(0,1)$ denotes a normally distributed random number with mean 0 and standard deviation 1. $N_j(0,1)$ indicates that the random number is generated anew for each value of j. The factors τ and τ' are set to $1/(2n^{1/2})^{1/2}$ and $1/(2n)^{1/2}$ respectively (these values were found experimentally in the literature, however other values can be tried) and δ_j is a Cauchy random variable with a scale of 1, and is also generated anew for each value of j.

4) Evaluate each offspring $\{(x_i', \eta_i'), i=1,...,\mu.\}$ according to Equation 6-6.

5) Generate a new population $P(g)$ using tournament selection and elitism to keep track of the best individual at each generation. Obviously, other selection approaches can also be used at this stage. Tournament selection has been chosen due to its simple implementation and its efficiency.

6) Stop if a maximum number of generations is reached ($g=g_{max}$) or a target error is met; otherwise, $g=g+1$ and go to step 3.

6.7 Demonstration on classification tasks

The supervised training approach described above was implemented using Matlab R13 and is demonstrated on classification tasks of some benchmark datasets, namely the famous XOR problem to first test the ability of the developed training approach to learn non-linearly separable problems, the IRIS dataset and the Breast Cancer data benchmark. The encoding schemes applied in each case along with the results obtained are presented and discussed in the following sections.

6.7.1 The non-linearly separable XOR problem

The table below shows the temporal encoding of the logical values of the XOR function truth table. The input logic value '0' is assigned an early firing time of '5ms' while a later firing time of '10ms' is assigned to the input logic value '1'. In order to classify both output classes represented by {0, 1} in the truth table, the network free parameters (i.e. the time constants of the dynamic synapses) are tuned using the evolutionary strategy (ES) approach as described in the previous section. The aim is to adapt the postsynaptic response at the output layer so that it reaches its maximum (or peak) early (around '10ms') for the class identified by the output logic value of '0' (CLASS 0), and reaches its peak a later (around 40ms) for the second class identified by the output logic value of '1' (CLASS 1). The resulting encoding scheme for the XOR truth table is illustrated in Table 6-1.

Digital inputs			Temporal codes		
Input 1	Input 2	Output	Input 1	Input 2	Output
0	0	0	5	5	10
0	1	1	5	10	40
1	0	1	10	5	40
1	1	0	10	10	10

Table 6-1. Temporal encoding of the XOR problem. At the output layer a logic value '0' is encoded by a later time to maximum postsynaptic response (around 40 ms), while a logic value of '1' is assigned an early time (around 10 ms). For the input values, logic values '0' and '1' are assigned firing times of 5ms and 10ms respectively.

A network of two input neurons, three hidden neurons and one output neuron (2x3x1) has been implemented (see Figure 6-8). The number of dynamic synapses amounts to 2*3+3*1=9, consequently each spiking network results in a genotype of 18 real values. The first 9 values represent the time constants of the dynamic synapses which are mapped according to the transform between a phenotype and a genotype as described previously in this chapter. The second part of the genotype, also consists of 9 real values (standard deviations), represents the strategy parameters which are co-evolved with the objective parameters (the first 9 synaptic free parameters) and contribute to the selection of desirable solutions and their survival throughout the evolutionary process.

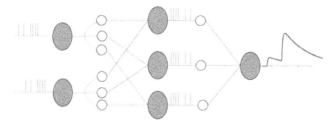

Figure 6-8 A network of 2x3x1 neurons implemented to solve the the XOR problem. The time of the maximum postsynaptic response at the output layer is considered to signal the detection of specific temporal patterns at the input layer.

The trained network shows perfect learning of the XOR problem. This is demonstrated by the illustrations in Figure 6-9 to Figure 6-13. The time of the maximum postsynaptic response at the output layer before and after the training are shown (superimposed) in Figure 6-9 to Figure 6-12 for

149

the XOR patterns (0,0), (1,1), (0,1) and (1,0) respectively. These figures illustrate how the time of the maximum postsynaptic response is almost similar for all input patterns (i.e. it is not selective to any XOR pattern) before the training, while after the training those times become adapted to each pattern and are pushed towards the neighbourhood of the desired times within a tolerated error (margin).

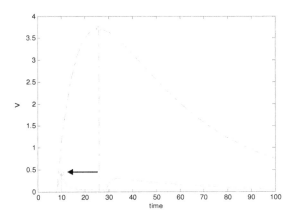

Figure 6-9 Input pattern (0,0) temporally encoded as (5ms, 5ms) and classified as CLASS 0 (temporally encoded as 10ms). Dashed line: it shows the time of the maximum postsynaptic response before training. Solid line: it shows the new time of the maximum response obtained after training. It is clear the time of the maximum postsynaptic response has been adapted by being advanced towards the desired time (10ms).

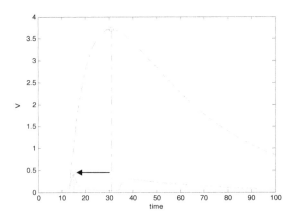

Figure 6-10 Input pattern (1,1) is temporally encoded as (10ms, 10ms) and classified as class 0 (temporally encoded as 10ms). Dashed line: shows the time of the maximum postsynaptic response before training. Solid line: shows the new time of the maximum response obtained after training.

150

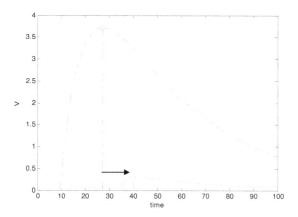

Figure 6-11 Input pattern (0,1) temporally encoded as (5ms, 10ms) and classified as CLASS 1 (temporally encoded as 40ms). Dashed line: it shows the time of the maximum response before training. Solid line: it shows the new time of the maximum response after training which has, this time, been delayed to match the desired time (40ms).

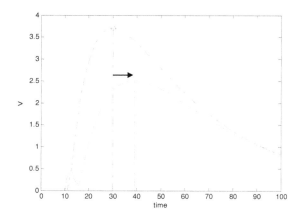

Figure 6-12 Input pattern (1,0) temporally encoded as (10ms, 5ms,) and classified as CLASS 1 (temporally encoded as 40ms). Dashed line: it shows the time of the maximum response before training. Solid line: it shows the new time of the maximum response after training (38ms) which has been delayed towards the desired time (40ms).

Figure 6-13 on the other hand shows the evolution of the time at which the postsynaptic response peak is attained in response to each XOR pattern during the iterative alteration of the dynamic synapse free parameters. Initially the postsynaptic response peaks are reached at random timings, and then they undergo a fluctuation when the synaptic free parameters are adjusted during the first 30 generations before they settle in the neighbourhood of the target times just before generation 120. It is observed from Figure 6-13 that the times of the postsynaptic response for patterns (0,0) and (0,1) have converged to the exact target times (i.e. 10ms and 40ms respectively), while those for the remaining patterns (1,0) and (1,1) did not converge to the exact target times but were rather close (38ms and 15ms respectively). Obviously the aim of the training is not to obtain an absolute zero error but it is rather to learn the training samples with a reasonable error tolerance as the ultimate goal is to obtain a good generalisation rather than simply memorising the training set.

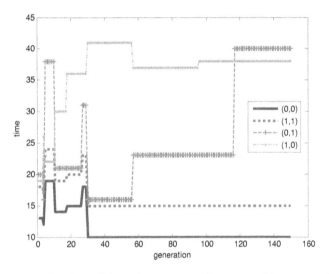

Figure 6-13 Evolution of the times of the maximum postsynaptic response of the neuron at the output layer during the iterative tuning of the synaptic free parameters. The x-axis denotes the generations for which the evolutionary strategy is run and the y-axis defines the timings of the maximum postsynaptic response at the output layer for each presented pattern at a particular generation/iteration.

6.7.2 The IRIS data benchmark

For comparison reason, the approach is also demonstrated on the classification of the IRIS data benchmark, which consists of learning three different classes of flowers. This dataset has already been described in the previous chapter (see section 5.7.2). Unlike the case of static synapse-based spiking network where both the sparse and the 1-D encoding schemes have been used, the 4-dimensional feature vectors representing the IRIS patterns are temporally encoded using only the linear 1-D encoding scheme due to its simplicity and efficiency. A spiking network of 4x10x1 is implemented to solve this task. Similarly to the work in the previous chapter, the 150 samples are split into a training set used to adjust the dynamic synapse parameters and a test set for testing the generalisation ability of the trained network. While the number of input neurons is driven by the dimensionality of the IRIS dataset and one output neuron suffices to encode the three classes, the number of hidden neurons is the result of trial and error and no rule of thumb is available for identifying the optimal size of the hidden layer. However, a different configuration could also been adopted for the output layer. For example, there could be three output neurons at the output layer such as each neuron is assigned to signal each class and the first neuron to reach its maximum response signals the presence of the class to which it is assigned. The encoding scheme in this case could be perceived as another version of time-to-first spike approach. This alternative will also result in more dynamic synapse being created and therefore an increase in the size of genotypes.

	IRIS data set		
	Net	Train	Test
Dynamic synapse based SNN	4x10x1	96%	97.3%
SRM based SNN (1-D encoding)	4x10x1	98.6%	97.3%
SRM based SNN (sparse coding)	16x10x1	98.67 %	96.00 %
Matlab BP	50x10x3	97.3%	94.6%
Matlab LM	50x10x3	98.6 %	96%
SpikeProp	50x10x3	97.5%	96.2%

Table 6-2. Comparison of the performance for the range of different approaches for the IRIS data set. The table lists the dimensions of each network architecture (Net), and the training (train) and test classification accuracies. Four receptive fields neurons are used with the SRM based network (sparse coding), which explains the 16 input neurons. For the last three approaches 50 neurons are used in the input layer to provide an exact comparison with the SpikeProp approach which employed 12 receptive field neurons (12*4+2=50) with extra two input neurons.

Table 6-2 shows the classification accuracies obtained for both the training as well as the test sets. These performances are also compared with those obtained from their static synapse-based counterparts developed in the previous chapter, Spikeprop and the classical multi-layer perceptron (MLP). The comparison is made in terms of the accuracies obtained and the network size used in each case. As can be seen from Table 6-2, the dynamic synapse based spiking network was able to successfully learn the IRIS dataset with comparable performances to the static synapse based network developed in the previous chapter and MLPs. This demonstrates the efficiency of evolutionary strategy-based supervised training in finding the optimal free parameters of dynamic synapses which underlie the learning of a classification tasks with multiple classes. It also shows that despite the smaller number of adjustable parameters, when compared to static-synapse-based networks, these biologically detailed models are capable of learning temporal patterns with satisfying performance.

6.7.3 The Breast Cancer data benchmark

This section describes the application of dynamic synapses-based networks to the Wisconsin Breast Cancer data benchmark (the reader is referred to section 5.7.3 of the previous chapter for a description of this dataset). Both the sample size of this dataset and its dimensionality are bigger than the IRIS dataset used in the previous section. This will help test the performance of spiking networks with dynamic synapse on slightly larger scale problems. A network of 9x6x1 is implemented. The number of inputs reflects the nine features used to represent the state of a tissue for cancer diagnosis, and one single output neuron is used to signal the presence of a malignant or a benign tissue. The mapping between this network, i.e. the phenotype, results in a genotype with a number of $9*6+6*1=60$ objective variables and another 90 strategy parameters (standard deviations). The integer features ($\in [1,10]$) of the 9-dimensional patterns are encoded using the linear 1-D encoding scheme and the total number of samples (699) are split into a training and test set. Table 6-3 shows the performance obtained and how it compares to other approaches. Again comparable classification accuracies were obtained and the dynamic synapse-based spiking network was able to generalise to newly unseen data. The training process has proved time consuming in this case due to the high number of required computations resulting from the step by step Euler integration of three dynamic variables modelling each dynamic synapse. However, the obtained performance demonstrates once again the capability of spiking networks with dynamic synapses in performing classification tasks for both small and large scale problems. It also shows the suitability of evolutionary strategies as a tool for supervised training of dynamic synapse-based network.

	BREAST CANCER data set		
	Net	Train	Test
Dynamic synapse based SNN	9x6x1	97.2%	97.3%
SRM based SNN	9x6x1	97.2%	98.2%
Matlab BP	64x15x2	98.5%	96.9%
Matlab LM	64x15x3	98.0%	97.3%
SpikeProp	64x15x3	97.8%	97.6%

Table 6-3. Comparison of the performance obtained from different approaches for the Breast Cancer data set. Network architecture, training and test classification accuracy are shown. Only the 1-D encoding scheme is applied, which maintains the data dimensionality at the input layer. Alternative approaches used receptive fields to encode the data resulting in increased neuron numbers in the input layer.

6.8 Discussion

The results presented in the previous section show that using time as a means of information representation and processing, biologically plausible models of dynamic synapses are capable of extracting relevant features through the transformation of input temporal patterns into another spatio-temporal pattern. This transformation is the result of synaptic transmission mechanisms based on the release of neurotransmitters caused by the arrival of each action potential. The obtained spatio-temporal patterns are then processed by the output neurons whose postsynaptic response is used to discriminate between different classes of input patterns. The performance obtained is comparable to those obtained with static synapses despite the number of free parameters is reduced in the case dynamic synapses. Although the use biologically detailed models of dynamic synapse offers a chance to investigate and capture the possible computation mechanisms of real neural circuitries, it suffers the drawback of being computationally intensive as more integrations are required to determine the state of neurons. This poses a real problem when very large scale networks are implemented. It also reflects on the application of evolutionary strategies in supervised training of such networks. ES are population based iterative algorithms; and the search for optimal parameters of dynamic synapses requires the evaluation of many individuals (i.e. several spiking networks) at each generation which results in a time consuming training process that runs for hours or even days. However, it is important to mention that it is not the aim of this work to claim that dynamic synapse-based spiking networks outperform the classical methods on all benchmark datasets as according to the 'no free lunch' theorem (Wolpert and and Macready, 1995, 1997) no search algorithm is on average better than any other. The aim was rather to investigate and demonstrate their learning mechanisms and capabilities and to help further our understanding of the way real neurons represent and communicate information.

6.9   More detailed versus more abstract: which model is best?

Learning and computing with spiking neural networks and dynamic synapses have been investigated in this chapter. On the other hand, static synapses in the form of a simple entity represented by a scalar weight were combined with spike response model-based neurons and their supervised training and their ability in performing classification tasks were presented in the previous chapter. Clearly there is a difference in the level of biological details between the two models. The question that arises is which model to use and why?

Shall more biologically detailed synaptic models be used as they help capture real mechanisms of synaptic transmission and investigate computation principles that are plausible and close to what happens in neural circuits of the nervous system, or shall we rather use more abstract models as they allow the simulation and analysis of large scale networks activity while the essential neural behaviour is retained?

The choice of a particular level of detail is driven by the objectives of the research work. If the objective is to study the nervous system at low level than the choice of more detailed neural and synaptic models is inevitable as a deep and thorough understanding can only be gained through the investigation of synaptic transmission and neural communication/behaviour at the cellular or even the molecular. However, there is a limit on the size of spiking networks that can be simulated using such detailed models due to time and resource (hardware/software) consumption. On the other hand, the study of the activity of large scale neural populations will only be feasible if more abstract neural and synaptic models are used. In order to maintain a certain level of plausibility, it is important that the chosen abstract models can still capture the essential neural behaviour

6.10   Summary

The contribution of this chapter consists of the implementation and application of an evolutionary strategy-based supervised training on spiking neurons with dynamic synapses. Neurons are based on the integrate-and-fire model and a phenomenological model of dynamic synapses was used. Unlike static synapses, dynamic synapses are weightless and their efficacy changes upon the arrival of spike trains and depends on the amount of neurotransmitters released at the synaptic cleft. Based on self-adaptable evolutionary strategies, the proposed supervised training searches for the optimal parameters of dynamic synapses which allow the postsynaptic response at the output layer reaches its maximum at different times for different classes of patterns presented at the input layer. A simple linear temporal encoding scheme was used to transform real valued features into spike events and the demonstration of the proposed approach on the classification of benchmark datasets yielded comparable performance with other static synapse based networks and classical MLPs. The suitability of unsupervised training in the form of spike-time-dependent plasticity rule has been explored and the question of choosing between more detailed and their abstract counterparts or abstract was discussed.

This chapter and the previous one investigated feed-forward architectures where no lateral connections employed. Also the encoding/decoding schemes were based on postsynaptic response times of individual neurons. The next chapter will investigate different architecture where lateral connections are used with a different type of neural model called neural oscillators. The activity of population of recurrent oscillators is simulated and the significance of neural synchronisation explored and applied to solve a real world problem, namely a colour image segmentation task.

CHAPTER 7

Computing with neural oscillators: application to colour image segmentation

7.1 Introduction

While computing and training of the integrate-and-fire (IAF) and spike response (SRM) models with different level of synaptic abstraction were investigated in the previous two chapters, this chapter investigates the computing capabilities and potential applications of another different model called 'neural oscillators'. Unlike the previous two chapters where neurons were interconnected in a feed-forward topology and the timing of the postsynaptic response (PSR) of single neurons was used for input/output temporal encoding, a different architecture is employed in this work where neurons are arranged in a two-dimensional grid and neurons are locally connected through excitatory connections and globally connected to a common inhibitor which receives excitation from each neuron and sends back inhibition to the entire network. In this approach, temporal encoding of different objects is based on the synchronisation and desynchronisation of the activity of populations of neurons.

In order to understand the behaviour of this neural model, Matlab simulations of the dynamics of single and coupled neural oscillators were performed, their phase plane representations examined and their convergence to limit cycles or to fixed points analysed. More importantly, the application of these neural models, which is the main focus of this work, to the segmentation of small and large sized grey scale images is investigated and a comparison with traditional image segmentation approaches is presented. A network of neural oscillators is built where each neuron is mapped to a pixel of the image and objects represented by homogenous areas are segmented through the synchronisation of the activity of neural oscillators that are mapped to pixels of the same object, and also through the desynchronisation of neural oscillators that belong to different objects in the image. This work also explores the synergy between networks of neural oscillators and Kohonen self-organising maps (SOM) and its application to segmentation of real world colour images where self-organising maps form the basis of a colour reduction pre-processing stage whose output is fed to a two dimensional grid of neural oscillators for temporal correlation-based object segmentation.

These points will be elaborated in the remaining parts of this chapter which is structured as follows. Section 7.2 briefly reviews neural oscillators and discusses their biological relevance and the current related research. Then, Section 7.3 presents the mathematical modelling of neural oscillators' dynamics where single and coupled neurons are simulated and their phase plane analysis is carried out. The feature binding problem, synchronous activity of neural oscillators and their relation to computer vision are discussed in Section 7.4 and Section 7.5. Section 7.6 presents the application of networks of neural oscillators to grey scale images and discusses two approaches for simulating the dynamics of networks of oscillators. The first one is used with small scale images and based on directly solving the neural oscillators differential equations through step-by-step integration, and the second is used with larger images and is based on an algorithmic approach which captures the essential properties of neural oscillator dynamics. Section 7.7 presents a system developed for colour image segmentation which combines networks of neural oscillators with a self-organising map-based colour reduction method. Section 7.8 discusses the findings of this research work before concluding the chapter in Section 7.9.

7.2 On neural oscillators

The model of neural oscillators used in this work represents an instance of a general model called 'relaxation oscillators' which represent a large class of dynamic systems that emerge from many physical systems (e.g engineering, mechanical and biological systems) (Grasman, 1987; Verhulst, 1990). The first observation of relaxation oscillators dates back to 1926 when Van Der Pol (1926) studied the characteristics of a triode circuit which show self-sustained oscillations. In his study, van der Pol realised that the observed oscillations were almost sinusoidal for a certain range of parameters and that abrupt changes were exhibited for a different range of parameters. The name of the model reflects the system time constants, also called relaxation times. A relaxation oscillator is characterised by a slow time scale needed to charge the capacitor and a fast time scale for its quick discharge. It was found that the period of oscillation is proportional to the relaxation time needed to charge the capacitor; hence the name of the model was derived.

Relaxation oscillators can be observed in a variety of biological phenomena such as heartbeat and neural activity. Some scientists, such as the physiologist Hill A.V (1933), went even further by stating that all physiological periodic phenomena are governed by this type of oscillations, i.e. relaxation oscillations. However, despite the existence of such models in a number of domains, the real motivation of exploring them in this work comes from their relevance to neurobiology (will be explained later); hence the focus of this study is oriented towards models that represent neural activity in the brain and the investigation of emerging behaviours from networks of such neural models (oscillators).

It has been recognised that relaxation oscillators are similar to their biological counterparts and were therefore used to model biological phenomena. They were used in 1928 by van der Pol (1928) to describe the heartbeat and to present an electrical model of the heart. Using a system of differential equations based on four dynamic variables, Hodgkin and Huxley have mathematically described the dynamics of the neuron membrane potential, ionic exchange and electric transmission of impulses along nerves (Hodgkin and Huxley, 1952). Their famous system for which they obtained the Noble prize in 'Physiology or Medicine' in 1963 [1], was later reduced to a system of two dynamic variables called Fitzhugh-Nagumo model (Fitzhugh, 1961; Nagumo et al., 1962) which represents a relaxation oscillator. A relaxation oscillator description of the burst-generating mechanism in the cardiac ganglion cells of the lobster was later developed by Mayeri et al. (Mayeri, 1973). Oscillations in cortical neurons were also modelled by Wilson-Cowan polynomial equations which model interactions between excitatory and inhibitory neurons (Wilson and Cowan, 1972, 1973; Pinto et al., 1996; Wilson, 1999). Their model consists of a two variable system of differential equations with a number of parameters which offer a variety of dynamics when carefully adjusted (Shannon and DeLiang, 1996). Another model was presented by Morris and Lecar and consists of a two variable relaxation oscillator which describe the voltage oscillation in the giant muscle fibre (Morris and Lecar, 1981).

Since coherent oscillations were discovered in the visual cortex and other areas of the brain (Gray et al., 1989; Eckhorn et al., 1988; Singer and Gray, 1995) and due to the neurobiological relevance of relaxation oscillators, they have attracted more research work where they have been studied as mathematical models representing the behaviour of neurons (Aronson, 1990; Cairns et al., 1993; Grasman and Jansen, 1995; Plant, 1995; Grossberg and Somers, 1991; Somers and Kopell, 1995; Terman and Wang, 1995). These research findings concluded that the observed oscillations are stimulus-dependent as they are triggered by appropriate sensory stimulus, that synchronisation of these oscillations emerges when the sensory stimuli appear to belong to a coherent object and that no such synchrony is observed otherwise, i.e. in the case where the stimuli are not connected by similarities or a common object. These findings are consistent with the principles of the theory of temporal correlation (von der Malsburg, 1981; von der Malsburg and Schneider, 1986) which explains how the perception of a coherent object is brought about by the brain through temporal correlation of the firing activity of various neurons which detect the features of the perceived object. This is also related to the binding problem which is explained later in Section 7.5.

Synchronisation of neural activity was observed in different areas of the brain (Phillips and Singer, 1997; Keil et al., 1999). It has been observed in mammals, amphibians and insects (Singer and Gray, 1995; Prechtl, 1994; MacLeod and Laurent, 1996) and has been measured across 14 mm in

---

[1] http://nobelprize.org/nobel_prizes/lists/1963.html

the monkey motor cortex (Murthy and Fetz, 1992) and across different hemispheres of the brain in the visual cortices of cats (Engel et al., 1991). One of the main concerns of this research work is to understand how synchrony is brought about in locally interacting groups of neural oscillators and how the emerging synchronised activity of populations of neural oscillators can be applied to image perception, particularly the important stage of image segmentation. This motivation is driven by the fact that the exhibition of synchronised neural activity in a wide range of brain areas and by a diversity of organisms indicate that neural synchronisation could be fundamental to information processing in the brain.

7.3 Modelling dynamics of neural oscillators

The objective of this section is to present a description of the dynamics of single and coupled neural oscillators through numerical simulations of a chosen mathematical model. Simulations are implemented in Matlab and a step-by-step discrete integration of the system of differential equations, which governs the behaviour of neural oscillators, is carried out using the Euler method. In order to keep the size of this chapter to a reasonable size, only the analyses of single and coupled oscillators in the phase plane are presented. However, because of the importance of the simulations and analysis of their temporal behaviours (both single and coupled neural oscillators) and synchronisation/desynchronisation in understanding their underlying principles, further details are provided in Appendix A.

7.3.1 Dynamics of single neural oscillators

The neural oscillator model used in this work is similar to the relaxation oscillator defined by Terman and Wand (1995) which is based on the neural oscillator model developed by Morris and Lecar (1981). However the chosen model is considerably simpler and has been shown to achieve synchrony more rapidly than other neural oscillators models (Somers and Kopell, 1993). According to this model, a neural oscillator consists of a feedback loop between two units, one excitatory (called x_i) and the other is inhibitory (called y_i) as illustrated in Figure 7-1.

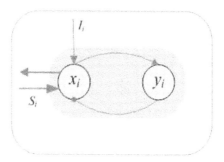

Figure 7-1 A single neural oscillator which consists of two coupled units x (excitatory) and y (inhibitory). While the x unit sends excitation (indicated by a triangle) to unit y, the unit y sends inhibition (indicated by a small circle) to unit x. I_i and S represent an external input and a possible coupling with other neural oscillators, respectively.

The dynamics of the temporal activity of the coupled units (x_i and y_i) are governed by the following system of first order differential equations:

$$\begin{cases} \dot{x}_i = 3x_i - x_i^3 + 2 - y_i + \rho + I_i + S_i \\ \dot{y}_i = \varepsilon[\lambda\,(1 + tanh(x_i\,/\,\beta)) - y_i] \end{cases}$$

Equation 7-1

where I_i represents an external input (eg. pixel features) and S_i defines the total coupling from other neurons. The parameter ρ represents the amplitude of a Gaussian noise added to the total oscillator input in order to test its robustness to noise, and also to contribute to the desynchronisation process when a neural oscillator is coupled with other neurons. The parameter ε is a small positive number whose value affects the time scales (which characterise relaxation oscillators) of the activities of units x and y. The parameter β controls the steepness of the y-nullcline which will be explained below when the dynamics of the neural oscillator are analysed in the phase plane. The role of the parameter λ is explained in Appendix A (Section 1.1) where the temporal behaviour of a neural oscillator is analysed. In order to better understand the dynamics of a neural oscillator defined by the system in Equation 7-1, the phase plane analysis approach is used where the oscillator nullclines, limit cycles and motion directions are examined. Phase plane analysis is a graphical method which helps understand the behaviour of a system of differential equations over time. The nullclines and limit cycle of the oscillator i defined in Equation 7-1 are examined first.

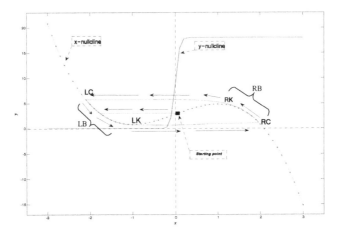

Figure 7-2 x- and y-nullclines with a periodic solution of the system in Equation 7-1 (limit cycle) represented in the phase plane. This oscillator trajectory jumps periodically between the left and the right branches of the limit cycle. LC, LB and LK indicate the upper left corner, left branch and left knee respectively. RC, RB and RK indicates lower right corner, right branch and right knee respectively. The starting point for this simulation is set to $(x_i, y_i)=(0, 3)$ and the values of other parameters are: $\lambda=9$, $\beta=0.1$, $\varepsilon=0.02$, $\rho=0.02$, I=+0.8. (Note: The parameter values are based on the range of values found in literature).

The x-nullcline is represented by the curve along which the derivative of the unit x_i function is nil (i.e. $\dot{x}_i = 0$). It is given by the function $y_i = 3x_i - x_i^3 + 2 + \rho + I_i + S_i$ and results in a cubic curve that is characterised by a left branch denoted by LB(which extends from the local minimum to -∞) and a right branch denoted by RB (which extends from the local maximum to +∞) as illustrated in Figure 7-2. This cubic curve has two crucial values (related to the dynamics of a neural oscillator) which are defined by the function values (i.e. the y-values) at the two local extrema and referred to by left knee (LK) and right knee (RK) (see Figure 7-2). On the other hand, the y-nullcline is determined by the curve along which the derivative of the unit y function is nil (i.e. $\dot{y}_i = 0$). It is given by the function $y_i = \lambda [1 + tanh(x_i / \beta)]$, a hyperbolic tangent function which results in a sigmoidal curve whose steepness is controlled by the parameter β such that a big value of β makes the sigmoidal curve close to a step function. Based on these nullclines, the dynamics of a neural oscillator depend on the external input and are described in Appendix A. In the case of a single oscillator, the coupling term does not exist, i.e. $Si=0$.

7.3.2 Dynamics of coupled neurons

In this section, the behaviour of two coupled neural oscillators is examined with particular focus on the emerging synchronisation and desynchronisation of their temporal activities which depends, amongst other parameters, on the coupling strength linking them together. The same model equations in the previous section are used for each neural oscillator with the addition, this time, of the coupling term (previously discarded in the case of a single oscillator). The connection between two neural oscillators is illustrated in Figure 7-3 which clearly shows that it is the unit x of the neural oscillator that sends (receives) output (input) to (from) another oscillator and that the role of unit y is only '*internal*' and consists of sending an inhibiting signal to the unit x of the same oscillator as explained in the previous section. As a result, the unit y has no interaction with other units of other oscillators.

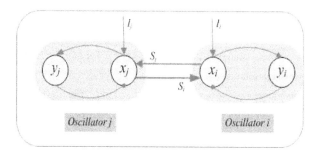

Figure 7-3 Example of two coupled neural oscillators. Besides the external input received and fed to each neural oscillator, both oscillators send/receive an output/input to/from each other.

The mathematical equations defining Oscillator i and Oscillator j are given, respectively, by Equation 7-2 and Equation 7-3 as follows:

$$\begin{cases} \dot{x}_i = 3x_i - x_i^{3} + 2 - y_i + \rho + I_i + S_i(x_j) \\ \dot{y}_i = \varepsilon[\lambda\,(1 + tanh(x_i / \beta)) - y_i] \end{cases}$$

$\qquad\qquad\qquad$ **Equation 7-2**

$$\begin{cases} \dot{x}_j = 3x_j - x_j^{3} + 2 - y_j + \rho + I_j + S_j(x_i) \\ \dot{y}_j = \varepsilon[\lambda\,(1 + tanh(x_j / \beta)) - y_j] \end{cases}$$

$\qquad\qquad\qquad$ **Equation 7-3**

Where S_i represents the coupling term received by Oscillator i from Oscillator j, and S_j represents the coupling term received by Oscillator j from Oscillator i. The general form of this coupling term (which applies to the case where a neural oscillator is connected to several oscillators) is given by the following equation:

$$S_i = \sum_{k \in Ni} W_{ik} H(x_k - \theta_x)$$

$\qquad\qquad\qquad$ **Equation 7-4**

where W_{ik} are positive synaptic weights (coupling strength) connecting neuron k and i, N_i represents the neighbourhood of neuron i, H is a Heaviside function and θ_x is a threshold that is applied to the received input from neighbouring neurons. From Equation 7-4, it can be seen that the application of the Heaviside function on the received input allows an oscillator to receive its neighbour input only if the latter is above a certain threshold θ_x. Other transform functions can also be used (instead of the Heaviside function) such as a sigmoidal function (which has a role of a 'squashing function'). Only positive weights are assumed for the coupling term which mimics the excitatory synapses. For the applications which will be discussed in the following sections, neural oscillators will be connected locally in an excitatory way while a global common inhibitor is used to allow competition between groups of neurons.

The x and y-nullclines of both neural oscillators and the convergence of their trajectories to a limit cycle are represented in the phase plane as illustrated in Figure 7-4. The threshold is represented by a vertical line with a circle on the x-axis. Three nullclines are obtained for this simulation as the same y-nullcline is common to both oscillators, however two different x-nullclines are obtained because the change in the parameter values only affects the equations of unit x while the unit y equations remain identical (this change is caused by the use of different initial parameters and also during the continuous interaction defined by the coupling term). The upper cubic is referred to as the 'excited x-nullcline/cubic' because it represents the excited neural oscillator (i.e. the neuron whose coupling term S_i is above the threshold). Likewise the lower cubic is referred to as the 'unexcited cubic' as it represents the neural oscillator without excitation (i.e. with a nil coupling term $S_i=0$).

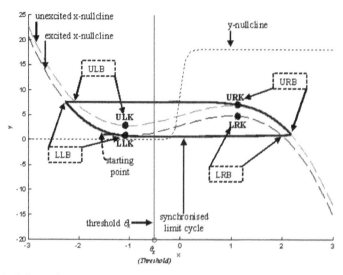

Figure 7-4 Nullclines of two coupled oscillators and the convergence of their temporal activity to a synchronised limit cycle which is represented by a thick solid line. The x-nullclines (cubic curves) of the system in Equation 7-2 and Equation 7-3 are represented by a dashed line and the y-nullcline (sigmoid curve) is represented by a dotted line. The excitation threshold (θ_x) is set between the left and the right branches of the limit cycle (vertical line with a circle end on the x axis). ULB (upper left branch), URB (upper right branch), LLB (lower left branch), LRB (lower right branch), ULK (upper left knee), LLK (lower left knee), URK (upper right knee), LRK (lower right knee). The parameters used for this simulation are: $W_{ij}=W_{ji}=3.0$, $\theta_x=-0.5$, $\lambda=9$, $\beta=0.1$; $\varepsilon=0.04$; $\rho=0.02$; I=+0.8.

Based on the coupling strength, the emerging behaviour is either a synchronisation or a desynchronisation of the neural oscillators' temporal activities. Increasing the coupling strength leads to an elevation of the x-nullcline (the cubic), on the other hand a decrease in the coupling strength will shift the cubic downwards. The example shown in Figure 7-4 illustrates the dynamics of strongly coupled oscillators which led to synchronised activities and to the neural oscillators' trajectories converging to a limit cycle. The temporal activities of coupled neural oscillators and the effect of the coupling strength on their synchronisation and their trajectories in the phase plane are described in Appendix A. The interactions between coupled oscillators, discussed in Appendix A, which result in either a synchronisation or a desynchronidation of their temporal activities, will form the basis of the following sections which describe the application of networks of neural oscillators to grey scale and colour image segmentation developed in this work. However, before discussing the developed system in sections 7.6, 7.7 and 7.8, it is important to introduce the problem of feature binding and highlight its relation to the temporal synchronisation in neural oscillators and how it relates to object segmentation and image analysis tasks. The following two sections will briefly address these issues.

165

7.4 The feature binding problem, synchrony and neural oscillators

Perhaps one of the most intriguing capabilities of the brain is its ability to organize the tremendous amount of information supplied by our senses in such a way that the world is not perceived as a chaotic stream of impressions, but as a well-structured set of entities (Ontrup et al., 2004). This issue is addressed by the controversial topic of feature binding, a problem that continues to receive attention among researchers at both theoretical and experimental levels (Roskies, 1999; Charles, 1999; Singer, 1999; Calvert et al., 2004). The binding problem can be defined as the question of how the unity of conscious perception is brought about by the distributed activities of the central nervous system (Revonsuo and Newman, 1999; Wolfe and Cave, 1999). It arises when the features, of a given object, that are represented or processed by distinct populations of neurons must be combined and linked together to form an object representation and achieve the perception of a coherent whole.

However, the large body of research carried out to date suggests two main competing hypotheses to explain how the brain binds together the distributed features of a perceived object. The first hypothesis, based on the so-called *neuron doctrine* (Barlow, 1972), suggests that information about a stimulus is conveyed by the average firing rate of a single neuron and that neurons at higher brain areas become more selective (Desimone et al., 1984; Perrett et al., 1987; Zeki, 1993) so that a single neuron may represent each single object (the grandmother-cell representation). Consequently, multiple objects in a visual scene would be represented by the co-activation of multiple units at some level of the nervous system. This hypothesis faces, however, major theoretical and neurobiological criticism which is rather in favour of another hypothesis based on the theory of temporal correlation (von der Malsburg, 1981; Abeles, 1991; Singer, 1993; Singer and Gray, 1995). This popular hypothesis suggests that it is the temporal correlation of the firing activities of distributed neurons that is used to create the binding between the features of an object. This means that an object is coded by a population of many neurons whose firing activity is synchronised. Unlike the first proposal, the neural firing times are considered as a means of stimulus representation. According to this hypothesis, different objects can be encoded by different populations of neurons each of which has different firing times. Evidence of this approach has been established through several neurophysiological experiments; a review of these experiments can be found in (Usrey and Reid, 1999; Singer, 1999).

7.5 Relation to digital image segmentation

Based on the second hypothesis and its theoretical and experimental supporting evidence, the work in this chapter attempts to understand and exploit the emerging synchronisation in networks of locally connected neural oscillators and apply such self-organising behaviour to colour image segmentation. Although the focus of this work is on visual scenes (images) only, the idea of temporal correlation-based feature binding can be exploited in the processing of other sensory modalities such as speech. The image features (pixel attributes) are distributed over a network of neural oscillators where each feature is represented by a single neural oscillator. Therefore, the synchronisation of a group of oscillators encodes the object which they represent and the desynchronisation of other neural oscillators indicates that they do not belong to the same object and might represent other objects of the scene. Figure 7-5 illustrates the idea of temporal scene segmentation where existing objects are segmented and emerge through time as the temporal activity of its corresponding neural oscillators synchronise with each other and desynchronise with other neural oscillators in other objects.

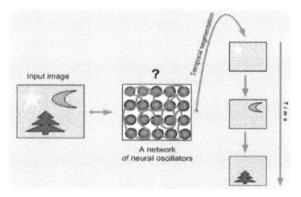

Figure 7-5: A colour image and its temporal segmentation using a network of neural oscillators. Neural oscillators which belong to the same object get their temporal activities synchronised with each other and desynchronised with other neurons from other different objects. This synchronisation and desynchronisation signal the detection an object.

The features of an image are referred to as 'pixel attributes' instead of pixel values because they depend on the type of the processed image. That is, in a black and white (binary) or grey scale image the pixel values could be directly used as features, although the use of other features based on the values of neighbouring pixels is also possible and sometimes might be unavoidable (such as in texture images). In a colour image, on the other hand, the situation is different and the colour of a pixel cannot be directly represented by a single oscillator as it is encoded by a triplet of integer values. Therefore the feature value should be determined by some mechanism or formula before being eventually fed to a neural oscillator. This work presents the self-organising maps of Kohonen (SOM) as a feature extraction (pre-processing stage) phase where the pixel values (triplets) of the original colour image are mapped to a new reduced space of colours where each pixel is assigned one value rather than a triplet of values. The creation of a new space and the mapping of original colours are based on the self-organising characteristic of Kohonen maps. The implementation details of this process are presented and thoroughly explained and illustrated in Section 7.7. The following section discusses the application of neural oscillators to image segmentation, starting initially with segmentation of grey scale images.

7.6 Application of neural oscillators to grey scale image segmentation

Image segmentation is a crucial problem in machine vision, as there is no generic method that can be applied to all types of images and the choice of a particular method is rather problem specific. The segmentation process consists of partitioning an image into its homogenous regions whose pixels share similar features. It has an important role in image understanding and object recognition systems. Although the human brain performs the task of image segmentation efficiently and with apparent ease, it is still a major challenge for computer vision systems and remains an open research field which encompasses a variety of applications such as pattern recognition, medical diagnosis, remote sensing, robotics, content-based information retrieval and search engines, etc. Over the last few decades of research in machine vision, many techniques have been produced, usually based on pixel classification, edge detection or region growing (Pal and Pal, 1993; Jain et al., 1995; Gonzalez, 2001), yet modelling the segmentation output in a network of neurons remains a challenging task. There is a large body of research work on image segmentation in different application fields and the number of publications is still growing every year. Obviously, it is beyond the scope of this work to provide a full survey of the various techniques developed in different application fields, and the reader is referred to the following references for a better review of the literature (Haralick and Shapiro, 1985; Pal and Pal, 1993; Skarbek and Koschan, 1994; Valentina et al., 2002). The work presented in this chapter presents a biologically inspired approach that is based on temporal correlation of neural oscillators with the aim to further our understanding of their dynamics through the simulation and analysis of their mathematical models, developed by neuroscientists, and more importantly (from a computing perspective) to exploit these dynamics in solving real world engineering problems.

As already stated in previous sections, it is hypothesised in neuroscience that segmentation of different objects in a visual scene is based on the temporal correlation of neural activity. Accordingly, a population of neurons which fire in synchrony, or in a highly correlated way, would signal attributes of the same object. Also, neurons with asynchronous activity would participate in the formation of different objects. Based on these principles and the dynamics of neural oscillators presented in previous sections, this work uses a network (grid) of neural oscillators that are locally connected through excitatory synapses and globally inhibited by a common inhibitor as defined in (Terman and Wang, 1995) and referred to by the acronym LEGION which stands for locally excitatory globally inhibitory oscillator networks. Such a network is first applied to grey scale images where the intensities of pixels are directly assigned to neural oscillators then to colour images.

7.6.1 Network architecture

The network consists of a grid (a 2D array) of neural oscillators which are locally connected through excitatory synapses represented by positive weights and a global neuron which receives excitation from each neuron and sends inhibition to all neurons in the grid (i.e. negatively connected to all neurons). Each neuron input is assigned a feature of the image pixel as illustrated in Figure 7-6. The local connections between each two neurons are reciprocal and each neuron is connected with its nearest four neighbouring neurons as shown in Figure 7-7. While a 4-connectedness is shown this figure, it is still possible to use alternative forms such as 8-connectedness where each neuron is reciprocally connected to its 8 nearest neighbours. The motivation behind local excitatory connections is that, besides its consistence with lateral synaptic connections in several areas of the brain, it is hoped that such connections will contribute to object segmentation by inducing synchronised activities amongst neurons which belong to the same region (i.e. neurons that are mapped to pixels with similar features).

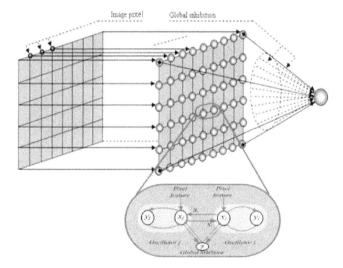

Figure 7-6 A grid (network) of competitive self-organising locally excitatory globally inhibitory neural oscillators. Each neural oscillator is connected to its four neighbours through excitatory synapses and receives inhibition from a global inhibitor. The latter helps create competition between neurons that belong to a single object (synchronised) and other neurons which belong to different objects (desynchronised). Note that only the coupling between oscillators x_i and x_j has been highlighted; the connections between each neuron and other neighbours are not shown for the sake of simplicity.

169

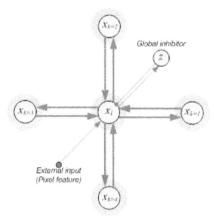

Figure 7-7 Connections between each neural oscillator, its four neighbours (x_1, x_2, x_3 and x_4) and the global inhibitor (z). Note that every neural oscillator in the grid is connected to the global inhibitor (these connections are not shown in this figure in order to keep the diagram simple). Each neuron is assigned to a pixel of the image whose features form the external input of the neural oscillator. Only the unit x of the oscillator is shown. Other forms of connectedness can also be used (e.g. 8-connectedness where each neuron is connected to its immediate surrounding neighbours).

The building block of the network is similar to the model in Equation 7-1 and Equation 7 2 with the slight modification of the external input term (will be explained below) and the integration of the added global inhibition in the coupling term S_i, the resulting equations are given by:

$$\begin{cases} \dot{x}_i = 3x_i - x_i^3 + 2 - y_i + I_i H(p_i - \theta) + S_i + \rho \\ \dot{y}_i = \varepsilon(\gamma(1 + tanh(x_i / \beta)) - y_i) \end{cases}$$

Equation 7-5

The coupling from other neighbouring neurons is represented by S_i and defined by:

$$S_i = \sum_{k \in Ni} W_{ik} H(x_k - \theta_x) - W_z zH(z - \theta_z)$$

Equation 7-6

Similarly to the coupling term defined in section 7.3.2 in relation to coupled oscillators, excitatory connections (W_{ij}) are used and they contribute to the propagation of the neuron activity to its neighbours. Also, an oscillator can receive its neighbour input only if the latter is above a certain threshold θ_x (set between LK and RC). The calculation of the connection weights of a neural oscillator is based on the value of its input (pixel feature) and those of its neighbours such as oscillators with similar pixel values are assigned strong weights while other oscillators belonging to different regions are given weaker connections. There is a new term added in this case to count for the global inhibitor whose inhibition weight is denoted by W_z. The activity of the global inhibitor is represented by the dynamic variable z defined as follows:

$$\dot{z} = \phi(\sigma - z)$$

Equation 7-7

where $\sigma = 1$ if at least one oscillator is on the active phase, and $\sigma = 0$ otherwise. When an oscillator is triggered, $z \rightarrow 1$, and ϕ is a parameter which determines the rate at which the inhibitor reacts to the stimulation from an active oscillator. According to Equation 7-6, the inhibitor activity is considered only when its value z is above a certain threshold θ_z (due to the Heaviside function), in which case the term W_z is subtracted from the total excitation from neighbouring neurons. The global inhibitor, which receives excitatory input from all the neurons and sends back inhibitory outputs to all neurons, contributes to the desynchronisation of other oscillators which does not belong to the object being segmented. It cannot affect synchronised oscillators as the sum of the inputs from synchronised neighbours is greater than W_z.

In addition, the function p_i, called the lateral potential, according to Terman and Wang model (1995), is introduced in Equation 7-5 in order to distinguish between small sparsed noisy fragments and coherent regions so that oscillations of noisy fragments are removed. Major coherent region contains at least one oscillator (called leader) with large enough lateral excitation ($> \theta_p$) from its neighbours, but such a leader oscillator does not exist in a noisy fragmented region. Therefore the function p_i determines whether or not an oscillator is a leader and also plays a role in 'ignoring' the noise in the input image. It is given by the following equation:

$$\dot{p}_i = \lambda(1 - p_i)H[\sum_{k \in Ni} W_{ik}H(x_k - \theta_x) - \theta_p] - \mu\, p_i$$

Equation 7-8

where λ is a constant. If the weighted sum of active neighbours (each of which should obviously exceed θ_x to make the inner Heaviside evaluate to 1) is above a certain threshold θ_p, then the outer Heaviside is activated (becomes 1) and p_i approaches one, otherwise it relaxes to zero on a time scale determined by a small value μ. Thus, only oscillators which are surrounded by a large number of active oscillators can maintain their p_i high.

7.6.2 Numerical simulations

In order to illustrate the separation of existing objects within a grey scale image through the synchronisation of neural oscillators belonging to the same object and desynchronisation of others belonging to different objects, a demonstration on a small scale synthetic image and a large scale real one is presented below. While discrete integration is used for the first test, an algorithmic approach (explained below) is used for the second.

7.6.2.1 Step-by-step equation integration for small scale images

A network of 10 by 10 neural oscillators, based on the models described above and the behaviour of the grid architecture explained in the section 7.6.1, was numerically simulated using Matlab© R13. The differential equations were first integrated using the Runge-Kutta 4th order to ensure a better accuracy. However the forward Euler method was also used and the same results were obtained. Therefore, as the Runge-Kutta method requires a bigger number of computations than its forward Euler counterpart, the latter is preferable as it offers a reduction in the computing time due to the smaller number of integrations implied. A 10 by 10 synthetic grey scale image, shown in Figure 7-8, is fed to a network of 100 neural oscillators. It consists of four separate rectangles, laid upon a black background, each of which has a different size and a different gray scale. Each pixel value is fed as an external input to the corresponding neural oscillator in the grid. The objects are labelled Obj 1, Obj 2, Obj 3 and Obj 4 for referencing in later discussions of the simulation results.

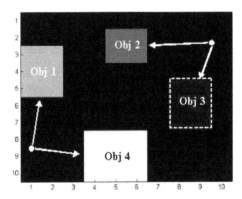

Figure 7-8 A 10x10 synthetic grey scale image, object number 3 manually highlighted with dashed line to be contrasted from the black background.

Figure 7-9 shows the temporal activity of all neural oscillators in the grid (only the first 1800 integration steps are shown, however the oscillations carry on indefinitely unless the input image is withdrawn). Neurons are arranged in a one dimensional array which represents a linear mapping (line by line) of the 2D format of the grid. It clearly shows the synchronisation and desynchronisation of the temporal activities of neural oscillators in the network. While some neurons are active and their temporal activity is synchronised, other neurons are inactive and therefore their temporal activity is desynchronised with those that are active and synchronised. At a given time, the active and synchronised neurons belong to the same object while those that are inactive belong to other different objects. However, the mapping between each neuron index and the object it belongs to may however not be straightforward from this graph. Although the 3D graph provides a better illustration of the activities of all the neurons in the grid and therefore the global picture of the network activity, it does not illustrate well which object is segmented each time a population of neurons is active and its temporal activity is synchronised. In order to emphasise the segmentation of different objects based on the synchronisation and desynchronisation of different neurons in the 2-dimensional networks, the neurons which belong to the same object are grouped together and their temporal activity is displayed on the same axis as shown in Figure 7-10.

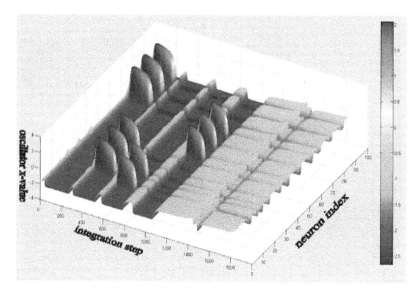

Figure 7-9 Temporal activity of the neural oscillators in the 10 by 10 grid. The z-axis represent the value of the x-unit of the neural oscillator (there are two units in an oscillator as described by the underlying differential equations, unit x and unit y). The x-axis represents the integration steps (only 1800 steps were shown here), and the y-axis represents the neurons' index (i.e. from neuron 1 which is associated with the top left corner pixel to neuron 100 which is associated with the bottom right corner pixel).

While the previous figure show the 3D visualisation of the temporal activity of all oscillators in the grid where each neural oscillator is mapped to a pixel in the image, Figure 7-10 illustrates the temporal activity of those neurons rearranged according to the different objects to which they belong. The indexes of neurons which belong to the same object are first determined (see Line2 to Line 6 of the Matlab code excerpt shown in Figure 7-11), then the corresponding waveforms of those neurons are plotted on the same axis one after the other. Each neuron's waveform is separated from the previous neuron by an offset to avoid any overlap between two consecutive waveforms (see Lines 7, 8 and Lines 9, 10 of the code in Figure 7-11 related to the plotting functions in the first and second 'for' loops). Ordering the waveforms according to the objects they belong to better

173

highlights which set of neurons are active at a given time and therefore indicate which object is detected at that time. For example at time T1 (see Figure 7-10) the neurons that belong to object 4 are active while other neurons are inactive. At time T2, it is object 1 neurons that are active and the other neurons that belong to other objects and the background are inactive. Similarly for time T3 and time T4, the neurons belonging to object 2 and object 3 are active respectively.

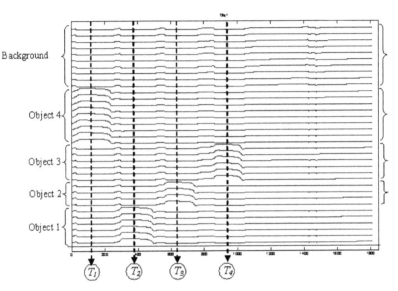

Figure 7-10 Temporal activity of neural oscillators ordered according to the objects they belong to. The x-axis represents integration steps and the y-axis represents neuron indexes. For example the first six neurons belong to object 1, the next four neurons belong to object 2, the following six neurons belong to object 3, then the following nine neurons represent object 4. Finally the remaining neurons (not all of them are drawn here for simplicity) represent the neurons that are mapped to the background pixels (there are [(10*10)-(6+4+6+9) =75] background neurons in total).

The following Matlab code excerpt (see Figure 7-11) illustrates the extraction of neurons indexes and the ordering of neural oscillators waveforms according to the objects they belong to in the input image. L and C represent the size of the grid which similar to the size of the input image expressed in terms of the number of lines (L) and columns (C). The function

ExistObjects(StartRow,EndRow,StartColumn,EndColumn,ImageRows,ImageColumns)

is written and used to determine the indexes of the neural oscillators located in a rectangular shape that is delimited by the row indices StartRow and EndRow, and the column indexes StartColumn and EndColumn. It is these returned indexes that are used to produce the waveforms in Figure 7-10 which correspond to neural oscillators associated with the four objects in the input image as well as its background.

174

```
L=10;C=10;                                          %Line 1

obj1=ExistObjects(3,5,  1,2,L,C);                   %Line 2
obj2=ExistObjects(2,3,  5,6,L,C);                   %Line 3
obj3=ExistObjects(5,7,  8,9,L,C);                   %Line 4
obj4=ExistObjects(8,10, 4,6,L,C);                   %Line 5
bkg=setdiff(1:C*L, [obj1 obj2 obj3 obj4]);          %Line 6

% Display temporal activities of oscillators associated with existing objects
% obj1, obj2, obj3 and obj4

offset=0;
for neur=[obj1 obj2 obj3 obj4 bkg(1:10)]    % neur is used as index
  plot(X(neur,:)'+offset*6);title('Obj1'); grid off ;hold on; %Line 7
  offset=offset+1;                                             %Line 8
end


% Display temporal activities of oscillators associated with the background
offset=0;
for neur=bkg
 plot(X(neur,:)'+offset*6);title('Obj1'); grid off ;hold on; %Line 9
  offset=offset+1;                                            %Line 10
end
```

Figure 7-11 Matlab code used to draw the temporal activities of neural oscillators grouped by the objects they belong to. The function ExistObjects(StartRow, EndRow, StartColumn, EndColumn, ImageRows, ImageColumns) determines the indices of neurons belonging to a rectangular shape delimited by the row indices StartRow and EndRow, and the column indices StartColumn and EndColumn in an image of size ImageRows by ImageColumns. An offset is used so that each curve is separated from the previous and the overlapping between two waveforms is avoided.

Using a 2D visualisation of the temporal activity of the neural oscillators of the network at selected points in time, the following figure illustrates further the segmented objects at the times shown in the previous Figure 7-10. Time T_1 corresponds to object 4 (see Figure 7-8 for initial object labelling). The neural oscillators associated with the pixel of this object are active and also synchronised. The x-values of all neural oscillators in the grid are mapped to a grey scale image. The obtained 2D visualisation clearly shows at T_1 the emergence of object 4, while other neurons representing the remaining objects are inactive (small values) and therefore the corresponding objects fade away. Likewise at time T_2, it is the neurons belonging to object 1 that are active and synchronised while other neurons are inactive. Similarly, at time T_3 and T_4 object 2 and object 3 have been temporally segmented, respectively.

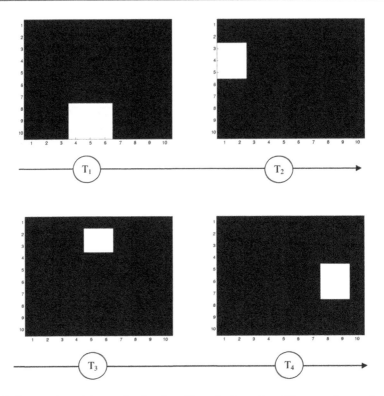

Figure 7-12 The value of the x-unit of each oscillator is shown in a 2D array where each element corresponds to one neural oscillator that is associated with a pixel of the image located at the same coordinates. The values of neural oscillators selected at different points in time (T1, T2, T3 and T4. These times correspond to those shown in Figure 7-10) clearly show that neurons belonging to the same object are active and their temporal activity is synchronised and that neurons belonging to different objects are inactive and therefore desynchronised with those that are active. The synchronisation of active neurons indicates which object is being segmented.

7.6.2.2 Algorithmic approach for large scale images

For larger images, the activity of the neuron oscillators is calculated using an algorithmic approach as solving hundreds or thousands of systems of ordinary differential equations (ODE), each of which assigned to an image pixel, is prohibitively costly in terms of computing time and may not be feasible unless their discrete integration is implemented on a hardware platform such as reconfigurable FPGAs (Field Programmable Gates Array). The algorithmic approach is based on the neural oscillators dynamics on the cubic branches and at jumping points (LK, RK) between left and right branches (LB, RB) (Terman and Wang, 1995). It produces the essential behaviours of coupled neural oscillators, namely the synchronisation and desynchronisation of their temporal activity as well as the exhibition of two time scales (i.e. the slow and fast motions on the left and

176

right branches, respectively). The use of an algorithmic approach considerably reduces the computation time induced by discrete integration of the resulting huge set of ODEs. Only the x value of an oscillator i is used and the algorithm is described below:

1. Initialisation
- set $z(0)=0$ and calculate the connecting weights

$W_{ik}=I_m/(1+|I_i-I_k|)$; where I_m is the maximum gray scale value, I_i and I_k represent the pixel value corresponding to neuron i and k.

- find leaders: $p_i = H(\sum_{k \in N_i} W_{ik} - \theta_p)$ and randomly start all the oscillators on the left

branch (i.e. set their the value of their units x to a random value in the interval [LCx, LKx], the points LC and LK has already been shown in Figure 7-2).

2. Selection
- Find the closest leader j to left knee (LK).
- Jump the found leader to right branch (RB), the other oscillators move towards LK

$x_j(t+1)=RK; z(t+1)=1$ {jump up};

$x_k(t+1)=x_k(t)+(LK-x_j(t)); for\ k \neq j$

3. Jumping
Iterate until stop

If $x_i(t)=RK$ and $z(t)>z(t-1)$

      $x_i(t+1)= x_i(t)$;   {stay on the RB}

elseif $x_i(t)=RK$ and $z(t)<=z(t-1)$

      $x_i(t+1)=LC; z(t+1)= z(t)-1$;   {jump down}

      if $z(t+1)=0$ go to Selection.

else

      {calculate input to neuron}

      $Si(t+1)=sum(w_{ik}.H(x_k(t)-LK)) -W_zH(z(t)-\theta_z)$;

      If $Si(t+1)>0$

           $x_j(t+1)=RK; z(t+1)=z(t)+1$ {jump up};

      else

           $x_j(t+1)= x_j(t)$;   {stay on LB}

The algorithm above is demonstrated on a 110 by 90 pixels image, which contains five chess pieces as shown in Figure 7-13 (left). A network of 110 by 90 oscillators is built, and each neuron is stimulated with its corresponding pixel value. Each neural oscillator is connected to its eight nearest neighbours, and the connecting weights are formed based on the image pixel values. Setting the coupling weights according to the expression $W_{ik}=I_m/(1+|I_i-I_k|)$ results in oscillators with similar pixel values being assigned large weights while the other oscillators belonging to different regions will be assigned weaker connections. The addition of 1 in the denominator is used to avoid a division by zero when both oscillators are assigned the same pixel values in which case the coupling term is assigned the maximum weight value. This will ensure the leaders will propagate their activity to the oscillators in the same group representing the same object. As the network activity evolves, the different objects (chess pieces) emerge one by one as shown in Figure 7-13. The emergence of each object is achieved through the synchronisation of the activities of neurons belonging to the same object (images (a) to (d)). The background is also separated from other objects as represented in Figure 7-13 image (f).

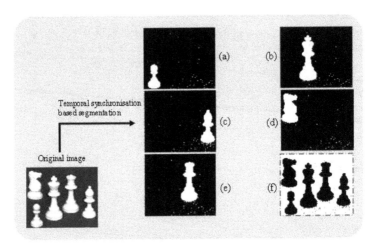

Figure 7-13 Segmented objects from 110x90 image containing five chess pieces. Left: original image. (a) to (e): segmented objects. (f) represents the image background.

7.7 Application of neural oscillators to colour image segmentation

A similar network of oscillators is applied to colour images where the HSV (hue, saturation, value) colour space is used and a self-organising map based colour reduction method is employed. The development of such a method for colour reduction allows the application of networks of oscillators to colour image segmentation. As each neuron in the grid of oscillators receives a one dimensional input value, there is a need for a mapping method between RGB triplets of an input colour image and corresponding feature values where colour similarity measurements are taken into account. To the best of the author's knowledge, this is the first time such neural models are applied to colour image segmentation. The HSV colour space, a liner transform of the RGB (red, green, blue) space (Gonzalez, 2001), has the advantage of specifying colours in an extremely intuitive manner as the luminance component is separated from the chrominance (i.e. colour) information (Jain et al., 1995; Ford and Roberts, 1998). The latter feature makes this colour space suitable for digital image processing applications because it is easy to select a desired colour (hue component) and to then

178

modify it slightly by adjustment of its saturation and intensity (saturation and value components) (Ford and Roberts, 1998). In addition, the components of the HSV colour space are normalised, which makes it suitable for the colour reduction method and the system of colour image segmentation developed in this work.

The colour reduction method exploits the colours of the pixels (chromatic features) as well as their spatial characteristics such as how the colour of each pixel is related to the colours of the neighbouring pixels. It is the newly obtained reduced space of colours that is eventually fed to a network of locally connected neural oscillators to achieve the segmentation of existing objects. The following sub-sections describe the use of Kohonen self-organising maps (SOM) for mapping the colours of pixels of an original image (given as input for segmentation) from the original colour space (available colours within the input image) to a new reduced space using the chromatic and spatial features of the image pixels.

7.7.1 Colour reduction using Kohonen self-organising maps

Given an RGB input image with a certain number of colours (16M colours with a 24-bit resolution), the final reduced set of colours is automatically selected using a Kohonen self-organising map (SOM) which is an unsupervised neural network devised by Tuevo Kohonen (1995). It is based on competitive learning and is a topology preserving map which can be adjusted to represent the distribution of the inputs (Kohonen, 1995; Haykin, 1999; Duda et al., 2001), a feature that is often used in the visualisation of high dimensional data and dimensionality reduction.

In this approach, the HSV components (chromatic components h, s and v) of each pixel are considered as chromatic features and are combined with additional spatial features that are extracted from neighbouring pixels (The mean and standard deviation are used here but there is no restriction on the type of possible spatial features that could be used). The goal is map the space of colour triplets (H,S,V) into a one dimensional space of colour indexes that can be used by the network of oscillators because the latter can only handle single valued inputs. Once the set of feature vectors of a given image is constructed, a SOM is built and trained according to Kohonen's competitive learning rule (Kohonen, 1995). The trained SOM is then used as a mapping system between the original image pixel values (triplets) and the newly created reduced colour space where each colour is represented by single value (or index). However, the main characteristic of this mapping is that it takes into account the chromatic and spatial similarities between neighbouring pixels. Eventually, the input image (with larger set of colours) is transformed into a new one with a limited number of colours and spatial characteristics similar to those defined by the adopted features. The implementation of the colour reduction method is fully described as follow:

7.7.1.1 RGB to HSV colour space transform

The RGB colour space $[0, 255]^3$ is mapped into the HSV colour space $[0, 1]^3$ where the input image is then represented. The RGB to HSV transform is performed using the Matlab function *rgb2hsv* routine. A new representation is obtained where each image pixel is still represented by a triplet (H, S, V) which determines its chromatic features. Should an input image be represented in a different format, it is easy convert it into an RGB image using Matlab image processing tool box. In this approach, it is assumed that the input image is represented in the RGB format.

7.7.1.2 Chromatic and spatial feature extraction

Thee chromatic features are taken from the previous RGB to HSV transform, hence each pixel in the image is associated with the three components H, S and V of its colour triplet. In order to form the final feature vector which describe each image pixel, the chromatic features are combined with the local spatial features of each pixel calculated for each chromatic plane, i.e. the H, S and V components (as shown later in Figure 7-15). The local spatial characteristics chosen in this work are the mean and the standard deviation of the pixel values within a window centred at the pixel being considered. Obviously other spatial feature can also be considered where other statistic measurements can be used. The local spatial features are calculated as follows:

Central location measurements (Mean values)

This spatial feature is based on statistical measurements of the central location of each pixel within the sample points selected from a given window, namely the mean value which is given by the following formula:

$$M_{ch}(i,j) = \frac{1}{M} \sum_{(k,l) \in Nij} Im_{ch}(i,j)$$

Equation 7-9

where *ch* represent the chromatic plane being considered $ch \in \{h,s,v\}$, *i,j* are the pixel coordinates for which the spatial feature is being calculated, N_{ij} is the neighbourhood of the pixel (i,j) (i.e. a window centred at the pixel (i,j)), and *M* is the total number of pixels within a that window in the input image *Im* (see illustration in Figure 7-14). For example, taking a 3 by 3 neighbourhood around pixel (i,j) yields:

$$M_{ch}(i,j) = \frac{1}{9} \sum_{k=i-1}^{i+1} \sum_{l=j-1}^{j+1} Im_{ch}(k,l)$$

Equation 7-10

Dispersion measurements (Standard deviation values)

Likewise, the standard deviation is computed for each chromatic component using the following formula:

$$STD_{ch}(i,j) = \sqrt{\frac{1}{M}\sum_{(k,l)\in Nij}(Im_{ch}(i,j) - M_{ch}(i,j))^2}$$

Equation 7-11

In this work, a window of size 3x3 is considered and the image is padded with zeros before the spatial characteristics are computed.

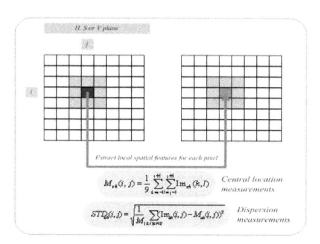

Figure 7-14 Extraction of local spatial features. The mean and standard deviation are calculated for each pixel in the three chromatic planes. Hence, each pixel in the image results in six different spatial features. These spatial features are calculated over a 3 by 3 window centred at the target pixel.

As a result of applying the previous stages, each pixel in the input image is described by a feature vector which includes both chromatic and spatial characteristics. The resulting feature vector consists of nine values representing the chromatic and spatial features of a pixel, i.e. three chromatic features and six spatial features (see Figure 7-15 for illustration). It is the size of the feature vector that will dictate the number of inputs of the Kohonen self-organising network. A set of these feature vectors will be created and used to build and train a Kohonen self-organising map as explained in the following section. Figure 7-15 summarises the previous stages involved in building a feature vector for each pixel in a given image.

181

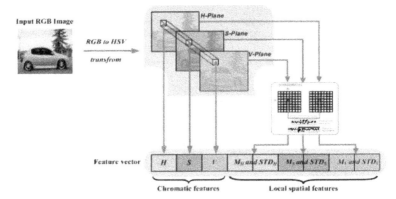

Figure 7-15 Building a feature vector for each pixel in the input image. both spatial and chromatic characteristics are considered.

7.7.1.3 Building and training of Kohonen Self-organising network

A one dimensional Kohonen SOM is designed, where the inputs represent the chromatic and the local spatial features of a pixel as calculated in the previous section. While the number of inputs is dictated by the dimensionality of the feature space (i.e. the size of feature vector), the number of output neurons represents the number of representative colours in the reduced colour space where each colour in the new space is indexed by the number of corresponding output neuron {$1, 2, ...j$} (see Figure 7-16). Once the network is built and a subset of feature vectors is randomly selected to form the training set, the SOM network is then trained and its final weights are adjusted using the Kohonen competitive learning rule and the final weight configuration is obtained. It is important to note that for each new image, a SOM is created anew and its weights are trained and adapted to the new image. Hence, the mapping between the original colour space and the reduced one is updated and adapted to the content of the image to be segmented.

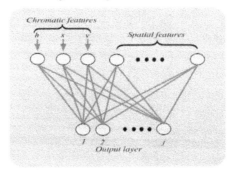

Figure 7-16 Self-organizing network map used for colour reduction and image transformation. The chromatic components and spatial features are used as inputs. The number of output neurons j represents the final number of reduced colours, which are represented in the weights of the output neurons.

182

7.7.1.4 Mapping

After training, the new reduced set of colours is represented by the final weights of the output neurons and the input image is transformed into a new one using the obtained SOM final weights. The new image contains only the representative colours selected by the Kohonen self-organising map and represented by its final weights. The resulting image contains fewer colours than the original image and each colour is represented by a single value as opposed to the RGB or HSV triplets usually used to represent images. As previously mentioned, it is the output neurons that represent the indexes (single values) of the new colours in the reduced space of colours. Each pixel in the image is assigned one value (represented by the index of selective output neuron) which represents its most similar colour. In order to map a given pixel to its closest colour in the new space colour, the features of the pixel are first extracted and then fed to the trained network. The closest colour is indicated by the index of the active neuron at the output layer and its calculation is carried out as follows:

An image pixel is represented by the (h,s,v) colour triplet representing its Hue, Saturation and Value in the original colour space. Its features are represented by the 9-dimensional feature vector $f=(f_1, f_2, ..., f_9)$ which are calculated as explained previously(see section 7.7.1.2). The resulting colour in the reduced colour space is the index of the active neuron resulting from the multiplication of the feature vector (a 1 by 9 vector) by the weight matrix W obtained after the training of the self-organising map. The SOM weight matrix W is a 9 by j matrix and is given by:

$$
W = \begin{bmatrix}
w_{11} & w_{12} & . & . & . & . & . & w_{1j} \\
w_{21} & w_{22} & . & . & . & . & . & w_{2j} \\
. & . & . & . & . & . & . & . \\
. & . & . & & & & & . \\
. & & . & & & & . & . \\
. & & . & & & . & & . \\
. & & & . & & & & . \\
. & & & & . & & & . \\
w_{91} & w_{92} & . & . & . & . & . & w_{9j}
\end{bmatrix},
$$

where j (number of columns) is the number of the output neurons of the SOM and number of rows is the number of pixel features. The closest colour is given by:

$$ClosestColour = IndexOfActiveNeuron(f * W),$$

where * represents the matrix multiplication operator and $ClosestColourIndex \in [1,j]$.

7.7.2 A neuro-system for colour image segmentation

The combination of the dynamics of networks of neural oscillators and the self-organising map based colour reduction approach, described in the previous section, results in a neuro-system for colour image segmentation. The original image is first converted into the HSV space, then the representative colours in a given image are automatically selected using a Kohonen self-organising map, which is newly trained for each input image, and the resulting image with a reduced number of colours is segmented using the temporal correlation of neural oscillators. An illustration of the proposed framework for colour image segmentation based on the combination of networks of neural oscillators and the colour reduction method described above is shown in the following figure:

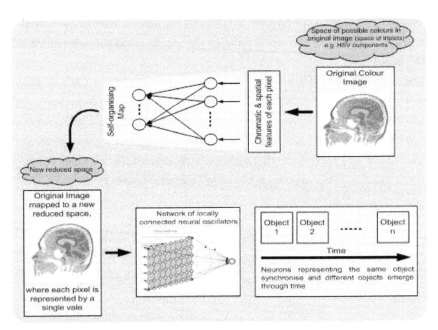

Figure 7-17 A framework for colour image segmentation. The output from a colour reduction stage is fed to a network of locally excited globally inhibited neural oscillators and objects are segmented one by one through temporal synchronisation of neurons belonging to the same coherent areas (objects).

7.7.3 MATLAB simulation results

The proposed approach has been implemented in Matlab R13 and demonstrated on 24-bit bitmap colour images (16 million colours as original space). The first image represents a car and contains 130x80 pixels (see Figure 7-18 bottom right corner), the second image represents a hand and has a size 100x129 pixels (see Figure 7-19) pixels and the third image which represents a cup has a size of 128x128 pixels (see Figure 7-20). The input images have a BMP format and are originally represented in the RGB space. A transformation to the HSV space is carried out using the Matlab *rgb2hsv* function which comes with the image processing toolbox. A self-organising network is built and trained for colour reduction, and its final weights are used to transform the input image into a new image with pixel values mapped to the newly obtained reduced space such that each pixel is represented by a single value instead of a triplet (original space). Finally, a network of neural oscillators (with a size equal to the input image size) is created, where the pixel values of the transformed image are used as external inputs to neural oscillators. The coupling weights are also determined according to the newly obtained pixel values. The segmentation results are illustrated in Figure 7-18, Figure 7-19 and Figure 7-20 where the main segmented objects are shown separated along with the original image. The assessment of the segmentation quality is subjective and based on human judgement which is a common practice in most segmentation applications.

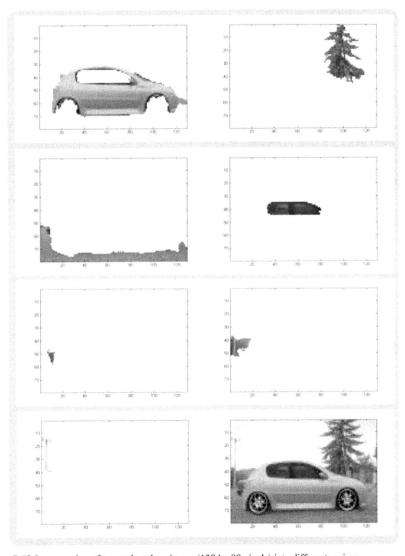

Figure 7-18 Segmentation of a sample colour image (130 by 80 pixels) into different regions.

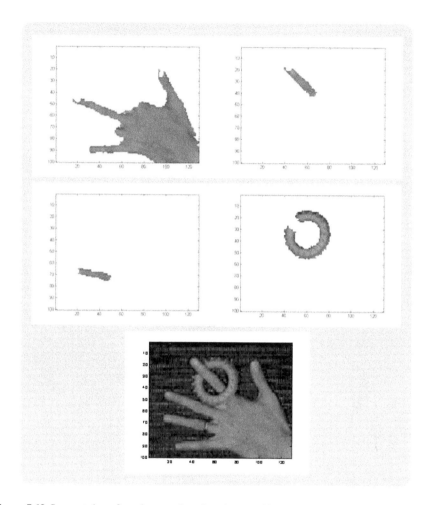

Figure 7-19 Segmentation of another sample colour image (100 by 129 pixels) into different regions. Fingers are separated due to the surrounding rings (the big blue ring and the small golden one). This is in accordance with the definition of an object as mentioned in early sections, i.e. a coherent region with similar pixels.

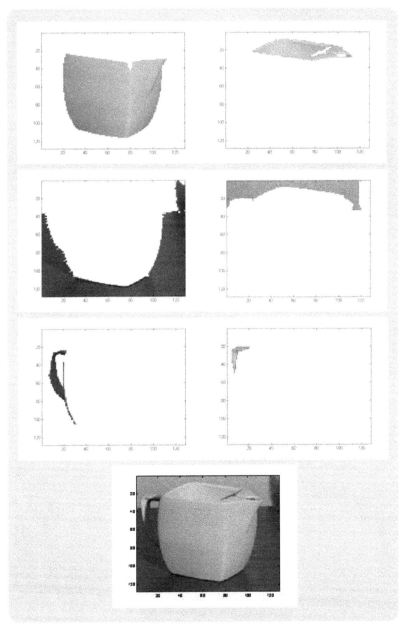

Figure 7-20 Segmentation of a third sample colour image (128 by 128 pixels) into different regions.

7.8 Discussion

Based on human visual assessment of the segmented images obtained from the previous simulations, one can judge the obtained segmentation to an acceptable quality, although it remains a subjective evaluation as mentioned earlier. This satisfactory judgement is based on the clear (always visually) separation of the existing objects within the input image. It can be seen from Figure 7-13 how all the existing objects (chess pieces and the background) are clearly and accurately segmented. Likewise, the segmentation of the synthetic image using the step-by-step integration of neural oscillators resulted in a perfect separation of the existing rectangles. The segmentation of the colour images in Figure 7-18, Figure 7-19 and Figure 7-20 clearly shows the segmentation of the coherent areas (objects) in the image (car frame, windows/glass, tree, grass, hand, ring, cup, etc). This subjective evaluation (also called visual evaluation) can be resembled to a comparison with what a manual segmentation should produce, as the latter is based on the human performance and is assumed as the ground truth (perfect reference segmentation). In fact the evaluation of segmentation quality is a problem on its own in the field of image segmentation applications, as often the latter do not produce a unique answer for the same input images and in the absence of accurate objective evaluations which do not need the intervention of human expertise, one will need to re-implement the existing methods and then compare their results, their constraints and algorithms in order to provide a fair comparison of both segmentation algorithms as well as their results.

However, the system developed above can be compared in terms of its computing principles and its advantages and disadvantages. First of all, the computing paradigm of this system can be compared to a region growing approach as more pixels are grouped within a given region (grown from a chosen seed) when their features satisfy some specified criteria. The system in this work remains different because of the inherent dynamics of synchronisation and desynchronisation of neurons' temporal activity and also the colour reduction method which is able to automatically select (i.e. pay attention to) a reduced number of representative colours judged as the most relevant for the segmentation of the image given at the input with these representative colours created anew for each input image (i.e. it is adaptable as it takes into account both the chromatic and local spatial features which are specific to each image being handled). However both approaches share the problem of subjective evaluation of the segmentation quality and being dependent on the system parameters as the outcome of segmentation depends on the model parameter values. The apparent differences and advantages of this system, is that it offers a biologically inspired approach (whose modules are not necessarily all plausible) which builds on the strengths (and also the limitations) of neural architectures and the computing principles of the brain, which is undoubtedly the *only* segmentation system that is perfectly working so far. The other advantage, a consequence of the previous one, resides in the parallelism and distributed computing of this approach as all the states of oscillators are computed locally and in parallel which makes it more suitable for hardware implementation (VLSI or reconfigurable computing platforms such as FPGAs) in order to dramatically reduce the computation time and achieve real time computations. This is a very desirable feature for segmenting large scale datasets (e.g. large scale images, grey or colour, for which a software-based segmentation may not be feasible). Moreover, this method is not specific to particular types of objects and requires less human intervention which is the case in a number of segmentation techniques where the user needs to specify initially the number of objects to be segmented (e.g clustering-based techniques). This approach can be extended to more specific domains where available a priori knowledge can be exploited to determine the most relevant features of pixels.

Finally, it is useful to comment on the computational complexity and biological plausibility of this system in terms of neuron models, the architecture used and the resulting dynamics. It is clear that there is a similarity between the neural oscillators used in the simulations above and many of the available plausible models used to model neural dynamics such as FitzHugh-Nagumo (FitzHugh, 1961) and the Morris-Lecar (Morris and Lecar, 1981) which are known for being a reduction of the famous detailed Hodgkin-Huxley model (Hodgkin and Huxley, 1952). Also while the locally excitatory connections reflect the various lateral connections found in the brain, the global common inhibitor which interacts with the entire network by receiving excitation from all neurons and sending back inhibition can be seen as a kind of global control. Moreover, the emerging synchronisation and desynchronisation behaviours in the presence of a homogeneous object closely relate to the principles of temporal correlation and features of the binding problem. The developed system is however computationally intensive when applied to large scale images such as high-resolution digital camera pictures which need to undergo a sub-sampling before being fed to the system.

7.9 Summary

Another biologically plausible neural model, called neural oscillators, and another computing paradigm have been investigated in this chapter. Also a new system for colour image segmentation was presented. The biological relevance of neural oscillators has been highlighted and their dynamics examined through simulations and analysis of single and coupled neurons as well as networks of neurons. Analysis of the behaviours of this type of neurons was carried out in the time domain as well as in the phase plane and an investigation of their application to segmentation of grey scale and colour images was presented. The problem of feature binding was discussed and its connection with neural oscillators has been highlighted. Also, a discussion of the established link between the binding problem and computer vision has been provided along with the role of temporal correlation in feature binding.

The main contribution of this chapter consists of the exploitation of the possibilities of computing and learning with neural oscillators in solving real world engineering problems. To the best of the author's knowledge, networks of neural oscillators have not yet been applied to the segmentation of colour images and the work presented in this chapter proposed a new system for colour image segmentation based on the combination of neural oscillators and Kohonen self-organising maps (SOM). A colour reduction method was developed and used as a feature extraction (pre-processing stage) whose outputs are fed to a network of neural oscillators with locally excitatory connections and global inhibition. The temporal correlation, i.e. synchronisation and desynchronisation, between different populations of neural oscillators is then exploited for segmenting existing objects with similar colours within a real world colour image.

In the absence of accurate objective assessment criteria, the segmentation quality was visually assessed (subjective evaluation). A comparison between the proposed approach and classical image segmentation counterparts was carried out in terms of computing paradigm and biological plausibility and both advantages as well as disadvantages were highlighted. The results obtained in this chapter show the emergence of neural oscillators, combined with self-organising maps as a selector of most representative colours in an image, as an efficient approach for colour image segmentation which differs from classical approaches and also presents the desirable feature of parallel computing. The latter feature can be exploited for hardware implementations in order to dramatically reduce the simulation times of the network dynamics and achieve real time computations. Mapping the system onto hardware platforms, will be a desirable extension of this work so that the segmentation of large scale colour images will be realisable and the segmentation outcome is exploited in different image understanding applications such as content image retrieval and object recognition.

APPENDIX

Dynamics of single and coupled neural oscillators

This appendix describes the temporal activities and phase plane analysis of the behaviour of single and coupled neural oscillators. The following simulations and analyses will help understand their underlying principles and the interactions between coupled neural oscillators which form the basis of networks of neural oscillators. Single oscillators are addressed first, followed by a description and analysis of the dynamics of coupled oscillators emphasising the occurrence of synchronisation and desynchronisation of their temporal activity. The following experiments should further illustrate the dynamics of neural oscillators which underlie the image segmentation systems presented in Chapter 7. They have been placed in an appendix to keep Chapter 7 to a reasonable size.

1   Dynamics of single neural oscillators

This section describes the dynamics of stimulated and unstimulated single neural oscillators. The model is similar to the one described in Chapter 7 (section 7.3.1) and an illustration of a single oscillator is shown in the following figure (repeated from Chapter 7, section 7.3.1):

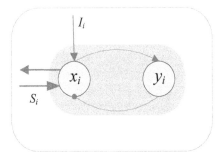

Figure A- 1 A single neural oscillator which consists of two coupled units x (excitatory) and y (inhibitory). While the x unit sends excitation (indicated by a triangle) to unit y, the unit y sends inhibition (indicated by a small circle) to unit x. I_i and S represent an external input and a possible coupling with other neural oscillators, respectively.

The following subsections describe the dynamics of stimulated and unstimulated single neural oscillators, therefore the coupling term is set to zero as no input is received from other neighbouring oscillators.

1.1   Dynamics of a stimulated neural oscillator (when I > 0)

An input is applied to the x-unit of the neural oscillator (i.e. the set of coupled x- and y-units) oscillator ad a neural oscillator is called stimulated in this case. The x and y-nullclines intersect at a unique point located in the middle branch of the cubic nullcline (see Figure A- 2). The trajectory of the oscillator defined in Chapter 7) will then converge to a periodic solution which is represented by a counter-clockwise attractor called limit cycle (see Figure A- 2). The limit cycle is bounded by four points –upper left corner LC, left knee LK, lower right corner RC, right knee RK- and indicated by oriented arrows to highlight its motion direction). The obtained periodic solution alternates between the right and left branch which are also called the *active* and *silent* phase, respectively. An oscillator is called active when it is found on the active phase (i.e. $x \in [$ RK, RC]), and is called silent when located on a silent phase (i.e. $x \in [$ LC, LK]). The positive parameter ε is set to a small value ($<<1$) which leads to two different time scales that characterise relaxation oscillators (Verhulst, 1996) and corresponds to different motion speeds along the periodic limit cycle. If the parameter ε is set otherwise, i.e. zero or bigger values are used, different regimes of the oscillator will then emerge and the system is not called a relaxation oscillator anymore. This case is not of interest to this work and will not be focused upon.

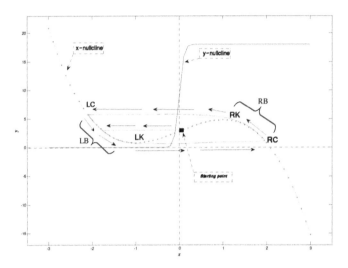

Figure A- 2 x- and y-nullclines with a periodic solution of the system in Equation 7-1 (limit cycle) represented in the phase plane. This oscillator trajectory jumps periodically between the left and the right branches of the limit cycle. LC, LB and LK indicate the upper left corner, left branch and left knee respectively. RC, RB and RK indicates lower right corner, right branch and right knee respectively. The starting point for this simulation is set to $(x_i, y_i)=(0, 3)$ and the values of other parameters are: $\lambda=9$, $\beta=0.1$, $\varepsilon=0.02$, $\rho=0.02$, $I=+0.8$. (Note: The parameter values are based on the range of values found in literature).

The motion of the neural oscillator along the two branches (being either active or silent) takes place on a slow time scale and the amount of the time spent on either phase is controlled by the parameter λ (a larger value leads to a shorter time spent on the active phase). However, the alternation between the two phases, which takes place at either the left knee (LK) or the right knee (RK), occurs on a fast time scale. This alternation is called a jump because of the speed at which it happens. An example of the convergence of the oscillator trajectories to a periodic counter-clockwise limit cycle simulated with two different starting points (0, 8) and (0, -3) is illustrated in Figure A- 3, left and right panel respectively. The temporal activity of the units x and y are also shown.

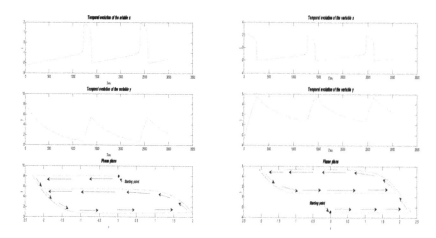

Figure A- 3 Dynamics of a single neural oscillator and its convergence to a periodic limit cycle. Left: Temporal activity of the excitatory unit *x* which represent the output of the neural oscillator (Top panel). Temporal activity of the inhibitory unit *y* (Middle panel). Trajectory of the neural oscillator with a starting point *(x,y)=(0,8)* (Bottom panel). Right: Temporal activity of the excitatory unit *x* (Top panel). Temporal activity of the inhibitory unit *y* (Middle panel). Trajectory of the neural oscillator with a starting point *(x,y)=(0,8)* (Bottom panel). It can be seen how the trajectory of the neural oscillator converges to the same stable periodic limit cycle. The same parameters in Figure A- 2 are used for this simulation.

Besides controlling the ratio of the times that a neural oscillator spend on both phases, the parameter λ also affects the shapes of the neural oscillator output, i.e. the temporal activities of its *x* units. Figure A- 4 illustrates this effect when different values of λ are used (the value of I is maintained constant for both cases). Note how, when λ is set to a higher value (λ=16), the shape of the temporal activity of the oscillator resembles that of an action potential or spike. Also it can be clearly seen from the widths of the two pulses in Figure A- 4 how the magnitude of the parameter λ affects the time spent by a neural oscillator in the *active* phase. Small values of λ (e.g. λ=4 as in Figure A- 4 -Top panel-) results in a narrow pulse (pulse means here the part of the signal with values falling in the active phase) and therefore a shorter active phase is obtained. On the other hand, large values of λ (λ=16 as in Figure A- 4 –lower panel-) generate a wider pulse which implies a longer time spent on the active phase.

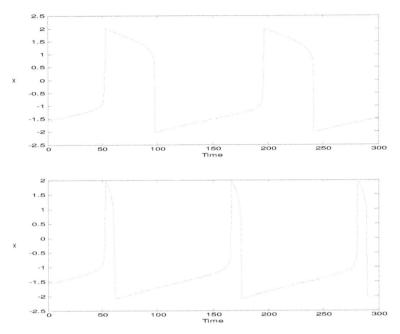

Figure A- 4 Effect of the value of λ on the shape of the neural oscillator output. The values 4, 16 of the parameter λ were used for the upper and lower panels. The remaining model parameters are: (β=0.1, ε=0.02, ρ=0.02, I=0.8).

1.2   Dynamics of an unstimulated neural oscillator (when I < 0)

In this case the neural oscillator is unstimulated and because the external input I is negative, the cubic (i.e. the x-nullcline) is shifted downwards and its left knee (LK) is brought below the left part of the sigmoidal curve (i.e. the y-nullcline). Consequently, the intersection between the cubic and the sigmoidal curves takes place on the left branch (LB) of the x-nullcline (instead of the middle branch as in the case where I>0) at two fixed points one of them is stable and no oscillation is produced as the trajectory of the neural oscillator converges to the stable fixed point as illustrated in Figure A- 5. A neural oscillator in such a state is called excitable. The convergence of the trajectory of the neural oscillator to a fixed point when different starting points are used is shown in Figure A- 6, Figure A- 7 and Figure A- 8. The temporal activities of units x and y are also shown where it can be clearly seen that whatever the values of initial conditions (starting point), the values of *x* and *y* converge to the same attractors and no oscillation is produced (temporal evolution of units *x* and *y*).

196

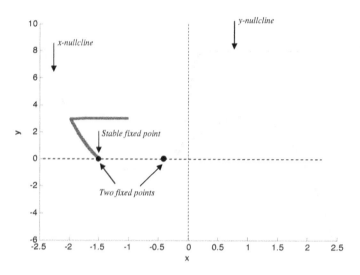

Figure A- 5 Nullclines of an unstimulated neural oscillator. Two fixed points are created on the left branch of the cubic and the trajectory of oscillator, represented by a thick line, converges to a stable fixed point and no oscillations produced. The model parameters are: (β=0.1, ϵ=0.02, ρ=0.02, I=-0.8) with a starting point set to (x, y)==(-1, 3).

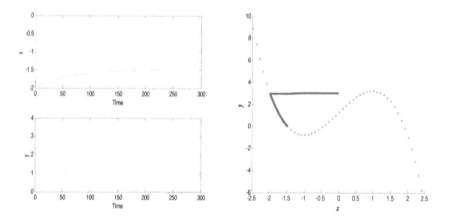

Figure A- 6. Activity of an unstimulated neural oscillator. (Left panel): Temporal activity of units x and y with initial conditions set to (x,y)=(0, 3). (Right panel): Convergence of the oscillator trajectory to a fixed point (instead of a periodic limit cycle). The parameters used in this simulation are as follows: (λ=4; β=0.1; ϵ=0.02; ρ=0.02; I=-0.8).

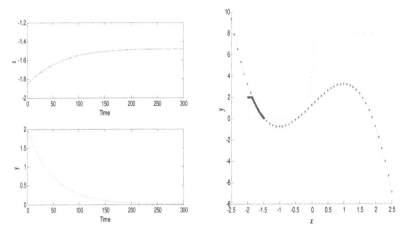

Figure A- 7 Another example of the same unstimulated neural oscillator in Figure A- 6 with a different starting point (x,y)=(-2,2).

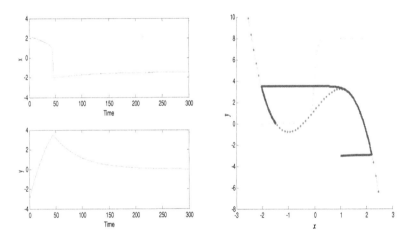

Figure A- 8 A third example of the same unstimulated neural oscillator in Figure A- 6 with a different starting point (x,y)=(1,-3).

2   Dynamics of coupled neurons

This section focuses on the occurrence of synchronisation and sesynchronisation of the temporal activities of coupled neural oscillators. An illustration of two coupled neurons is shown in Figure

A- 9 (repeated from Chapter 7) and the underlying model of these oscillators is based on Equations 7-2 to 7-4 as described in Chapter 7. The effect of the coupling strength on the synchronisation or desynchronisation of two coupled neural oscillators is described.

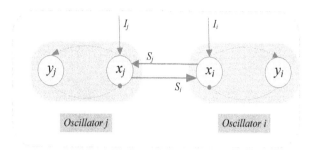

Figure A- 9 Example of two coupled neural oscillators. Besides the external input received and fed to each neural oscillator, both oscillators send/receive an output/input to/from each other.

2.1 Synchronisation of coupled neurons

The interaction threshold denoted by θ_x is set between the left and the right branch of the x-nullcline (the cubic) and the use of a Heaviside function makes the interaction between coupled oscillators binary, i.e. its activation (on or off) depends on the oscillator being on the active (which implies the its x-value is above the threshold) or on the silent phase (which implies the its x-value is below the threshold). When an oscillator crosses the interaction threshold, it jumps up from the silent to the active phase and, as a result, excites the other oscillator (interaction is activated). When a neuron is excited its x-nullcline is elevated by an amount equal to the coupling strength W (becomes the excited x-nullcline) and its behaviour is then based on the modified cubic (see Figure A- 10). The behaviour of the two coupled oscillators is based on their nullclines and their coupling strength.

However, before describing this behaviour, it is useful to define some pertinent points on the excited and unexcited nullclines as they will be used as references. These points (ULK, LLK, URK and LRK) are the four local extrema of the two cubics as shown in   Figure A- 10 (U for upper, L for left, R for right and K for knee). Also, four branches are distinguished on the two cubics, namely the upper left and right branches (ULB and URB) related to the upper cubic, and the lower left and right branches (LLB and LRB) related to the lower cubic. It can be seen from Figure A- 10 that the points ULK and LLK are on the same vertical line and the distance between them is equal to the coupling strength W, i.e. ULK=(LLK$_x$, LLKy+W). Similarly for the points URK and LRK, they share the same x-coordinate and their y-coordinates are linked, i.e. URK=(LRK$_x$, LRKy+W). These two relationships explain why the two x-nullclines have not been attributed to a specific oscillator, as the changes caused by continuous interaction dynamically modify each oscillator nullcline such as each time an oscillator gets excited, its nullcline is elevated (i.e. becomes the upper cubic) and when the oscillator does not receive interaction its nullcline becomes the lower cubic again.

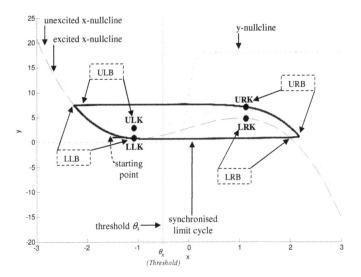

Figure A- 10 Nullclines of two coupled oscillators and the convergence of their temporal activity to a synchronised limit cycle which is represented by a thick solid line. The x-nullclines (cubic curves) of the system in **Error! Reference source not found.** and **Error! Reference source not found.** (Chapter 7) are represented by a dashed lines and the y-nullcline (sigmoid curve) is represented by a dotted line. The excitation threshold (θ_x) is set between the left and the right branches of the limit cycle (vertical line with a circle end on the x axis). ULB (upper left branch), URB (upper right branch), LLB (lower left branch), LRB (lower right branch), ULK (upper left knee), LLK (lower left knee), URK (upper right knee), LRK (lower right knee). The parameters used for this simulation are: $W_{ij}=W_{ji}=3.0$, $\theta_x=-0.5$, $\lambda=9$, $\beta=0.1$; $\varepsilon=0.04$; $\rho=0.02$; I=+0.8.

Now the interaction of the two coupled oscillators the evolution of their trajectories are explained through an example where a synchronised activity has emerged. The temporal activity of both oscillators is shown in Figure A- 11 which clearly shows their convergence to a synchronised activity.

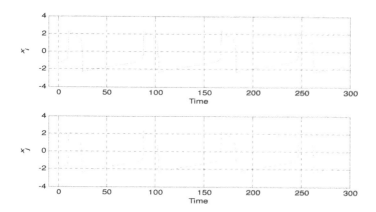

Figure A- 11 Synchronisation in a pair of oscillators. When the coupling between two neural oscillators is strong enough, a synchronisation between their temporal activity is obtained. Same parameters of Figure A-10 are used with a starting point for oscillator i at $(x_i, y_i)=(-2.3, 1)$ and $(x_j, y_j)=(-2.3, 3)$ for oscillator j.

Initially, both neural oscillators start at two different times before reaching the lower left branch (LLB) as shown in Figure A- 11 panel A. Oscillator i is depicted with a thick solid line while oscillator j corresponds to the thin solid line. The oscillator i is leading oscillator j and it is the first one to jump up its active phase (i.e. the lower right branch LRB) as shown in Figure A- 11 panel B. The oscillator j gets excited as soon as oscillator i crosses the excitation threshold (-0.5 here). By the time oscillator j jumps up, it excites this time the oscillator i which makes a hop to the upper right branch (although it might appear in Figure A- 12 panel B that oscillator i jumped directly to the URB, it has in fact reached the LRB first before it hopped to the URB. This hopping process does not clearly appear in this example because the jumping to the active phase occurs so quickly and there is not much of a gap between the jumping times of the two oscillators. The hopping from the lower to the upper nullcline and vice versa will be clearly shown in the next example overleaf where the starting point of the non leading oscillator is set above the left local extremum of the upper cubic, i.e. the ULK). This hopping results in a reduction in the time difference between the coupled oscillators. This reduction referred to as time compression (Somers and Kopell, 1993). Once both oscillators are on the active phase (i.e. both are on the URB), they both move along the URB before jumping almost together to the lower left branch (LLB) as shown in Figure A- 12 panel C . They jump to the LLB instead of the ULB because by jumping from the URB they will both cross the threshold again (from above) and therefore both become unexcited which impies their x-nullclines get shifted downwards to the lower cubic. Then the two oscillators will both move along the LLB before jumping for the second time to the URB which terminates one cycle of the periodic solution (limit cycle).

201

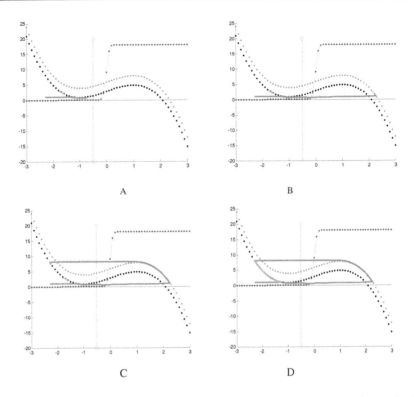

Figure A- 12 Snapshots of the evolution of the trajectories of two coupled oscillator towards a synchronised limit cycle (order is A, B, C then D). Initially (Panel A) starting from two different points (-2.3, 1) and (-2.3, 3), both oscillators are on the left branch and their x values are below the threshold θ_x=-0.5, i.e. both of them are not excited and are located on the unexcited x-nullcline (lower x-nullcline). Then (Panel B) the oscillator with a thick line crosses the threshold first and jumps up to the right branch (therefore the other oscillator gets excited). In (Panel C), both oscillators have jumped to the left branch and they are again found in and unexcited state (as their values are below the threshold θ_x). Finally, (Panel D) shows the convergence to a synchronous limit cycle. apart from the starting points, the same parameters of Figure A- 10 are used.

The next simulation example of coupled oscillators' convergence to a limit cycle clearly shows the hopping between the two nullclines (see Figure A- 13). Oscillator j (depicted by a thin solid line) is initially found on LLB, and it makes its first hop to the ULB when oscillator i (depicted with a thick solid line) jumps up to the RLB (note this time how it is clearly shown that oscillator jumped to the RLB and not directly to the RUB, because oscillator j was still on the LLB below the threshold when oscillator i jumped up, i.e. after the jump oscillator i stays unexcited as no excitation received from oscillator j). When oscillator i jumps down to the LLB, oscillator j makes it second hop back to the LLB, because oscillator i has just jumped to the silent phase (below the threshold) and does not send excitation to oscillator j anymore. The temporal activity of the two oscillators is shown in Figure A-14 and the two hops are highlighted.

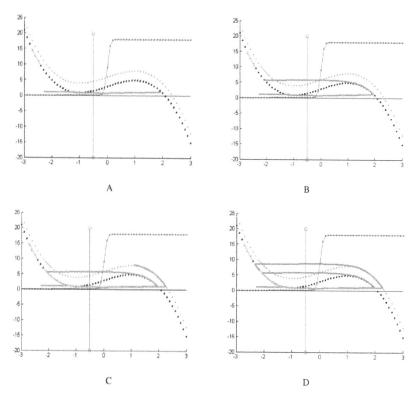

A

B

C

D

Figure A- 13 Another example of coupled oscillators where the starting point of the non-leading oscillator is placed above the upper left knee (ULK). The order of snapshots is A, B, C then D. Initially (Panel A) both oscillators are unexcited, they start from two different points such as oscillator i (thick line) is below the ULK and oscillator j (thin line) is above it. The leading oscillator jumps up first to the LRB and oscillator j hops to the upper nullcline. (Panel B) The leading oscillator has finished moving along the RLB and jumped down to the LLB because it is unxcited as oscillator j is still on the unexcited ULB. Oscillator j then hops again back to the LLB as it is not excited by oscillator I anymore. (Panel C) both oscillators move along the LLB before they jump up to the URB and finally (Panel D) stay moving along the limit cycle.

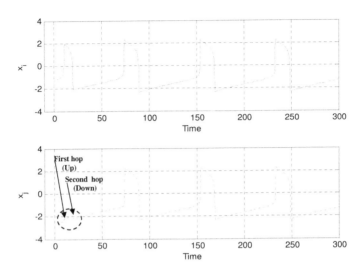

Figure A-14 Synchronisation of the temporal activity of coupled oscillators in Figure A- 13. The two hops are reflected on the temporal activity of oscillator j in the form of small fluctuations before it gets synchronised with oscillator i.

2.2 Desynchronisation of coupled neurons

The examples shown in the previous section represents cases where the two coupled oscillators exhibit a synchronisation in their temporal activity and their trajectories converge to a periodic stable limit cycle. Such synchronisation was obtained when the coupling used was strong enough. In this section, a desynchronisation case is shown where a weaker coupling is applied and the dynamics of the two coupled oscillators are observed both in the temporal domain and the phase plain. It has already been shown in the single oscillator case that if the input is negative ($I<0$, unstimulated neuron) no oscillation is obtained and the neuron trajectory converges to a fixed point (no limit cycle). This situation also applies to coupled neurons, i.e. if both neurons are unstimulated no synchronisation is applied and both neurons converge to the same fixed point even in the presence of a strong coupling. The temporal dynamics of two unstimulated neurons and the convergence of their trajectories to a fixed point are illsutrated in Figure A- 15.

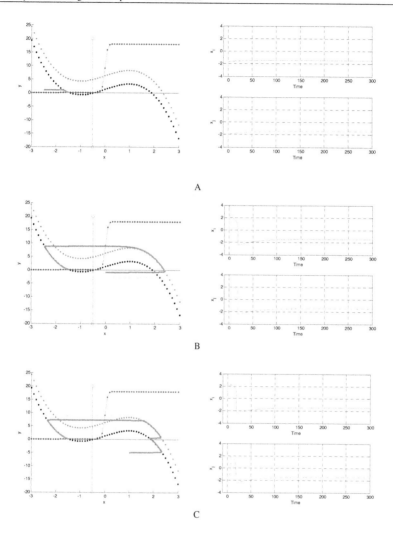

Figure A- 15 Temporal activities and convergence of unstimulated neurons to a fixed point. Neuron *i* is represented by the thick solid line and neuron *j* is represented by a thin solid line. A strong coupling value is used (W=5) but with different starting points for each panel as follows. (Panel A): [(i=(-2.5, 1) and j=(-2.5, 3)]. (Panel B) [i=(0,-1) and j=(0,-3)]. (Panel C) [i=(1,-5) and j=(-1,5)]. Temporal activity and phase plane representation are shown on the right and left of each panel, respectively.

Desynchronisation is not only caused by neural oscillators being unstimulated. The application of a weak coupling between two neurons also produce a desynchronisation of their temporal activity despite their trajectories converging to stable cycle (two different cycles in this case). The temporal activity of two coupled oscillators with a coupling strength of W=0.5 is shown in Figure A- 16 and their trajectories reprented in the phase plane is shown in Figure A- 17. In this figure, Panel A shows that the two oscillators have started from two different points and that while the leading oscillator (depicted by a thick solid line) has already traversed through the LRB the other oscillator is still on the URB (after making a hop from the LRB when the leading oscillator jumped up). Panel B shows the non-leading oscillator jumped up to the LRB and is traversing it, while the leading oscillator is on the URB (after hopping from the LRB when the non-leading oscillator jumped up). In order to show, in the phase plane, that both oscillators converge to a periodic cycle and that the two cycles are different, Panels C and D shows the limit cycle of the leading and non-leading oscillators, respectively.

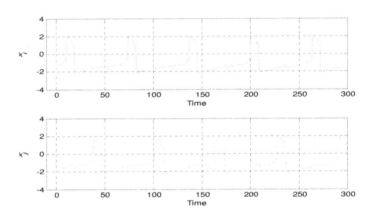

Figure A- 16 Desynchronisation in a pair of oscillators. A weak coupling ($W_{ij}=W_{ji}=0.5$) between two neural oscillators is applied. Other parameters of the two neurons remain similar to those used in Figure A- 11.

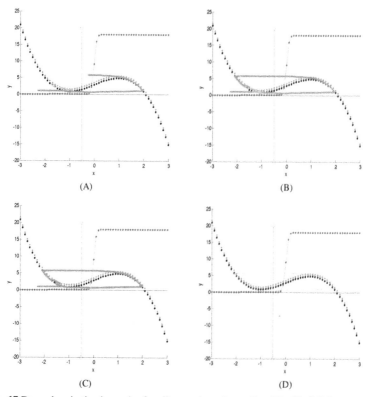

Figure A- 17 Desynchronisation in a pair of oscillators. A weak coupling ($W_{ij}=W_{ji}=0.5$) between two neural oscillators is applied. Other parameters of the two neurons remain similar to those used in Figure A- 11.

REFERENCES

Abbott, L. F., Varela, J. A., Sen, K. & Nelson, S. B. Synaptic depression and cortical gain control. Science, 275, 220-224, 1997.

Abbott, L., & Nelson, S., Synaptic plasticity: Taming the beast. Nat. Neurosci., 3, 1178–1183, 2000.

Abeles M., Bergman, H., Margalit, E., & Vaadia, E., Spatiotemporal firing patterns in the frontal cortex of behaving monkeys. J Neurophysiol, 70(4), 16291638, 1993.

Abeles M., Corticonics: neural circuits of the cerebral cortex, Cambridge, university press, 1991

Abeles, M., & Gat, I.. Detecting precise firing sequences in experimental data. Journal of Neuroscience Methods, 107(1–2), 141–154, 2001.

Adrian E. and Zotterman Y., The impulses produced by sensory nerve endings: Part II:The response of a single end organ. Journal of Physiology (London), 61:151–171, 1926.

Adrian E. and Zotterman Y., The impulses produced by sensory nerve endings: Part III: Impulses set up by touch and pressure. Journal of Physiology (London), 61:465–83, 1926.

Adrian E. D., The Basis of Sensation: The Action of the Sense Organs. Christophers, London, 1928.

Adrian E., The impulses produced by sensory nerve endings: Part I. Journal of Physiology (London), 61:49–72, 1926.

Ahmed M. S., Neural-net-based Direct Adaptive Control for a Class of Nonlinear Plants, IEEE Trans. Automat. Contr., Vol.45, Na. 1, pp. 119-124, Jan. 2000.

Akay, Y.M.; Akay, M.; Welkowitz, W.; Kostis, J., Noninvasive detection of coronary artery disease; IEEE Engineering in Medicine and Biology Magazine, Vol. 13, Issue 5, pp.761–764, Nov-Dec. 1994.

Anderson J. R., Induction of augmented transition networks. Cognitive Science, 1, 125--157. 1977.

Andreon, S., Gargiulo, G., Longo, G., Tagliaferri, R., & Capuano, N., Wide field imaging. I. Applications of neural networks to object detection and star/galaxy classification. Monthly Notices Royal Astronomical Society, 319, 700-716, 2000.

Angeline P. J., Evolving basis functions with dynamic receptive fields, in Proc. IEEE Int. Conf. Systems, Man, and Cybernetics, Part 5, pp. 4109–4114. 1997.

Arabshahi P., Choi J. J., Marks R. J., and Caudell T. P., Fuzzy control of backpropagation, IEEE Int. Conf. on Fuzzy Systems, pp.967–972, San Diego, CA, USA, 1992.

Arbib M. A., The handbook of brain theory and neural networks, MIT Press, Cambridge, 1995.

Arbib, M.. Levels of modeling of mechanisms of visually guided behaviour. Behavioural and Brain Sciences, 10, 407–465, 1987.

Aronson, D., Ermentrout, G., and Kopell, N., Amplitude response of coupled oscillators. Physica D, 41:403–449, 1990.

Artsen A., brain theory : spatiotemporal aspects of brain function, Elsevier, 1993.

Atiya, A.; Talaat, N.; Shaheen, S., An efficient stock market forecasting model using neural networks, International Conference on Neural Networks, vol. 4, pp.2112 – 2115, 9-12 June 1997.

Baccigalupi, C., Bedini, L., Burigana, C., De Zotti, G., Farusi, A., Maino, D., Maris, M., Perrotta, F., Salerno, E., Toffolatti, L., & Tonazzini, A.. Neural networks and the separation of cosmic microwave background and astrophysical signals in sky maps. Monthly Notices Royal Astronomical Society, 318, 769-780, 2000.

Bäck T., Fogel D. B., Michalewicz Z., andbook on Evolutionary Computation. IOP Publishing Ltd and Oxford University Press, 1997.

Bäck T., Hoffmeister F., and Schwefel H. A survey of evolution strategies. In R. K. Belew and L. B. booker, editors, Proceedings of the 4th International Conference on Genetic Algorithms, pages 2-9, San Diego, CA, Morgan Kaufmann. 1991.

Bäck T., Schwefel H. An Overview of Evolutionary Algorithms for Parameter Optimization, Evolutionary computation, Vol 1, Issue 1, 1993.

Bäck T., Schwefel H. Evolutionary computation: an overview, proc. Int. Conf. on Evolutionary Computation, pp.20-29, 1996.

Bäck, T.; Hammel, U.; Schwefel, H.-P.: Evolutionary computation: comments on the history and current state. IEEE Transactions on Evolutionary Computation, Vol 1 Issue 1, pp 3–17, 1997.

Bailer-Jones C. A. L., Gupta R., & Singh H. P., Automated data analysis in astronomy, In Gupta (Ed.), Astro-ph/0102224, 2001.

Baker J. E. Reducing bias and inefficiency in the selection algorithm. In J. J. Grefenstette, editor, Proceedings of the 2nd International Conference on Genetic Algorithms, pages 14-21, Hillsdale, New Jersey,. Lawrence Erlbaum, 1987.

Baker J., "Adaptive Selection Methods for Genetic Algorithms," presented at The First International Conference on Genetic Algorithms and Their Applications, J. J. Grefenstette Eds., Lawrence Erlbaum Associates (Hillsdale), pp. 101-111, 1985.

Barlow H., Single units and cognition: A neurone doctrine for perceptual psychology. Perception, 1:371–394, 1972.

Barnard, E., Cole, R.A., Vea, M.P. & Alleva, F.A. Pitch detection with a neural-net classifier. IEEE Trans. on Signal Processing, 39(2), pp.298-307, 1991.

Baxter J. The evolution of learning algorithms for artificial neural networks. Complex Systems, pages 313-326, 1992.

Baxter J., The evolution of learning algorithms for artificial neural networks, in Complex Systems, D. Green and T. Bossomaier, Eds. Amsterdam, The Netherlands: IOS, pp. 313–326, 1992.

Beale R, Finlay J. Neural Networks and Pattern Recognition in Human-Computer Interaction. Ellis Horwood, 1992.

Bebis, G.; Georgiopoulos, M.; Lobo, N.V., Using self-organizing maps to learn geometric hash functions for model-based object recognition; IEEE Transactions on Neural Networks, Volume 9, Issue 3, pp.560 – 570, May 1998.

Belatreche A, Maguire L.P. McGinnity T.M, Advances in Design and application of Spiking Neural Networks, Springer, Special Issue of Soft-Computing, published online March 2006, (print to appear) Vol.11, pp. 239-248, 2007.

Belatreche A, Maguire L.P. McGinnity T.M, Neuronal Synchronisation-Based Colour Image Segmentation, 2nd International Workshop on Bio-Inspired Systems and Brain-Like Computer, in conjunction with 8th Joint Conference on Information Sciences (JCIS'05), Salt Lake City, Utah, USA, July 21 - 26, 2005.

Belatreche A, Maguire L.P. McGinnity T.M, Temporal patterns classification using spiking neural networks: a biologically motivated approach, Proceedings of PREP'2004, Hertfordshire, , United Kingdom, 5th - 7th April 2004.

Belatreche A, Maguire L.P. McGinnity T.M, Wu Q.X, A method for supervised training of spiking neural networks, Proceedings of IEEE Cybernetics Intelligence - Challenges and Advances (CICA'03), Reading, United Kingdom, pp 39-44, Sep 2003.

Belatreche A, Maguire L.P. McGinnity T.M, Wu Q.X, Evolutionary design of spiking neural networks. Journal of new mathematics and natural computing, 2006.

Belatreche A, Maguire L.P. McGinnity T.M, Wu Q.X, An Evolutionary Strategy for Supervised Training of Biologically Plausible Neural Networks, Proceedings of The 7th Joint Conference on Information Sciences, North Carolina, USA, pp.1524-1527, September 26-30,2003.

Belatreche A., Maguire L.P., McGinnity M., Pattern Recognition with Spiking Neural Networks and Dynamic Synapses, in Applied Computational Intelligence, Proceedings of the 6th international FLINS conference, Belgium, pp 205-210, World Scientific, 2004.

Bengio S., Bengio Y., Cloutier J., and Gecsei J., On the optimization of a synaptic learning rule, in Preprints Conf. Optimality in Artificial and Biological Neural Networks, Univ. of Texas, Dallas, 1992.

Bengio Y. and Bengio S., Learning a synaptic learning rule, Dep. Informatique et de Recherche Opérationelle, Univ. Montréal, Canada, Tech. Rep. 751, Nov. 1990.

Berlich R. and Kunze M., Comparison between the performance of feed forward neural networks and the supervised growing neural gas algorithm, Nuclear Instrum. Methods in Phys. Res., Section A: Accelerators, Spectrometers, Detectors and Associated Equipment, vol. 389, nos. 1–2, pp. 274–277, 1997.

Beyer H.G., Toward a theory of evolution strategies: Self-adaptation, Evolutionary Computation 3 (3), 311 –34, 1996.

Bi, G. and Poo, M.. Synaptic modification of correlated activity: Hebb's postulate revisited.Ann. Rev. Neurosci., 24:139-166, 2001.

Bi, G. and Poo, M.. Synaptic modifications in cultured hippocampal neurons: dependence on spike timing, synaptic strength, and postsynaptic cell type. J. Neuroscience., 18:10464-10472, 1998.

Bialek W, Rieke F, reliability and information transmission in spiking neurons, trends in neuroscience, vol. 15, pp428-434, 1992.

Bibitchkov D., Herrmann J. M., & Geisel T.. Pattern storage and processing in attractor networks with short-time synaptic dynamics. Network, Comput. Neural Syst., 13(1), 115–129, 2002.

Blickle T. and Thiele L. A comparison of selection schemes used in genetic algorithms. Technical Report 11, Computer Engineering and Communications Networks Lab (TIK), Swiss Federal Institute of Technology (ETH), Gloriastrasse 35, 8092 Zurich, 1995.

Bliss, T.V.P. and Gardner-Medwin, A.R., Long- Lasting potentiation of synaptic transmission in the dendate area of unanaesthetized rabbit following stimulation of the perforant path. J. Physiol. (Lond), 232:331-356, 1973.

Bofill-i-Petit, A.; Murray, A.F., Synchrony detection and amplification by silicon neurons with STDP synapses, Neural Networks, IEEE Transactions on Volume 15, Issue 5, pp:1296-1304, Sept. 2004.

Bohte, S. M., Kok, J. N., and Poutre, J. A. L., Error-backpropagation in temporally encoded networks of spiking neurons. Neurocomputing, 48(1-4):17—37, 2002.

Borda, F., Roberto, A., Mininni, P. D., Mandrini, C. H., Gómez, D. O., Bauer, O. H., & Rovira, M. G., Automatic Solar flare detection using neural network techniques. Solar Physics, 206, 347-357. 2002.

Bornholdt S. and Graudenz D., General asymmetric neural networks and structure design by genetic algorithms," Neural Networks, vol. 5, no. 2, pp. 327–334, 1992.

Bower, J., & Beeman, D.. The book of GENESIS: Exploring realistic neural models with the General NEural SImulation System. Springer-Verlag. 1998.

Brescia, M., D'Argenio, B., Ferreri, V., Longo, G., Pelosi, N., Rampone, S., & Tagliaferri, R.. Neural net aided detection of astronomical periodicities in geologic records. Earth and Planetary Science Letters, 139, 33-45, 1996.

Bressloff P.C., Dynamic synapses, a new concept of neural representation and computation, Phys. Rev. E, 60(2), 2160–2170, 1999.

Broomhead D.S., Lowe D., "Multivariate functional interpolation and adaptive networks". Complex Systems, 2:321-355, 1988.

Brunel N., Chance F., Fourcaud N., and Abbott L. F, Effects of synaptic noise and filtering on the frequency response of spiking neurons. Phys. Rev. Lett., 86:2186-2189, 2001.

Buckley J. J., Reilly K. D., and Penmetcha K. V., Backpropagation and genetic algorithms for training fuzzy neural nets. In: Herrera F., Verdegay J. L.: Genetic Algorithms and Soft Computing. Physica-Verlag, Heidelberg, 505-531. 1996.

Buckley J.J., Ayashif Y. H., Fuzzy Neural Networks: A survey. Fuzzy Sets and Systems, volume 66, issue 1, pp. 1-13, 1994.

Burkitt A.N., Meffin, H., Grayden, D.B, Spike-timing-dependent plasticity: the relationship to rate-based learning for models with weight dynamics determined by a stable fixed point, Neural Computation, v 16, n 5, p 885-940, 2004.

C. Panchev, S. Wermter, and H. Chen. Spike-timing dependent competitive learning of integrate-and-fire neurons with active dendrites. In Lecture Notes in Computer Science. Proc. of the Int. Conf. on Artificial Neural Networks, pp.896–901, Madrid, Spain, Springer, 2002.

Cairns, D., Baddeley, R., and Smith, L., Constraints on synchronizing oscillator networks. Neural Comp., 5:260–266, 1993.

Calvert, G., Spence, C., & Stein, B. E.. The handbook of multisensory processes. Cambridge, MA: MIT Press, 2004

Cariani, P.. Temporal coding of sensory information. In J. M. Bower (Ed.), Computational neuroscience: Trends in research, pp. 591–598, New York: Plenum. 1997.

Carlson N. Foundations of Physiological Psychology. Needham Heights, Massachusetts: Simon & Schuster, 1992.

Caruna R. A., Eshelman L. J. & Schaffer J. D. Representation and hidden bias II: Eliminating defining length bias in genetic search via shuffle crossover. In N. S. Sridharan (Ed.), 11th international joint conference on artificial intelligence, pp. 750–755. Morgan Kaufmann, 1989.

Chaker F., Braham R., Ghorbel F., A new method for invariant hand-written digit recognition using neural networks, Seventh International Conference on Image Processing And Its Applications, Volume: 1 , pp. 460 -464 vol.1, 1999.

Chalmers D. J. The evolution of learning: An experiment in genetic connectionism. In D. S. Touretzky, J. L. Elman, and G. E. Hinten, editors, Proceedings of the Connectionist Models Summer School, pages 81-90, San Mateo, CA,. Morgan Kaufmann, 1990.

Chalmers D. J., "The evolution of learning: An experiment in genetic connectionism," in Proc. Connectionist Models Summer School, D. S. Touretzky, J. L. Elman, and G. E. Hinton, Eds. San Mateo, CA: Morgan Kaufmann, , pp. 81–90. 1990.

Charalambous, C.; Charitou, A.; Kaourou, F., Comparative analysis of artificial neural network models: application in bankruptcy prediction; International Joint Conference on Neural Networks IJCNN '99, Vol. 6, pp. 3888 – 3893, , 10-16 July 1999

Charles M. Gray: The Temporal Correlation Hypothesis of Visual Feature Integration: Still Alive and Well; Neuron 24: 31, 1999.

Chen, C.H., Neural networks for financial market prediction, IEEE World Congress on Computational Intelligence., IEEE International Conference on Neural Networks, vol.2, pp.1199-1202, 1994..

Cho J. M., Chromosome classification using backpropagation neural networks; IEEE Engineering in Medicine and Biology Magazine, Volume 19, Issue 1, pp.28 – 33, Jan.-Feb. 2000.

Chowdhury F. N., "Ordinary and Neural Chi-Squared Tests for Fault Detection in Multi-Output Stochastic Systems", IEEE Pans. Contr. Syst. Tech., Vol. 8, No. 2, pp. 372-378, Mar. 2000.

Chowdhury F.N., Wahi P., Raina R., Kaminedi S., A survey of neural networks applications in automatic control, Proc. of the 33rd Southeastern Symposium on System Theory, 18-20 March, pp.349 – 353, 2001.

Darwin C. R., On the Origin of Species. John Murray, London, 1859.

Dayan P. and Abbott L. F., Theoretical Neuroscience. MIT Press, Cambridge, MA, 2001.

de Garis H., GenNets: Genetically programmed neural nets—Using the genetic algorithm to train neural nets whose inputs and/or outputs vary in time, in Proc. IEEE Int. Joint Conf. Neural Networks (IJCNN), Singapore, vol. 2, pp. 1391–1396, 1991.

De Jong, K. & Spears, W. Learning concept classification rules using genetic algorithms. Proceedings of the 12th International Joint Conference on Artificial Intelligence, pp 651-656. Sydney, Australia, Morgan Kaufmann, 1991.

De Jong, K. A. An analysis of the behavior of a class of genetic adaptive systems. Doctoral Thesis, Department of Computer and Communication Sciences. University of Michigan, Ann Arbor, 1975.

De Jong, K. A. Are genetic algorithms function optimizers? Proceedings of the 2nd International Conference on Parallel Problem Solving from Nature, 1992.

Deb K. and Goldberg D. E. An investigation of niche and species formation in genetic function optimisation. In J. D. Schaffer, editor, Proceedings of the 3rd International Conference on Genetic Algorithms, pp 42-50, Morgan Kaufman, 1989.

Desimone, R., Albright, T. D., Gross, C. G., and Bruce, C., Stimulus-selective properties of inferior temporal neurons in the macaque. J. Neurosci., 4:2051–2062, 1984.

Destexhe A., Mainen Z., and Sejnowski T., Kinetic models of synaptic transmission. In C. Koch & I. Segev (Eds.), Methods in neuronal modeling . Cambridge, Massachusetts: MIT Press, 1998.

Dibazar A.A., Namarvar H.H., Berger T.W., A new approach for isolated word recognition using dynamic synapse neural networks, Proceedings of the International Joint Conference on Neural Networks, Vol 4, pp 3146–3150, , 2003.

Duda R.O., Hart P.E., Stork D.G., "Pattern Classification." Wiley-Interscience, 2nd ed., 2001.

Dugast, C.; Devillers, L.; Aubert, X., Combining TDNN and HMM in a hybrid system for improved continuous-speech recognition; IEEE Transactions on Speech and Audio Processing, Vol. 2, Issue 1, Part 2, pp. 217 – 223, Jan. 1994.

Eckhorn R., Bauer R., Jordan W., Brosch M., Kruse W., Munk M., and Reitboech H.J., Coherent oscillations: A mechanism of feature linking in the visual cortex. Biol. Cybern., 60: 121-130, 1988.

Eiben A.E. and Smith J.E., Introduction to Evolutionary Computing. Springer Verlag, Berlin, Heidelberg, New York, 2003.

Engel, A. K., König, P., Kreiter, A. K., and Singer, W., Interhemispheric synchronization of oscillatory neuronal responses in cat visual cortex. Science, 252:1177–1179, 1991.

Er M. J., Wu S., Lu J., Toh H.L, Face recognition with radial basis function (RBF) neural networks, IEEE Transactions on Neural Networks, Volume 13, Issue 3, pp.697 – 710, May 2002.

Eshelman L. J. Genetic Algorithms, in Evolutionary Computation 1. Basic Algorithms and Operators, T. Back, B. D. Fogel, and T. Michalewicz, Eds. New York: Institute of Physics Publishing, pp. 64-80, 2000.

Eshelmann L. J., Caruana R. A., and Schaffer J. D., Biases in crossover landscape. In J. D. Schaffer, editor, Proceedings of the 3rd International Conference on Genetic Algorithms, pp 10-19, 1989.

Fels, S.S.; Hinton, G.E., Glove-Talk: a neural network interface between a data-glove and a speech synthesizer;, IEEE Trans. on Neural Networks Vol. 4, Issue 1, pp.2 - 8,Jan. 1993.

Feng J., and, Zhang P. The behaviour of integrate-and-fire and Hodgkin-Huxley models with correlated input Phys. Rev. E. vol. 63, 051902: 1-11, 2001.

Feng J., Brown D., Wei G., and Tirozzi B. Detectable and undetectable input signals for the integrate-and-fire model? J. Phys. A. vol. 34, 1637-1648, 2001.

Fisher R.A., The use of multiple measurements in taxonomic problems, Annals of Eugenics Vol. 7, No. 2, pp. 179-188, 1936

FitzHugh, R.. Impulses and physiological states in models of nerve membrane. Biophys. J., 1:445-466, 1961.

Fogel D. B., Fogel L. J. and Porto V. W. Evolving neural networks, Biological Cybern., vol. 63, no. 6, pp. 487–493, 1990.

Fogel D. B., Wasson E. C., and Boughton E. M., "Evolving neural networks for detecting breast cancer," Cancer Lett., vol.96, no. 1, pp. 49–53, 1995.

Fogel D. B., Wasson E. C., and Porto V. W., A step toward computer-assisted mammography using evolutionary programming and neural networks, Cancer Lett., vol. 119, no. 1, p.93, 1997.

Fogel D.B, an analysis of evolutionary programming, In Fogel D. B and Atmar W., editors, proceedings on 1st annual conference on evolutionary programming, pages 43-51, La Jolla, CA, Evolutionary programming Society, 1992.

Fogel, editor. Evolutionary Computation: The Fossil Record. IEEE Press, 1998.

Fogel, L. J., Owens, A. J., and Walsh, M. J. Artificial Intelligence through Simulated Evolution. John Wiley & Sons, 1966.

Fontanari J. F. and Meir R., Evolving a learning algorithm for the binary perceptron, Network, vol. 2, no. 4, pp. 353–359, Nov. 1991.

Ford A. and Roberts A., Colour space conversions, Westminster University, London, 1998.

Foresti, G.L.; Pellegrino, F.A., Automatic visual recognition of deformable objects for grasping and manipulation; IEEE Transactions. on Systems, Man and Cybernetics, Part C, Volume 34, Issue 3, pp.325–333, Aug. 2004.

Foster, D.; McCullagh, J.; Whitfort, T., Evolution versus training: an investigation into combining genetic algorithms and neural networks, , 1999. Proceedings of the 6th International Conference on Neural Information Processingm, ICONIP'99. Volume 3, 16-20 Page(s):848-854 vol.3, Nov. 1999.

Freisleben B, Kunkelmann T., Combining Fuzzy Logic and Neural Networks to Control an Autonomous Vehicle, Proceedings of IEEE International Conf on Fuzzy Systems, 1993.

Froemke R.C., and Dan Y., Spike-timing-dependent synaptic modification induced by natural spike trains. Nature 416,433–438, 2002.

Fu L.M., Knowledge discovery by inductive neural networks; IEEE Trans. on Knowledge and Data Engineering, Vol. 11, Issue 6, pp.992 – 998, Nov.-Dec. 1999.

Fuentes, O., Automatic determination of stellar atmospheric parameters using neural networks and instance-based machine learning. Experimental Astronomy, 12, 21-31. 2001.

Fuhrmann G., Segev I., Markram H. & Tsodyks M., Coding of temporal information by activity dependent synapses, Journal of Neurophysiology, 87, 140-148, 2002.

Fukuda T. and Ishigami H., Structure optimization of fuzzy neural network by genetic algorithm. In Proc. Fifth International Fuzzy Systems Association World Congress (IFSA'93), Seoul , pp. 964--967, 1993.

Gawne, T., Kjaer, T., & Richmond, B.. Latency: another potential code for feature binding in striate cortex. Journal of Neurophysiology, 76(2), 1356–1360, 1996.

George F. L., William A. S. , "Artificial Intelligence: Structures and Strategies for Complex Problem Solving", Addison Wesley Longman Inc., - 824 p, 1998.

George S., Dibazar A., Desai V., Berger T.W., Using dynamic synapse based neural networks with wavelet preprocessing for speech applications,. Proceedings of the International Joint Conference on Neural Networks, pp 666 – 669, vol.1, 2003.

Gerstner W., Kistler W. Spiking Neuron Models: Single Neurons, Populations, Plasticity, Cambridge University Press, 2002.

Gerstner, W., Kempter, R., van Hemmen, J.L., and Wagner, H., A neuronal learning rule for sub-millisecond temporal coding. Nature, 383, 76–81, 1996.

Gerstner, W., Population dynamics of spiking neurons: fast transients, asynchronous states and locking. Neural Comput., 12:43-89, 2000.

Gerstner, W.. Spiking neurons. In W. Maas & C.M.Bishop (Eds.), Pulsed neural networks, MIT Press, pp.3–53, 1999.

Gerstner, W.. Time structure of the activity in neural network models. Phys. Rev. E, 51(1):738—758, 1995.

Godfrey, K.R.L.; Attikiouzel, Y. Applying neural networks to colour image data compression, TENCON. "Technology Enabling Tomorrow: Computers, Communications and Automation towards the 21st Century.' IEEE Region 10 Int. Conf., pp.545 -549 vol.1, 1992.

Goldberg D. E.. Genetic Algorithms in Search, Optimization and Machine Learning. Addison Wesley Longman Inc., 1989.

Goldberg D. E. and Richardson J. Genetic algorithms with sharing for multimodal function optimisation, In J. J Grefenstette, editor, Proceedings of the 2nd International Conference on Genetic Algorithms, pp 41-49, Lawrance Erlbaum Associates, 1987.

Goldberg D.E., Real-coded genetic algorithms, virtual alphabets, and blocking, Complex Systems 5 (2), 139 –167, 1991.

Goldberg, D. E, Sizing populations for serial and parallel genetic algorithms. Proceedings of the 3rd International Conference on Genetic Algorithms, pp 70-79. Fairfax, Morgan Kaufmann, 1989.

Goldberg, D. E. Genetic Algorithms in Search, Optimization & Machine Learning. Reading, MA: Addison-Wesley, 1989.

Goldberg, D. E., Deb, K., & Korb, B. Don't worry, be messy. Proceedings of the Fourth International Conference on Genetic Algorithms, pp 24-30. La Jolla, CA, Morgan Kaufmann, 1991.

Gonzalez R. C., Richard E. W., Digital Image Processing, Digital Image Processing, 2001.

Gonzalez-Seco, J., A genetic algorithm as the learning procedure for neural networks, International Joint Conference on Neural Networks, IJCNN, Volume 1, Page(s):835 - 840 vol.1, June 1992.

Grasman J., Asymptotic Methods for Relaxation Oscillations and Applications. New York: Springer-Verlag, 1987.

Grasman, J. and Jansen, M. J. W., Mutually synchronized relaxation oscillators as prototypes of oscillating systems in biology. J. Math. Biol., 7:171–197, 1979.

Grasman, J. and Jansen, M. J. W.. Mutually synchronized relaxation oscillators as prototypes of oscillating systems in biology. J. Math. Biol., 7:171–197, 1979.

Gray C.M., König P., Engel A.K., Singer W., Oscillatory responses in cat visual cortex exhibit intercolumnar synchronization which reflects global stimulus properties. Nature, 338: 334-337, 1989.

Greenwood G. W. Training partially recurrent neural networks using evolutionary strategies, IEEE Trans. Speech Audio Processing, vol.5, pp. 192–194, Feb. 1997.

Grossberg S., Adaptive Pattern Classification and Universal Recoding, I: Parallel Development and Coding of Neural Feature Detectors. Biological Cybernetics, 23(2): 121-134, 1976.

Grossberg S., Neural Networks and Natural Intelligence. Cambridge, MA: MIT Press, 1988.

Grossberg S., Studies of Mind and Brain: Neural Principles of Learning, Perception, Development, Cognition, and Motor Control. Boston: Reidel, 1982.

Grossberg, S. and Somers, D., Synchronized oscillations during cooperative feature linking in a cortical model of visual perception. Neural Networks, 4:453–466, 1991.

Gulati, R. K., & Altamirano, L.. Artificial neural networks in stellar astronomy. In Aguilar (Ed.), Focal points in Latin American astronomy, Revista Mexicana de Astronomia y Astrofisica. Serie de Conferencias, Vol. 85, pp. 85, 2001.

Gupta M. and Ding H. Fuzzy neuronal networks and genetic algorithms. In Proc. Third International Conference on Fuzzy Logic, Neural Nets and Soft Computing, pages 187--188. Iizuka, 1994.

Gurgen, F., Neural-network-based decision making in diagnostic applications; IEEE Engineering in Medicine and Biology Magazine, Volume 18, Issue 4, pp.89 – 93, July-Aug. 1999.

Gurney, K. ``An Introduction to Neural Networks''. University of Sheffield Press, London, UK, 1997.

Halgamuge S. K., Mari A. and Glesner M., Fast perceptron learning by fuzzy controlled dynamic adaptation of neural parameters, In R. Kruse et al. (Eds.), Fuzzy Systems in Computer Science'' Ch. 3.4, Wiesbaden. Germany: Verlag Vieweg, pp.129–140, 1994.

Hanes, M.D.; Ahalt, S.C.; Krishnamurthy, A.K., Acoustic-to-phonetic mapping using recurrent neural networks; IEEE Transactions on Neural Networks, Volume 5, Issue 4, pp.659 – 662, July 1994.

Hassoun M. H. ``Fundamentals of Artificial Neural Networks''. The MIT Press, Bambridge, MA, 1995.

Haykin, S. ``Neural Networks: A Comprehensive Foundation, second edition''. Prentice-Hall, Upper Saddle River, NJ, 1999.

Hebb D. O, Organization of behavior. Wiley, New York, 1949.

Hecht-Nielsen R., Applications of Counterpropagation Networks, Neural Networks, 1, pp. 131-139, 1988.

Heittmann A., Ramacher U., An architecture for feature detection utilizing dynamic synapses, The 47th Midwest Symposium on Circuits and Systems, MWSCAS '04, pp 373-6 vol.2, 2004.

Hill A.V., Wave transmission as the basis of nerve activity. Cold Spring Harbour Symp. Quant. Biol., vol. 1: 146-151, 1933.

Hines M. and Carnevale N., NEURON: a tool for neuroscientists. The Neuroscientist, 7, 123–135. 2001.

Hines, M.. NEURON–a program for simulation of nerve equations. In F. Eeckman, Neural systems: Analysis and modeling. Norwell, Massachusetts: Kluwer, 127–136, 1993.

Hines, M.. The neurosimulator NEURON. In C. Koch & I. Segev, Methods in neuronal modelling, 129–136. MIT Press, 1998.

Hintz, K.J.; Spofford, J.J., Evolving a neural network, Proceedings of the 5th IEEE International Symposium on Intelligent Control, Page(s):479 - 484 vol.1, Sept. 1990.

Hodgkin, A. L. and Huxley, A. F.. A quantitative description of membrane current and its application to conduction and excitation in nerve", Journal of Physiology, vol 117, pp500-544, 1952.

Holland, J. H., Adaptation in Natural and Artificial Systems. University of Michigan Press, 1975.

Holland, J. H., outline for a logical theory of adaptive systems, Journal of the association of computing machinery, 3, 1962.

Hopfield J.J , pattern recognition computation using action potential timing for stimulus representation, nature, vol. 376, pp 33-36, 1995.

Hopfield J.J., "Neural networks as physical systems with emergent collective computational abilities", Proc. National Academy of Sciences of USA, vol.72, pp.2554-2558, 1982.

Hsin-Chia F.; Hung-Yuan C.; Yeong Y. X.; Pao H., User adaptive handwriting recognition by self-growing probabilistic decision-based neural networks Neural Networks, IEEE Transactions on , Volume: 11 Issue: 6 , Page(s): 1373 –1384, Nov. 2000.

Hunt K. J., Sbarbaro D., Zbikowski R., and P. J. Gawthorp, "Neural networks for control systems-A survey," Automatica, vol. 28, no. 6, pp. 1083--1112, 1992.

Hutchins R. G. Identifying nonlinear dynamic systems using neural nets and evolutionary programming, in Proc. 28th Asilomar Conf. Signals, Systems & Computers. Part 2. Los Alamitos, CA: IEEE Computer Soc., pp. 887–891. 1994.

Ishibuchi H., Fujioka R., and Tanaka H., "Neural networks that learn from fuzzy-if-then rules," IEEE Transactions on Fuzzy Systems, Vol. 1, pp. 85-97, 1993.

Ishibuchi H., Kwon K., Tanakaa H., A learning algorithm of fuzzy neural networks with triangular fuzzy weights. Fuzzy Sets and Systems 71, pp. 277-293, 1995.

Izhikevich, E , Which Model to Use for Cortical Spiking Neurons?, IEEE Trans. on Neural Networks, vol. 15, no. 5, 1063-1070, 2004.

Izhikevich, E. Neural excitability, spiking and bursting. International journal of bifurcation and chaos, 10, 1171-1266, 2000.

Izhikevich, E., Resonate-and-fire neurons. Neural Networks, 14, 883–894, 2001.

Izhikevich, E.M, Relating STDP to BCM, Neural Computation,v15, n 7, pp1511-23, 2003.

Jain R., Kasturi R., Schunck B. G., Machine Vision, McGraw-Hill, 1995.

Jamil, N.; Iqbal, S.; Iqbal, N, Face recognition using neural networks. Multi Topic Conference, IEEE INMIC. Technology for the 21st Century. Proceedings. IEEE International , Page(s): 277 –281, 2001.

Jander M., Luciano D. F. C., Neural-based color image segmentation and classification using self-organizing maps, Anais do IX Sibgrapi, 47-54, 1996.

Janson D. J. and Frenzel J. F. Training product unit neural networks with genetic algorithms, IEEE Expert, vol. 8, pp. 26–33, May 1993.

Jonston S., Prasad G., Maguire L.P, Belatreche A., Investigation into the pragmatism of phenomenological spiking neurons for hardware implementation onto FPGAs, IEEE Systems man and cybernetics, 3rd Workshop on Intelligent Cybernetic Systems (ICS'04), , Londonderry, UK, 7- 8 September 2004.

Kandel, E. R., Schwartz J. H., Jessell, T.M., (Eds.). Principles of neural science. McGraw Hill. 2000.

Karmarkar, U.R., and Buonomano, D.V.. A model of spike timing dependent plasticity: one or two coincidence detectors? J.Neurophysiol. 88, 507–513, 2002.

Keil A, Mueller M. M., Ray W. J., Gruber T., Elbert T., Human gamma band activity and perception of a Gestalt. J. Neurosci., 19, 7152. 7161, 1999.

Kepecs A, van Rossum MC, Song S, Tegner J., Spike timing dependent plasticity: common themes and divergent vistas, Biological Cybernetics 87, 446-458, 2002.

Kewley R.H.; Embrechts M.J.; Breneman C., Data strip mining for the virtual design of pharmaceuticals with neural networks; IEEE Trans. on Neural Networks, Vol.11, Issue 3, pp.668-679, May 2000.

Khoshgoftaar T.M., Allen E.B., Hudepohl J.P., Aud S.J., Application of neural networks to software quality modeling of a very large telecommunications system; IEEE Transactions on Neural Networks, Vol. 8, Issue 4, pp.902 – 909, July 1997.

Kim Y. H. and Lewis F. L., "Reinforcement Adaptive Learning Neural Net Based Friction Compensation Control for High Speed and Precision", IEEE Trans. Contr. Syst. Tech., Vol. 8, No. 1, pp. 118, Jan. 2000.

Kinnear K. E., editor, Advances in Genetic Programming. The MIT Press, Cambridge, MA, 1994.

Kistler W. M. and van Hemmen J. L., Modeling Synaptic Plasticity in Conjunction with the Timing of Pre- and Postsynaptic Action Potentials Neural Computation, 12, 385-405, 2000.

Kistler W. M. and van Hemmen J. L., Short-Term Synaptic Plasticity and Network Behavior Neural Computation, 11(7): 1579-1594, 1999.

Kistler W. M., van Hemmen, J. L. Short-term synaptic plasticity and network behavior. Neural Comput., 11(7), 1579–1594, 1999.

Kistler W., Gerstner W., Van Hemmen J. L., Reduction of the Hodgkin-Huxley Equations to a Single-Variable Threshold Model ,Neural Computation, 9:1015-1045, 1997.

Kistler W.M, Spike-timing dependent synaptic plasticity: a phenomenological framework, Biological Cybernetics, v 87, n 5-6, pp 416-27, 2002.

Kobayashi, K., and Poo, M.M.. Spike train timing-dependent associative modification of hippocampal CA3 recurrent synapses by mossy fibers. Neuron 41, 445–454, 2004.

Koch, C. Biophysics of computation: Information processing in single neurons. New York: Oxford University Press, 1999.

Koch, C., & Segev, I. (Eds.). Methods in neuronal modeling: From ions to networks (Second edition), MIT Press. 1998.

Kohonen T., Oja E., Simula O., Visa A., Kangas J., Engineering applications of the slef-oragnising map, proceedings of the IEE, vol.84, no. 10, pp. 1358-1385, 1996.

Kohonen T., Self-Organizing Maps. Springer-Verlag, 1995.

Kohonen, T. Physiological interpretation of the self-organizing map algorithm. Neural Networks, vol. 6, pp.895-905, 1993.

Kohonen, T. Self-organized formation of topologically correct feature maps. Biological Cybernetics, 43:59-69, 1982.

Konig, A., Interactive visualization and analysis of hierarchical neural projections for data mining; IEEE Transactions on Neural Networks, Volume 11, Issue 3, pp.615–624, May 2000.

Kopell, N. and Ermentrout, G. B., Symmetry and phase locking in chains of weakly coupled oscillators. Comm. Pure Appl. Math., 39:623–660, 1986.

Kopell, N. and Somers, D., Anti-phase solutions in relaxation oscillators coupled through excitatory interactions. J. Math. Biol., 33:261–280, 1995.

Kosko, B.: Neural networks and Fuzzy systems, NJ, USA: Prentice Hall, 1991.

Koza J. R. and Rice J. P., Genetic generation of both the weights and architecture for a neural network, in Proc. IEEE Int. Joint Conf. Neural Networks (IJCNN'91 Seattle), vol. 2, pp. 397–404, 1991.

Koza J. R., "Genetic Programming: A Paradigm for Genetically Breeding Populations of Computer Programs to Solve Problems," Stanford University Computer Science Department STAN-CS-90-1314, 1990.

Koza J. R., Bennet F. H., Andre D., and Keane M. A.. Genetic Programming III - Darwinian Invention and Problem Solving. Morgan Kaufmann Publishers, San Francisko, CA, USA, 1999.

Koza J. R., Genetic Programming On the Programming of Computers by Means of Natural Selection Complex Adaptive Systems The MIT Press, Cambridge MA, 1992.

Kumar, V.P.; Manolakos, E.S, Unsupervised statistical neural networks for model-based object recognition.; IEEE Transactions on Signal Processing, Volume 45, Issue 11pp. 2709 – 2718, Nov. 1997.

Lei J., He G., and Jiang J.-P., State estimation of the CSTR system based on a recurrent neural network trained by HGA's, in Proc. IEEE Int. Conf. Neural Networks. Part 2 (of 4), pp. 779–782, 1997.

Leung, F.H.F.; Lam, H.K.; Ling, S.H.; Tam, P.K.S., Tuning of the structure and parameters of a neural network using an improved genetic algorithm, IEEE Transactions on Neural Networks, Volume 14, Issue 1, Page(s):79 – 88, Jan. 2003.

Li G. Ye W.; Lin L.; Yu Q.; Yu X., An artificial-intelligence approach to ECG analysis; IEEE Engineering in Medicine and Biology Magazine, Volume 19, Issue 2, pp.95–100, March-April 2000.

Liaw J. S., & Berger T. W., computing with dynamic synapses, a case study of speech recognition, proceedings of ICNN'97, pp 350-355, 1997.

Liaw J. S., & Berger T. W., Dynamic synapses, a new concept of neural representation and computation. Hippocampus, 6, 591–600, 1996.

Likothanassis S. D., Georgopoulos E., and Fotakis D., Optimizing the structure of neural networks using evolution techniques, in Proc. 5th Int. Conf. Application of High-Performance Computers in Engineering. Ashurst, U.K.: Computational Mechanics, pp.157–168. 1997.

Lin S.H.; Kung S. Y.; Lin L. J., Face recognition / detection by probabilistic decision-based neural network; IEEE Transactions on Neural Networks, Volume 8, Issue 1, pp.114 – 132, Jan. 1997.

Lu H.; Setiono R.; Liu H., Effective data mining using neural networks; IEEE Trans. on Knowledge and Data Engineering, Vol. 8, Issue 6, pp. 957 – 961, Dec. 1996.

Maass W and Zador A.M. Dynamic stochastic synapses as computational units. Neural comput 11: 903–917, 1999.

Maass W., Networks of spiking neurons: the third generation of neural network models. Neural Networks, 10:1659-1671, 1997.

Maass W., Paradigms for computing with spiking neurons. In Leo van Hemmen, editor, Models of Neural Networks, volume 4. Springer (Berlin), to appear, 1999.

Maass, W., On the computational complexity of networks of spiking neurons. Advances in neural information processing systems, Vol.7, pp. 183–190, MIT Press, 1995.

MacLeod, K. and Laurent, G., Distinct mechanisms for synchronization and temporal patterning of odor-encoding neural assemblies. Science, 274:1868–1871, 1996.

Mahfoud S. W., Niching methods for genetic algorithms. PhD Thesis, 1995.

Mainen, Z., & Sejnowski, T., Modeling active dendritic processes in pyramidal neurons. In C. Koch & I. Segev, Methods in neuronal modelling, 171–210, MIT Press. 1998.

Mandischer M., Evolving recurrent neural networks with nonbinary encoding, in Proc. IEEE Int. Conf. Evolutionary Computation, Part 2 (of 2), pp. 584–589. 1995.

Mangasarian O. L. and Wolberg W. H., Cancer diagnosis via linear programming, SIAM News, Volume 23, Number 5, pp 1-18, 1990.

Mark F. B., Barry W. C., Michael A. P., Neuroscience- exploring the brain, Williams and Wilkins, 1996.

Markram H. & Tsodyks M., Redistribution of synaptic efficacy between pyramidal neurons, Nature, 382, 807-810, 1996.

Markram H., Lübke J., Frotscher M.and Sakmann B.. Regulation of synaptic efficacy by coincidence of postsynaptic APs and EPSPs. Science, 275:213-215. 1997.

Matveev V., Wang X. J. Implications of all-or-none synaptic transmission and short-term depression beyond vesicle depletion: a computational study. J Neurosci 20: 1575–1588, 2000.

Mayeri, E.. A relaxation oscillator description of the burst-generating mechanism in the cardiac ganglion of the lobster, homarus americanus. J. Gen. Physiol., 62:473–488, 1973.

McCulloch W. S., Pitts W. "a logical calculus of the ideas imminent in nervous activity", Bull. Maath. Biophy. 5:115-133, 1943.

Mel, B.. Information processing in dendritic trees. Neural Computation, 6, 1031–1085, 1994.

Mendel J.M., McLaren R.W. Reinforcement learning control and pattern recognition systems. In: Adaptive, Learning and Pattern Recognition Systems: Theory and Applications, edited by J.M. Mendel & K.S. Fu, pp. 287--318. New York: Academic Press, 1970.

Meng J. E., Shiqian W., Juwei L., Hock L. T., Face recognition with radial basis function (RBF) neural networks Neural Networks, IEEE Transactions on , Vol.13 Issue: 3 , Page(s): 697 –710, May 2002.

Michalewicz Z., Genetic Algorithms + Data Structures = Evolution Programs, 3rd ed. New York: Springer-Verlag, 1996.

Min Qi, Forecasting real time financial series, Proceedings of the 2002 International Joint Conference on Neural Networks IJCNN '02, Vol. 1, pp.377 – 381, 12-17 May 2002.

Minsky M.L., "Neural Nets and the Brain Model Problem," Ph.D. dissertation, Princeton University, 1954.

Minsky M.L., Papert S.A., "Perceptrons: An introduction to computational geometry", Cambridge, Mass, MIT press, 1969.

Montana D. and Davis L. Training feedforward neural networks using genetic algorithms, in Proc.11th Int. Joint Conf. Artificial Intelligence. San Mateo, CA: Morgan Kaufmann, pp.762–767, 1989.

Morris, C. and Lecar, H.. Voltage oscillations in the barnacle giant muscle fiber. Biophys. Journal, pp. 193-213, 1981.

Mozer, M.C.; Wolniewicz, R.; Grimes, D.B.; Johnson, E.; Kaushansky, H., Predicting subscriber dissatisfaction and improving retention in the wireless telecommunications industry; IEEE Transactions on Neural Networks, Vol.11, Issue 3, pp.690 – 696, May 2000.

Murthy, V. N. and Fetz, E. E.. Coherent 25- to 35-Hz oscillations in the sensorimotor cortex of awake behaving monkeys. Proc. Natl. Acad. Sci. USA, 89:5670–5674, 1992.

Nagumo, J. S., Arimoto, S., and Yoshizawa, S.. An active pulse transmission line simulating nerve axon. Proc. IRE, 50:2061-2070. 1962.

Nakao M., Yamamoto M., Modeling neuronal dynamics-transition during sleep; IEEE Engineering in Medicine and Biology Magazine, Volume 18, Issue 3, pp.99 – 107, May-June 1999.

Narendra K. S. and Parthasarathy K., "Identification and Control of Dynamical Systems Using Neural Networks", IEEE trans. On Neural Networks, Vol. 1, pp. 4-27, Mar. 1990.

Nasrabadi, N.M.; Li, W., Object recognition by a Hopfield neural network; IEEE Transactions on Systems, Man and Cybernetics, Volume 21, Issue 6, pp.1523–1535, Nov.-Dec. 1991.

Natschläger T., Maass W., & Zador A.. Efficient temporal processing with biologically realistic dynamic synapses. Network, Computation in Neural Systems, 12(1), 75–87, 2001.

Nauck N., Fuzzy Neuro Systems: An Overview. In: Rudolf Kruse, Jörg Gebhardt and Rainer Palm (eds.): Fuzzy Systems in Computer Science, pp. 91-107. Vieweg, Braunschweig, 1994.

Nordstrom, E.; Carlstrom, J.; Gallmo, O.; Asplund, L., Neural networks for adaptive traffic control in ATM networks; IEEE Communications Magazine, Vol. 33, Issue 10, pp.43 – 49, Oct. 1995.

Ontrup, J., Wersing H., Ritter H., A computational feature binding model of human texture perception, Cognitive Processing 5,32–44, 2004.

Oster M.; Shih-Chii Liu, A winner-take-all spiking network with spiking inputs; Proc. of 11th IEEE Int. Conf. on Electronics, Circuits and Systems (ICECS), pp 203-206, 2004.

Pal N.R. and Pal S.K., "A review on image segmentation techniques", Pattern Recognition, vol. 26, pp. 1277-1294, 1993.

Panchev C., Wermter S., Spike-timing-dependent Synaptic Plasticity: From Single Spikes to Spike Trains. Neurocomputing, Vol. 58-60, pp.365-371, 2004.

Pantic, L., Torres, J.J., & Kappen, H.J., "Coincidence detection with dynamic synapses" Network: Computation in Neural Systems, 14 (1), 17-34, 2003.

226

Pantic, L., Torres, J.J., & Kappen, H.J., Gielen Stan C.A.M, Associative Memory with Dynamic Synapses, Neural Computation 14, 2903–2923, 2002.

Pavlidis, I.; Morellas, V.; Papanikolopoulos, N., A vehicle occupant counting system based on near-infrared phenomenology and fuzzy neural classification; IEEE Transactions on Intelligent Transportation Systems, Volume 1, Issue 2, pp.72 – 85, June 2000.

Pazzani M.J., Bilsus D., Learning and revising user profiles: The identification of interesting web Sites. Machine Learning, 27(3), 1997.

Pengyu Hong; Zhen Wen; Huang, T.S., Real-time speech-driven face animation with expressions using neural networks; IEEE Transactions on Neural Networks, Volume 13, Issue 4, pp.916 – 927, July 2002.

Perez C. A. and Holzmann C. A., "Improvements on handwritten digit recognition by genetic selection of neural network topology and by augmented training," in Proc. IEEE Int. Conf. Systems, Man, and Cybernetics, Part 2 (of 5), pp. 1487–1491. 1997.

Perret D. I., Rolls E. T, Caan W. C, visual neurons responsive to faces in the monkey temporal cortex, experimental brain research, vol. 47, pp 329-342, 1982.

Perrett, D. I., Mistin, A. J., and Chitty, A. J.. Visual neurones responsive to faces. Trends in Neuroscience., vol. 10, issue 9, pp. 358–364, 1987.

Peter H. Raven, George B. Johnson, Biology, 6th ed., McGraw-Hill, Boston, ISBN-0071122613 , 2002.

Petrowski A., a clearing procedure as niching method for genetic algorithms. In T. Fukuda, editor, proceedings of the 3rd IEEE international conference on evolutionary computation, pp 798-803, 1996.

Phan, F.; Micheli-Tzanakou, E.; Sideman, S., Speaker identification using neural networks and wavelets; IEEE Engineering in Medicine and Biology Magazine, Volume 19, Issue 1, pp.92-101, Jan.-Feb. 2000.

Phillips W. A., Singer W., In search of common foundations for cortical computation. B Behavioral and Brain Sciences, 20 (4), pp. 657-722, 1997.

Pinto, D. J., Brumberg, J. C., Simons, D. J., and Ermentrout, G. B.. A quantitative population model of whiskers barrels: re-examining the Wilson-Cowan equations. J. Comput. Neurosci., 3:247-264, 1996.

Plant R. E., A fitzhugh differential-difference equations modeling recurrent neural feedback. SIAM J. Appl. Math., 40:150–162, 1981.

Plant, R. E., A fitzhugh differential-difference equations modeling recurrent neural feedback. SIAM J. Appl. Math., 40:150–162, 1981.

Porto V. W., Fogel D. B. and Fogel L. J. Alternative neural network training methods, IEEE Expert, vol. 10, pp. 16–22, 1995.

Prechtl, J. C., Visual motion induces synchronous oscillations in turtle visual cortex. Proc. Natl. Acad. Sci. USA, 91:12467–12471, 1994.

Principe J. C., Euliano N. R., Curt W. L. 'Neural and Adaptive Systems: Fundamentals through Simulations', John Wiley & Sons, Inc, 2000.

R.M. Haralick and L.G. Shapiro, "Survey- image segmentation techniques", Computer Vision Graphics and Image Processing, vol. 29, pp. 100-132, 1985.

Rachid, S., Niki, N., Nishitani, H., Nakamura, S., Mori, S., Segmentation of sputum color image for lung cancer diagnosis Proc. Int. Conference on Image Processing,Vol. 1, pp. 243 –246, 1997.

Ragg T. and Gutjahr S. Automatic determination of optimal network topologies based on information theory and evolution, in Proc. 23rd EUROMICRO Conf, IEEE Computer Soc., pp.549–555. 1997.

Rana S. and Whitley D., "Search, Binary Representations, and Counting Optima," presented at the Workshop on Evolutionary Algorithms, Springer, vol. 111, pp. 177-190, New York, 1999.

Recce, M., Encoding information in neuronal activity. In W. Maass & C. Bishop (Eds.), Pulsed neural networks. MIT Press, 1999.

Rechenberg, I. Evolution strategie: Optimierung Technischer Systeme nach Prinzipien der Biologischen Evolution. Frommann-Holzboog, Stuttgart, 1973.

Revonsuo, A. and Newman, J., Binding and Consciousness. Consciousness and Cognition, vol. 8, issue 2, pp. 123-127, 1999.

Rieke F., Warland D., Van Stevenik R., Bialek W., SPIKES: exploring the neural code, MIT Press, Cambridge, 1996.

Rojas I., Pomares H., Gonzáles J., Bernier J. L., Ros E., Pelayo F. J. and Prieto A., Analysis of the Functional Block Involved in the Design of Radial Basis Function Networks, Neural Processing Letters, Vol. 12 no. 1, pp. 1-17, Aug 2000.

Rolls E. T., brain mechanisms for invariant visual recognition and learning, behavioural processes, vol. 33, pp 113-138, 1994.

Rolls E. T., Tovee M. J., Processing speed in the cerebral cortex, and the neurophysiology of visual backward masking, proc. Roy. Soc. B., vol. 257, pp 9-15, 1994.

Rosenblatt F, The perceptron: a probablistic model for information storage and retrieval in the brain. Psych. Rev, (65):386-408, 1958.

Roskies Adina L. The Binding Problem. Neuron. Vol. 24:7-9, September, 1999.

Rovithakis G.A., Maniadakis M., Zervakis M., Filippidis G., Zacharakis G., Katsamouris A.N., Papazoglou T.G., Artificial neural networks for discriminating pathologic from normal peripheral vascular tissue; IEEE Transactions on Biomedical Engineering, Vol. 48, Issue 10, pp.1088–1097, 2001.

Rudolph G. Convergence of evolutionary algorithms in general search spaces. In Proceedings of the IEEE Conference on Evolutionary Computation, pp 50-54, Piscataway, NJ, IEEE Press, 1996.

Rudolph G.. Convergence Properties of Evolutionary Algorithms. Verlag Dr. Kova C, Hamburg, 1997.

Ruf B., Schmitt M., "Hebbian learning in networks of spiking neurons using temporal coding", Proc. of the Int. Work-Conference on Artificial and Natural Neural Networks IWANN'97, Lecture Notes in Computer Science, vol. 1240, pp 380--389, Springer, Berlin, 1997.

Rumelhart D.E. and McClelland J.L. Parallel Distributed Processing, volume 1. MIT Press, 1986.

Ryan C., Collins J.J and Michael O.N, Grammatical evolution: evolving programs for an arbitrary language, Vol.1391 of LNCS, pp. 83-96. Springer Verlag, 1998.

Sala D.M. and Cios K.J., Self-organization in networks of spiking neurons. Australian Journal of Intelligent Information Processing Systems, 5(3): 161-170, 1998.

Sala D.M. and Cios K.J., Solving graph algorithms with networks of spiking neurons, IEEE Transactions on Neural networks, vol.10, issue 4, pp. 953-957, 1999.

Saravanan N. and Fogel D. B., Evolving neural control systems, IEEE Expert, vol. 10 No 3, pp. 23–27, Mar. 1995.

Sarkar M. and Yegnanarayana B. Evolutionary programming based probabilistic neural networks construction technique, in Proc. IEEE Int. Conf. Neural Networks, Part 1 of 4, pp.456–461, 1997.

Saudargiene A., How the shape of pre- and postsynaptic signals can influence STDP: a biophysical model, Neural Computation, v 16, n 3, p 595-625, 2004.

Schaffer J. D., Caruana R. A., Eshelman L. J., & Das R. A study of control parameters affecting online performance of genetic algorithms for function optimization. pp. 51–60, 1989.

229

Schultz A. and Wechsler H., Data fusion in neural networks via computational evolution, in Proc. IEEE Int. Conf. Neural Networks. Part 5, pp.3044–3049. 1994.

Schwefel H. P, Kybernetische evolution als strategie der experimentellen forschung in der stromungstechnik. Technical university of Berlin,. Dipl-Ing Thesis, 1965.

Schwefel H. P, Numerische optimierung von computer-modellen mittels der evolution strategie. Interdisciplinary systems research, 26, 1977.

Schwefel H. P., Evolution and Optimum Seeking. New York: John Willey and Sons, 1995.

Segev I. and Burke R, Compartmental models of complex neurons. In C. Koch & I. Segev, Methods in neuronal modeling: From ions to networks , MIT Press, 1998.

Senn W., Wyler K., Streit J., Larkum M., Luscher H. R., Mey H., Muller L., Stainhauser D., Vogt K., Wannier T., Dynamics of a random neural network with synaptic depression. Neural Networks, vol. 9 issue 4, pp. 575–588, 1996.

Senowski T. J., Time for a new neural code, Nature, vol. 376, pp 21-22, 1995.

Shannon C, DeLiang W., Synchronization and Desynchronization in a Network of Locally Coupled Wilson-Cowan Oscillators, IEEE transactions on Neural networks, Vol.7 No.3, 1996.

Shen S.; Chung-Ju Chang; ChingYao Huang, Qi Bi, Intelligent call admission control for wideband CDMA cellular systems; IEEE Transactions on Wireless Communications, Vol. 3, Issue 5, pp.1810-1821, 2004.

Shepherd, G. and Koch C Introduction to synaptic circuits. In: The Synaptic Organization of the Brain. G. Shepherd, ed., pp. 3-31, third edition, Oxford University Press, 1990.

Shin C.K.; Ui Tak Yun; Huy Kang Kim; Sang Chan Park, A hybrid approach of neural network and memory-based learning to data mining, IEEE Transactions on Neural Networks, Vol. 11, Issue 3, pp. 637–646, May 2000.

Singer W., Neuronal synchrony: a versatile code for the definition of relations? Neuron 24:49–65, 1999.

Singer W., Synchronization of cortical activity and its putative role in information processing and learning. Ann. Rev. Physiol. 55, 349-374, 1993.

Singer, W. and Gray, C. M.. Visual feature integration and the temporal correlation hypothesis. Ann. Rev. of Neurosci., 18:555–586, 1995.

Skarbek W. and Koschan A., Colour image segmentation: A survey. Technical report, Institute for Technical Informatics, Technical University of Berlin, October 1994.

Somers, D. and Kopell, N., Waves and synchrony in networks of oscillators of relaxation and non-relaxation type. Physica D, 89:169–183, 1995.

Somers, D. and Kopell, N.. Rapid synchronization through fast threshold modulation. Biol. Cybern., vol 68, pp. 393–407, 1993.

Song, S., Miller, K., & Abbott, L.. Competitive hebbian learning through spike-timingdependent synaptic plasticity. Nature Neuroscience, 3(9), 919–926. 2000.

Spears W. M. and De Jong K. A. On the virtues of parametrized uniform crossover, Proc. of the 4th Int'l Conf on Genetic Algorithms, pp 230-236, 1991.

Spears W. M., Evolutionary Algorithms: the role of mutation and recombination, Springer-Verlag, 1998.

Srinivas M. and Patnaik L. M. Learning neural network weights using genetic algorithms—Improving performance by search-space reduction, in Proc. IEEE Int. Joint Conf. Neural Networks IJCNN, Singapore, vol. 3, pp. 2331–2336,1991.

Stacey D, Calvert D, Carey T. Artificial neural networks for analysis user interaction. In: Beale R, Finlay J (eds), Neural Networks and Pattern Recognition in Human-Computer Interaction. Ellis Horwood, pp.103–113, 1992.

Stevens, C. F., & Zador, A., Neural coding: The enigma of the brain. Current Biology, vol. 5, issue 12, 1370–1371, 1995.

Stevens, C. F., & Zador, A.M., Novel integrate-and-fire-like model of repetitive firing in cortical neurons.In Proceedings of the 5th Joint Symposium on Neural Computation. La Jolla, California.1998.

Su H. T. and McAvoy T. J., "Artificial Neural Networks for Nonlinear Process Identification and Control", in Nonlinear Process Control, Ed. M. A. Henson and D. E. Seborg, pp. 371-428, Englewood Cliffs, NJ: PrenticeHall, 1997.

Sun Y.N., Horng M.H., Lin X.Z., Wang J.-Y., Ultrasonic image analysis for liver diagnosis; IEEE Engineering in Medicine and Biology Magazine, Volume 15, Issue 6, pp.93 – 101, Nov.-Dec. 1996.

Suri, R.E., and Sejnowski, T.J., Spike propagation synchronized by temporally asymmetric Hebbian learning. Biol. Cybern, 87, 440–445, 2002.

Syswerda G., Uniform crossover in genetic algorithms. In Schaffer J. D., editor, Proceedings of the 3rd Int'l Conf. on Genetic Algorithms, pp 2-9, San Francisco, Morgan Kaufmann, 1989.

T. Kohonen, Associative Memories: A System Theoretical Approach, Springer-Verlag, Berlin, 1977.

Tagliaferri R., Longo G., Milano L, Acernese F, Barone F., Ciaramella A., De Rosa R., Donalek C, Eleuteri C., Raiconi G, Sessa S., Staiano A. and Volpicelli A., Neural networks in astronomy, Special issue: Neural network analysis of complex scientific data: Astronomy and geosciences, Volume 16 , Issue 3-4, pps: 297 - 319 , 2003.

Tang K. S., Chan C. Y., Man K. F., and Kwong S., Genetic structure for NN topology and weights optimization, in Proc. 1st IEE/IEEE Int. Conf. Genetic Algorithms in Engineering Systems: Innovations and Applications (GALESIA'95), U.K., pp. 250–255, 1995.

Tegner, J., Kepecs A., An adaptive spike-timing-dependent plasticity rule, Neurocomputing, v 44-46, pp189-94, 2002.

Teller A., Manuela V., PADO: A new learning architecture for object recognition. In Katsushi Ikeuchi and Manuela Velso, editors, Symbolic Visual Learning, pp.81-116, Oxford University Press, 1996.

Terman, D. and Lee, E., Partial synchronization in a network of neural oscillators. SIAM J. Appl. Math., 57(1):252–293, 1997.

Terman, D. and Wang, D., Global competition and local cooperation in a network of neural oscillators. Physica D, 81:148–176, 1995.

Thomson A. M. & Deuchars J., Temporal and spatial properties of local circuits in neocortex. Trends in Neurosci., 17, 119–126, 1994.

Thorpe S.T, Imbert M., Biological constraints on connectionist modelling, in Connectionism in perpective, Pfeifer R., Schreter Z., Fogelman-Soulié, Steels L., eds, Elsevier, pp 63-92, 1989.

Thorpe, S., & Gautrais, J.. Rank order coding. In Computational neuroscience: Trends in research 1998 (pp. 113–118). New York: Plenum Press, 1998.

Thorpe, S., & Gautrais, J.. Rapid visual processing using spike asynchrony. Advances in neural information processing systems, Vol.9, pp.901–907, MIT Press, 1997.

Thorpe, S., Fize, D., & Marlot, C.. Speed of processing in the human visual system. Nature, vol. 381, pp. 520–522, 1996.

Tikovic, P., Durackova, D.: An Integrate-and-Fire Neuron Implementation, In: Electronic Devices and Systems Y2K - Proceedings, Brno, pp. 93-98, 2000.

Tikovic, P., Voros, M., Durackova, D.: Implementation of a learning synapse and a neuron for pulse-coupled neural networks,In: Journal of Electrical Engineering,Vol.52, No.3-4, , pp.68- 73. 2001.

Tillmann, B., Bharucha, J. J., & Bigand, E., Implicit Learning of Tonality: A Self-Organizing Approach, Psychological Review, 107, 885¬913, 2000.

Torreele J., Temporal processing with recurrent networks: An evolutionary approach, in Proc. 4th Int. Conf. Genetic Algorithms, R. K. Belew and L. B. Booker, Eds. San Mateo, CA: Morgan Kaufmann, pp. 555–561. 1991.

Trentin, E.; Gori, M., Robust combination of neural networks and hidden Markov models for speech recognition; IEEE Trans. on Neural Networks, Volume 14, Issue 6, pp.1519 – 1531, Nov. 2003.

Trippi R. R., Efraim T., Neural Networks in Finance and Investment, Irwin Professional Pub; 2nd edition, ISBN: 1557389195, 1996.

Tsaih, R., Sensitivity analysis, neural networks, and the finance, International Joint Conference on Neural Networks IJCNN '99, Vol. 6, pp:3830 - 3835, 10-16 July 1999.

Tsodyks M., Pawelzik K. & Markram H., Neural networks with dynamic synapses. Neural Computations, 10, 821-835, 1998.

Tsodyks, M. V., & Markram, H.. Plasticity of neocortical synapses enables transitions between rate and temporal coding. Lect. Notes Comput. Sci., 1112, 445–450, 1996.

Tsodyks, M. V., & Markram, H.. The neural code between neocortical pyramidal neurons depends on neurotransmitter release probability. Proc.Nat'l Acad. Sci. USA, 94, 719–723, 1997.

Tsodyks,M., Uziel, A.,&Markram, H.. Synchrony generation in recurrent networks with frequency-dependent synapses. J. Neurosci., 20(1), 50, 2000.

Usrey W.M, Reid R.C., Synchronous activity in the visual system. Annu Rev Neurosci 61:194–214, 1999.

Valentina Zharkova, Stan Ipson, Jean Aboudarham and Bob Bentley, "Survey of Image Processing Techniques", EGSO internal deliverable, Report No: EGSO-5-D1_F03-20021029, 2002.

van der Pol, B. and van der Mark, J.. The heartbeat considered as a relaxation oscillation, and an electrical model of the heart. Phil. Mag., 6:763–775, 1928.

van der Pol, B.. On "Relaxation Oscillations". Phil. Mag., 2 (11) :978–992, 1926.

Van Rullen, R., & Thorpe, S., Rate coding versus temporal order coding: what the retinal ganglion cells tell the visual cortex. Neural Computation, 13, 1255–1283. 2001.

Verhulst F., Nonlinear Differential Equations and Dynamical Systems. Berlin: Springer-Verlag, 1990.

Verhulst F., Nonlinear Differential Equations and Dynamical Systems. Berlin,Germany, ISBN-3540609342, Springer, 1996.

Vetter P., Roth A., and Hausser M., Propagation of action potentials in dendrites depends on dendritic morphology. Journal of Neurophysiology, 85, 926–937, 2001.

von der Malsburg C. and Schneider W., A neural cocktail-party processor, Biological Cybernetics, vol. 54, pp. 29–40, 1986.

von der Malsburg C., The correlation theory of brain function, Max-Planck-Institute for Biophysical Chemistry, Internal Rep. 81-2, 1981.

Vose M. D., The Simple Genetic Algorithm: Foundations and Theory. Cambridge, Massachussets, MIT Press, 1999.

Wang C. J.; Weissler P.N.; The use of artificial neural networks for optimal message routing, IEEE Network, Vol. 9, Issue 2, pp.16 – 24, March-April 1995.

Whitley D. , Starkweather T., and Bogart C., "Genetic algorithms and neural networks: Optimizing connections and connectivity," Parallel Comput., vol. 14, no. 3, pp. 347–361, 1990.

Whitley D. and Rana S., "Representation, Search, and Genetic Algorithms," presented at the 14th National Conference on Artificial Intelligence (AAAI-97), AAAI Press/MIT Press, 1997.

Whitley D. The GENITOR algorithm and selection pressure: Why rank based allocation of reproductive trials is best. Proc. of the 3rd Int. Conf. on Genetic Algorithms, pages 116-121. Morgan Kaufmann, 1989.

Widrow B., Hoff M. E., Adaptive switching circuits. IRE WESTCON Convemtion Record, pp. 96-104. New York, 1960.

Wilson H. R., "Simplified dynamics of human and mammalian neocortical neurons," J. Theor. Biol., vol. 200, pp. 375–388, 1999.

Wilson H.R. and Cowan J.D., "Excitatory and inhibitory interactions in localized populations of model neurons", Biophys. J., vol. 12, pp. 1-24, 1972.

Wilson, H. R. and Cowan, J. D., A mathematical theory of the functional dynamics of cortical and thalamic nervous tissue. Kybernetik, 13:55-80, 1973.

Woldberg W.H, Mangasarian O.L., Multisurface method of pattern separation for medical diagnosis applied to breast cytology. Proc. of the National Academy of Sciences, v 87, No 23, pp 9193-9196, 1990.

Wolfe, J.M., and Cave, K.R., The psychophysical evidence, for a binding problem in human vision, Neuron Vol.24, pp 11–17, 1999.

Wolpert D.H. and Macready W.G., No free lunch theorems for optimization. IEEE Transactions on Evolutionary Computation, 1997.

Wolpert D.H. and Macready W.G., No Free Lunch Theorems for Search, Technical Report SFI-TR-95-02-010. Sante Fe, NM, USA: Santa Fe Institute, 1995.

Wu Q, T.M. McGinnity, L.P Maguire, A. Belatreche and B. Glackin, Adaptive Co-ordinate Transformation Based on a Spike Timing-Dependent Plasticity Learning Paradigm, Lecture Notes in Computer Science, Springer-Verlag, Vol.3610, pp.420-429, 2005.

Xu H. Y., Wang G. Z. and Baird C. B., A fuzzy neural networks technique with fast back propagation learning, Int. J. Conf. on Neural Networks (IJCNN'92), Baltimore, MA, USA, pp.214–219, 1992.

Yao S., Wei C. J., and. He Z. Y, Evolving wavelet neural networks for function approximation, Electron. Lett., vol. 32, no. 4, pp.360–361, 1996.

Yao X., ``Evolving artificial neural networks," Proceedings of the IEEE, 87(9):1423-1447, 1999.

Yao X., Evolutionary computation: A gentle introduction, Kluwer Academic Publishers, Boston, ISBN 0-7923-7654-4, pp.27-53, 2002.

Yao X., Liu Y. and Lin G., Evolutionary Programming Made Faster, IEEE Transactions on Evolutionary Computation, Vol. 3, No. 2, pp. 82–102, July 1999.

Yao, H., and Dan, Y.. Stimulus timing-dependent plasticity in tentiation in the CA1 region of rat hippocampal slices. Neuroscience cortical processing of orientation. Neuron 32, 315–323, 2001.

Yasdi R., A Literature Survey on Applications of Neural Networks for Human-Computer Interaction, Neural Comput & Applic, Springer-Verlag London Limited, 9:245–258, 2000.

Yin X. and Germay N. A fast genetic algorithm with sharing scheme using cluster analysis methods in multimodal function optimisation. In artificial neural networks and genetic algorithms, pp. 450-457, Wien, Springer Verlag, 1993.

Yonghong Y., Understanding speech recognition using correlation-generated neural network targets; IEEE Transactions on Speech and Audio Processing, Volume 7, Issue 3, pp.350 – 352, May 1999.

Zador, A and Dobrunz, L., "Dynamic synapses in the cortex", Neuron Vol 19, 1-4, 1997.

Zahorian, S.A.; Nossair, Z.B., A partitioned neural network approach for vowel classification using smoothed time/frequency features; IEEE Transactions on Speech and Audio Processing, Volume 7, Issue 4, pp.414 – 425, July 1999.

Zeki, S., A Vision of the Brain. Blackwell Scientific Publications, Oxford, 1993.

Zhang, L. I., Tao, H. W., Holt, C. E., Harris, W. A., and Poo, M.-M.. A critical window for cooperation and competition among developing retinotectal synapses. Nature, 395:37-44, 1998.

Zhenquan Li , Vojislav K., Ichikawa A, Fuzzified neural network based on fuzzy number operations, Fuzzy Sets and Systems, v.130 n.3, p.291-304, September 16, 2002.

Zurada, J. M. `Introduction to Artificial Neural System". West Publishing Company, St. Paul, MN, 1992.

INDEX

www.ingramcontent.com/pod-product-compliance
Lightning Source LLC
LaVergne TN
LVHW042332060326
832902LV00006B/126